NERVOUS ILLS
THEIR CAUSE AND CURE

BORIS SIDIS

The Project Gutenberg EBook of Nervous Ills, by Boris Sidis

This eBook is for the use of anyone anywhere in the United States and most other parts of the world at no cost and with almost no restrictions whatsoever. You may copy it, give it away or re-use it under the terms of the Project Gutenberg License included with this eBook or online at www.gutenberg.org. If you are not located in the United States, you'll have to check the laws of the country where you are located before using this ebook.

Title: Nervous Ills
       Their Cause and Cure

Author: Boris Sidis

Release Date: April 2, 2018 [EBook #56893]

Language: English

*** START OF THIS PROJECT GUTENBERG EBOOK NERVOUS ILLS ***

Produced by Turgut Dincer, John Campbell and the Online Distributed Proofreading Team at http://www.pgdp.net (This file was produced from images generously made available by The Internet Archive)

TRANSCRIBER'S NOTE

Footnote anchors are denoted by [number], and the footnotes in a chapter have been placed at the end of that chapter.

Some minor changes to the text are noted at the end of the book.

WORKS BY BORIS SIDIS

NERVOUS ILLS, THEIR CAUSE AND CURE.

THE FOUNDATIONS OF NORMAL AND ABNORMAL PSYCHOLOGY.

SYMPTOMATOLOGY, PSYCHOGNOSIS, AND DIAG-NOSIS OF PSYCHOPATHIC DISEASES.

THE CAUSATION AND TREATMENT OF PSYCHO-PATHIC DISEASES.

HUMAN PROGRESS.

THE PSYCHOLOGY OF SUGGESTION.

MULTIPLE PERSONALITY.

PSYCHOPATHOLOGICAL RESEARCHES.

AN EXPERIMENTAL STUDY OF SLEEP.

PHILISTINE AND GENIUS.

THE PSYCHOLOGY OF SUGGESTION.

A STUDY OF GALVANOMETRIC DEFLECTIONS.

THE NATURE AND CAUSATION OF THE GALVANIC PHENOMENON.

NERVOUS ILLS

THEIR CAUSE AND CURE

BY

BORIS SIDIS, M.A., Ph.D., M.D.

MEDICAL DIRECTOR, THE SIDIS PSYCHO-
THERAPEUTIC INSTITUTE, PORTS-
MOUTH, NEW HAMPSHIRE

Author of "The Foundations of Normal and Abnormal Psychology," "The Causation and Treatment of Psychopathic Diseases," "Symptomatology, Psychognosis and Diagnosis of Psychopathic Diseases," etc., etc.

BOSTON
RICHARD G. BADGER
THE GORHAM PRESS

Copyright, 1922, by Richard G. Badger

All Rights Reserved
Made in the United States of America

Press of J. J. Little & Ives Company, New York, U. S. A.

"*The thing in the world I am most afraid of is fear.*"

Montaigne.

INTRODUCTION

In this volume I give a brief, popular account of some of my work in Psychopathology, or Abnormal Psychology for the last quarter of a century. I do not refer to my work on psychopathic reflexes, moment-consciousness, moment-thresholds, multiple personality and other subjects. The reader will find all these subjects in my other works. In this volume I make an attempt to simplify matters. I lay stress on the main factors and principles of that part of Abnormal Psychology that deals with the subject of nervous ills.

It is to be regretted that some physicians, and among them many neurologists of excellent standing, hesitate to accept the work accomplished in the domain of Psychopathology, confusing the latter with what parades at present under the name of psychoanalysis. Thus a well known physician writes to me:

"I think that the majority of men in general work (medical) do not separate Psychopathology from Psychoanalysis. Freud's theories and the whole trend of psychoanalysis have been so turned into channels of distorted and perverted sexual life that it has blinded people to the fact that there are many dominant phases in mental life which are not sexual. The ordinary, healthy minded, and vigorous practitioner sees a lot of motives in life that are not sexual, and where everything is twisted and turned to one side, to one 'complex,' he becomes indignant and disgusted, and condemns the whole broad subject of Psychopathology." I think that the physician is right in his attitude.

As a matter of fact psychoanalysis, by which Freud and his adherents have baptized their sexual theories and metaphysical wish-speculations, should be regarded as savage and barbaric. Psychoanalysis is a sort of Astrology, full of superstitious symbolizations, dream vagaries, and idle interpretations, foisted on the credulous, on those obsessed by sexual inclinations, and on those suffering from sexual perversions. It is idle and credulous to search in adults for "unconscious" memories of babies a few months old. Many take up psychoanalysis as a sort of mental masturbation which in the long run is sure to play havoc with their nerve and mind.

Psychoanalysis excites the curiosity of the vulgar just as for thousands of years Astrology held the interest of semi-civilized nations to the detriment of the science of Astronomy. Psychoanalysis belongs to the class of dangerous superstitions, harmful to health, both social and individual. Psychoanalysis, like Palmistry or Oneiroscopy, that is, "interpretation of dreams," imposes on the uncritical sense of the credulous public. Freudian psychoanalysis should be openly declared as a fraud.

Lecky points out that superstitions are not destroyed by discussion. To start a discussion in an earnest way a common ground is required. What common ground is there between science and superstition? Superstition should be left alone to die of inanition. There is no common ground between psychoanalysis and psychopathology. That is why it is just as impossible to argue with a psychoanalyst as with a Mormon or a Mohammedan. Anyone who does not accept the dogmas and superstitions of psychoanalysis is accused of "resistance of hidden complexes," just as pious believers accuse sceptics of evil thoughts.

A famous professor of a well known eastern college asked me to continue my "good work" against psychoanalysis. But criticism of psychoanalysis is a thankless task. It is futile to discuss psychological and medical matters with psychoanalysts. For psychoanalysts care for nothing else but the fulfillment of sexual wishes. It is useless to argue with psychoanalysts, who as a rule possess no more critical sense than Mormon saints. Psychoanalysis is a sort of Mormonism. In the far West psychoanalysis is preached from the pulpits in churches. Psychoanalysis is a sex religion. One should combat it with ridicule and scorn. Psychoanalysis needs a Voltaire, a Molière, or a Swift.

The so-called present civilized humanity, and especially our populace, lives in an age of vulgarity. Success *per se* is the sole aim in life. Books by the thousands tell how to achieve "success," how to fool the nerves, or how to deceive the mind. "Efficiency" and "success" fill home and school with all sorts of lucubrations and advertisements. Mental tests are supposed to help to success. Business success is the slogan. And success is only to the mediocre and the vulgar. Mediocrity writes for mediocrity, and is applauded by mobs of mediocrity. To teach the truth is a great privilege, but to deceive the ignorant and to debauch the young and inexperienced is a serious offence.

When science, literature, and art sink to the movie stage, why wonder at their triviality? When Government experts take seriously Freudian "Sublimation," why blame the credulity of the layman? When the Bureau of Education spreads far and wide pamphlets on mental tests, why wonder at the gullibility of the populace?

The tendency towards the rule of mediocrity in the twentieth century was observed by Tolstoy:

"About twenty years ago Matthew Arnold wrote a beautiful article on the purpose of criticism. According to his opinion, it is the purpose of criticism to find what is most important and good in any book whatever, wherever, and whenever written, and to direct the reader's attention to what is important and good in them.

"Such a criticism seems to me indispensable in our time of newspapers, periodicals, books, and advertisements. Such a criticism is requisite for the future of the cultured world.

"Printing has for some time served as the chief instrument for the diffusion of ignorance among the well-to-do (the middle classes, especially the so-called new women).

"Books, periodicals, especially the newspapers, have in our time become great financial undertakings for the success of which the largest possible number of purchasers is needed. The interests and tastes, however, of the largest possible number of purchasers are always low and vulgar. For the success of the press it is necessary that the productions should respond to the demands of the great majority of the purchasers, that is, that they should touch upon the low interests and correspond to the vulgar tastes. The press fully satisfies these demands, which it is quite able to do, since among the number of workers for the press there are many more people with the same low interests and vulgar tastes as the public than men with high interests and refined taste.

"The worst thing about it is that the reading of poor works corrupts the understanding and taste. Good works can no longer be appreciated.

"In proportion as newspapers, periodicals, and books become more and more disseminated, the value of what is printed falls lower and lower, and the class of the so-called cultured public sinks more and more into a most hopeless, self-contented, incorrigible ignorance...."

"A striking example is that of the English prose writers. From the great Dickens we descend at first to George Eliot, then to Thackeray, to Trollope; and then begins the indifferent manufacture of a Rider Haggard, Kipling, Hall Caine, and so forth.

"Still more striking is this fall noticed in American literature. After the great galaxy, Emerson, Thoreau, Lowell, Whittier, and others, everything breaks off suddenly, and there appear beautiful editions with beautiful illustrations and with beautiful stories and novels which are impossible to read on account of absence of all meaning.

"The ignorance of the cultured crowd of our times has reached such a pass that great thinkers and writers of former times no longer satisfy the highly refined demands of new men (and new women).

"The last word of philosophy is the immoral, coarse, inflated, disconnected babbling of Nietzsche. Senseless, artificial conglomeration of words of decadent poems is regarded as poetry of the highest rank. The theatres give dramas, the meaning of which is not known to any one, not even to the author."

What would Tolstoy have said had he witnessed the full blown art of our movies?

What the movies and literature accomplish in the world of art and letters, that is what psychoanalysis and mental tests achieve in normal and abnormal psychology.

The mediocrity of the modern man is akin to the vulgarity of the ancient freedman, so well described by Petronius in his type of Trimalchio. Both, the greedy freedman and the "efficient" freeman, have the same deleterious influence on the course of civilization.

Our age is not the age of Democracy, but of Mediocrity. It is in such an age that sensationalism, movies, and psychoanalysis are apt to flourish like green bay trees.

The reader will find that I often turn to Social Psychology. This is requisite. As I carry on my work on nervous ills I become more and more convinced that a knowledge of Social Psychology is essential to a clear comprehension of nervous ills.

The number of cases given in the volume will, I am sure, be of great help to the reader. For the concrete cases, carefully studied by me, bring out distinctly the mechanism, the factors, and the main principles of nervous ills.

I address this volume to the reader who wishes to learn the truth, not to those who are in search for ever new amusements, or for the "best seller" of the year. I hope that this work will prove of value to the thoughtful physician and of interest to the cultured layman.

I further hope that my reader will not be offended by my statements about superstitions. *I address myself to the liberal-minded reader who does not care to follow the herd.*

BORIS SIDIS

Maplewood Farms,
Portsmouth, New Hampshire.

CONTENTS

		PAGE
	INTRODUCTION	7

CHAPTER

I	SELF-PRESERVATION AND FEAR	19
II	STAGES OF FEAR	27
III	THE PRIMACY OF FEAR	32
IV	FEAR AND SUPERSTITION	38
V	THE POWER OF FEAR	45
VI	FEAR AND DISEASE	56
VII	FORMS OF NEUROSIS	61
VIII	FEAR AND THE HYPNOIDAL STATE	66
IX	HEALTH AND MORBIDITY	73
X	THE SUBCONSCIOUS	77
XI	THE CONDITIONS AND LAWS OF SUGGESTION	81
XII	IS THE SUBCONSCIOUS A PERSONALITY?	86
XIII	THE CHARACTER OF THE HYPNOIDAL STATE	91
XIV	HYPNOIDAL PSYCHOTHERAPY	101
XV	EGOTISM AND FEAR	115
XVI	NEUROTIC PARASITISM	131
XVII	FUNDAMENTAL PRINCIPLES	137
XVIII	ILLUSTRATIONS, NEUROTIC HISTORIES	149
XIX	HYPNOIDAL TREATMENT	164
XX	FEAR CONFESSIONS	183
XXI	TRANCE APPARITIONS	211
XXII	RECURRENT FEAR STATES—PSYCHOLEPSY	216
XXIII	APHONIA, STAMMERING, AND CATALEPSY	234
XXIV	SUGGESTED HALLUCINATIONS	250
XXV	TRANCE SERVILITY	258

XXVI	THE HYPNOIDAL STATE AND SUPERSTITIONS	264
XXVII	NEUROSIS AND HEREDITY	271
XXVIII	NEUROSIS AND EUGENICS	276
XXIX	PRIMITIVE FEARS	287
XXX	THE HERD AND THE SUBCONSCIOUS	303
XXXI	MYSTICISM, PRAYER, CONVERSION, AND METAPHYSICS	312
XXXII	FEAR SUGGESTIONS	324
XXXIII	LIFE ENERGY AND THE NEUROTIC	332
XXXIV	DYNAMIC ENERGY	339
XXXV	FEAR VARIETIES	347
XXXVI	CONTROL OF THE NEUROTIC	358
XXXVII	REGAINED ENERGY AND MENTAL HEALTH	369
	INDEX	377

NERVOUS ILLS

THEIR CAUSE AND CURE

NERVOUS ILLS

CHAPTER I

SELF-PRESERVATION AND FEAR

The impulse of self-preservation is at the basis of all animal life. From the simplest lump of protoplasm constituting a microbe to the highest form of life, such as man, one meets with the same primitive life tendency,—the impulse of self-preservation. Throughout all animal creation one important purpose runs, and that is the preservation of life.

When a creature is launched into the world, it is animated with one central, innate mission,—to live; and to fight for its living. For this purpose,—if purpose it really be, the creature, however small and insignificant, is provided with a rich arsenal of armour for defense and attack. When a biologist demonstrated the anatomical structure of a caterpillar, a bystander exclaimed in surprise: "Why, I always thought that a caterpillar was nothing but skin and squash!"

The simple living creatures, swarming in the waters of stagnant ponds and murky pools, the bits of living matter, inhabiting by the million the little world of a hanging drop of water, are supplied with the most complicated reactions, mechanical and more especially chemical, for the maintenance of their life existence. Simple as a cell, a minute particle of protoplasm, may appear, it is none the less a most wonderful laboratory where toxins, anti-toxins, and an infinite variety of secretions, highly poisonous and protective, are being produced, for the keeping in existence of that insignificant, microscopic bit of living matter. *Self-preservation is the central aim of all life-activities.*

The tendency of all organic processes is the maintenance of the life of each particular individual organism. It is this aspect that I wish to impress on the minds of my readers. Self-preservation is the nucleus of organic life. It is the mainspring of organic activities and functions. *The tendency of life is not the preservation of the species, but solely the preservation of each individual organism, as long as it is in existence at all, and is able to carry on its life processes.*

Every living thing, from the ultra-microscopic to the highest and most complex multicellular organism, man included, has only one fundamental tendency, the maintenance and defense of its *individual* existence. The claim that the individual counts for little or nothing, and that the species is everything, is not true to facts. "Nature cares not for the individual, but for the species" is a glittering generality of a metaphysical character.

It is the maintenance of its individual existence and the *struggle for this individuality* and its preservation, whether in defense or aggression, that form the main object of organic life in all its aspects. *The aim of life activities is the individual, the species is a secondary matter.* It is only when we keep this fundamental truth in mind that we begin to understand life in general, and human life in particular.

The struggle for existence of which so much is heard in modern science, theoretical or applied, means really the preservation of the individual organism, or the self-preservation of individuality. We may say that the *struggle for existence in the biological and social worlds means nothing else but the Struggle for Individuality.*

Wherever the organism forms a whole as to its vitality, whether it be an amoeba or a man, the struggle is for the maintenance of that whole or of that particular individual organism. All the structures and functions go to the preservation of that individuality, or of that individual organic self, constituting the impulse of self-preservation in the total activity of the particular individual organism. The great number of physico-chemical and mechanical processes, adaptations and adjustments of inner structures and functions, as well as the different reactions to the stimuli of external environment, even in the lowest of micro-organisms, are for the *whole* of the individuality.

When organisms take to forms of social life the fundamental aim is still the protection or self-preservation of the individual. The community is an additional defense of the individual against a hostile environment. Thus the herds of Damara cattle, or of social aggregates of other animals, offer greater protection to each individual animal. The individual wolf running in packs has more power for attack and defense. The individual man has more forces for aggression and for protection by living in a social medium which provides the individual with more sensory organs for observation of danger and with more organs for defense and attack, than in isolated states. The herd, the pack, the horde, the society are for the self-preservation of the individual.

It has been shown on good grounds that the very sense of external reality has become intensified in the individual by his capacity of living in a social aggregate. The social aggregate strengthens each individual member of the group. The individual is not for the group, but the group is for self-preservation of the individual. Should the individual lose his self-protection, or even have his impulse of self-preservation lowered, the whole aggregate faces ultimate destruction. That is why when in a social aggregate the impulse of self-preservation becomes limited, inhibited, and lowered by tyranny of social commandments, society is sure to decline, degenerate, and finally dissolve; or fall a victim to an external invader,— the fate of tribes, communities, and nations in the past and the present. *The moving power of life is self-preservation of the individual.*

A close study of life in general and of animal life in particular brings one to the inevitable conclusion that life in all its forms has self-preservation as its fundamental principle. *Self-preservation is the main impulse, the prime mover of life.* The prime mover of life is not the impulse of species preservation, or of sex, but the impulse of self-preservation of the individual organism.

Self-preservation has two aspects, the positive and the negative. In the positive form the primitive impulse is to keep the individual alive, to keep the functions and structure in normal condition, to conduce to the full development and harmonious activity of the individual. The negative form of the preservative impulse is the preservation from injury, degeneration, destruction, and death. This negative aspect of the impulse of self-preservation expresses itself in the higher animals in the form of fear.

The fear instinct is an essential constituent of the impulse of life. We may call the fear instinct the guardian of all sentient being. Wherever there is the least scent or even the least suggestion of danger, there the instinct of fear is aroused. Fear is the companion following close on the heels of the impulse of self-preservation.

Since every animal is always surrounded by enemies, and since every strange thing or strange occurrence is a menace or possible signal of danger, the fear instinct is aroused on all strange occasions. The fear instinct requires the slightest stimulus to start into function.

While most of the instincts require special conditions, and are usually *periodic*, the fear instinct is *ever present* and can be awakened on all occasions, and under any circumstances. Anything unfamiliar,—darkness, a state of exhaustion, weakness, fatigue, arouses the fear instinct, startling the animal into running, hiding, crouching, and preparation for attack or defense.

The fear instinct stays with us, and watches over us day and night. It follows us closely in our active, waking life, attends us in our resting hours, and watches over us in our sleeping periods. The fear instinct is the last to fall asleep, and the first to awake. The fear instinct follows us like our shadow, with the only difference that it constantly affects our actions, hardly ever leaves us alone, and keeps steady vigilance over our life activities. The reason for this apparently strange companionship is the fact that the fear instinct is the primitive instinct of the life impulse, the impulse for self-preservation.

The overwhelming intensity of the fundamental impulse of self-preservation is well described by the great writer Dostoevsky, whose insight into the psychology of human life and especially into abnormal mental life transcends that of any other writer: "Where is it I have read that someone condemned to death says or thinks, an hour before his death, that if he had to live on some high rock, on such a narrow ledge that he had only room to stand, and the ocean, everlasting darkness, everlasting solitude, everlasting tempest around him, if he had to remain standing on a square yard of space all his life, a thousand years, eternity, it were better to live so than to die at once! Only to live, to live, and live! Life whatever it may be!"

Just as the touch and pain nerves enmesh closely our body, warning us against hurtful stimulations, so we may say that fear, through our distant receptors of sight, hearing and smell, surrounds us, warning us against enemies, or inimical, suspicious objects, and forces. Were it not for the fear instinct, directly awakened, the animal threatened with danger would not have the time and the strong impulse to get ready for defense or for escape, by running or by hiding.

The fear instinct is of the utmost importance in animal life. Looked at from this standpoint the fear instinct is as important in animal economy as the skin which covers our body, which, by pain and hurts, warns of external injurious objects, and has an important function of warding off incessant invasion of disease-bearing organisms. In nervous ills we find the same fundamental factors:—*self-preservation and the fear instinct.*

CHAPTER II

STAGES OF FEAR

The fear instinct in its course of development passes through three stages:
I. The Stimulating Stage
II. The Arrestive, or Inhibitory Stage
III. The Paralyzing Stage.

In its milder forms when the fear instinct is but nascent, it serves as a sort of trigger to the activities of the organism. The animal may for a moment stop whatever activities and pursuits in which it happens to be engaged, and have its interest turn in the direction of the particular new stimulus, whether it be of an auditory, visual, or olfactory character. The fear instinct is just strong enough to suspend present interests, and direct its activities to the new source of the unknown stimulus.

When the source is unfamiliar, the animal becomes prepared for action. The energies are aroused for attack, or for hiding, freezing, or running, according to the mode of defense to which the animal has been adapted in its adjustments to the stimulations of its environment. The lion, the tiger, the skunk, the snake, the bird, the rabbit, the squirrel will act differently, according to their natural disposition in response to external objects and stimuli.

While the motor system may react differently in various animals, the fear instinct is alike in all of them. This stage of the fear instinct should be regarded as the healthy physiological reaction to strange and new stimuli, and is essentially protective, inasmuch as it serves for the arousal of energy and proper reactions of self-defense, characteristic of the particular individual.

In its milder forms the fear instinct is *normal, physiological,* and healthy in its reactions. In fact, the absence of it is rather pathological. It is quite natural that under the influence of some danger, the organism may feel the urging of this vital instinct, the consequent of the fundamental life impulse, and feel it as a stimulus rather than as a deterrent experience, feel fear as the key for the unlocking of energies in defense or attack. Such a reaction is healthy and strictly requisite in the total economy of life.

When I advanced the theory that the fear instinct is at the bottom of functional psychosis, or of psychopathic maladies, some jumped to the conclusion that I regarded the fear instinct as abnormal, giving rise to pathological states under all conditions and circumstances. This is not correct. *The fear instinct in its initial stages is perfectly normal, and is as indispensable to life as hunger and thirst.* It is only in the more advanced and extreme stages that the fear instinct becomes pathological, and is apt to give rise to psychopathic states.

In the arrestive or inhibitory state, the innervation of the voluntary and the involuntary muscular systems is arrested, or weakened. There is tremor and even convulsive contractions, the voluntary reactions are affected, and are carried out with some difficulty; there is cardiac arrhythmia, the respiration is irregular; there may be chattering of the teeth; the various bodily secretions are interfered with, and the vaso-motor nerves as well as the general vascular structures are thrown into disorder. Peristalsis, intestinal secretions, and the innervation of the sympathetic nervous system may become affected, first by inhibition, and then by irregular functioning. Associative mental or cerebral activity becomes arrested, confused; memory is disturbed, and the whole personality or individuality appears in a state of dissociation, accompanied by a lack of precision and lack of exactness of neuromuscular adaptations. The delicate reactions and adaptations are specially affected.

If this stage of fear instinct does not become intensified, the organism recovers its control,—many of the disturbances pass away, and the following reaction may come with a greater release of energy, developing a greater output of activity than under normal conditions. In short, the fear instinct may still serve as a stimulation to greater effort, but the chances of such a result are far smaller than in the first stage, which is essentially of a stimulating, useful, and healthful character.

The second stage of the fear instinct is the possibility of a pathological state, and, if persistent, leads directly to the third stage with consequent paralysis and danger of destruction. The first stage of fear is fully normal, helpful, and self-defensive. The second stage is harmful, but with the possibility of recovery and restitution of normal function. The third stage leads to destruction and death.

In the third stage there is paralysis of function of most of the muscular, secretory, excretory, circulatory, intestinal, and nervous systems. The animal is petrified with fear, and falls into a state of paralysis, rigidity, cataplexy, or in a state simulating death. This last stage of the effects of the fear instinct is pathological, and instead of conducing to the good of the individual, really leads to his destruction and death. The fear instinct in its extreme cases is not a help to the organism, but is distinctly a hindrance, and is felt as such by the organism which experiences it.

The fear instinct, which originally is a stimulating agent for self-defense, when in excess becomes a danger hastening the dissolution of the animal organism into its constituent parts. The intensity of the fear instinct is the expression of the fact that the organism is in imminent danger of destruction. The fear instinct in its extreme state is decidedly to the disadvantage of the animal.

Of course, it may be claimed that the paralysis and inhibition stages might have been of service or of protective value in the lower forms of life, when mimicking death or freezing prevented the animal from being noticed. This may possibly hold true in the cases of lower forms, but in the higher forms the fear instinct in its third stage, by bringing about inhibitions and paralysis of the vital functions, is decidedly of disservice to the organism, and leads to its destruction and death.

CHAPTER III

THE PRIMACY OF FEAR

The fear instinct is intimately related to the innermost principle, characteristic of all life, namely the impulse of self-preservation. When, however, the fear instinct becomes deranged by being too intense, and especially when reaching the extreme stage, the instinct becomes pathological, and its functioning leads to degeneration, destruction, and death. Even in its initiatory stages the fear instinct may become abnormal, when associated with objects, situations, and sensori-motor reactions which are otherwise normal and beneficial, or actually requisite in the total economy of life activity of the particular organism. Under such conditions the fear instinct is decidedly pathological.[1]

In fact we may say that the fear instinct is the main source of functional, psychopathic diseases. This also holds true of the individual in his aggregate capacity. If the impulse of self-preservation is at the basis of life, the fear instinct is its intimate companion. We may unhesitatingly assert that the fear instinct is one of the most primitive instincts of animal life. We are sometimes apt to overlook the power of fear, because our life is so well guarded by the protective agencies of civilization that we can hardly realize the full extent, depth, and overwhelming effects of the fear instinct. Fear is rooted deep in the nature of animal life, in the impulse of self-preservation.

The fear instinct is the earliest instinct to appear in child life. Preyer observed definite manifestations of the fear instinct on the twenty-third day after birth. Perez and

Darwin put its appearance somewhat later. In my observations of child life I found the manifestation of the fear instinct during the first couple of weeks, Ribot and other psychologists regard the fear instinct as "the first in chronological order of appearance."

"The progress from brute to man," says James, "is characterized by nothing so much as the decrease in the frequency of the proper occasion for fear. In civilization in particular it has at last become possible for large numbers of people to pass from the cradle to the grave without ever having had a pang of genuine fear. Many of us need an attack of mental disease to teach us the meaning of the word. Hence the possibility of so much blindly optimistic philosophy and religion. (James refers here to the blind optimism and cheerful metaphysical mysticism handed out to the uncultured classes.) Fear is a genuine instinct, and one of the earliest shown by the human child."

The fear of the unknown, of the unfamiliar, of the mysterious, is of the utmost consequence in the life history of children, savages, and barbaric tribes, and even in the social life of civilized nations. The fear of coming mysterious, unknown evil is a source of great anxiety to the young, or to the untrained, uncultivated minds. All taboos of primitive societies, of savages, of barbarians, and also of civilized people take their origin, according to anthropological research, in the perils and salvation of the soul, or in the fear of impending evil. As an anthropologist puts it: "Men are undoubtedly more influenced by what they fear than by what they love."

The civilized nations of antiquity used to be terrorized by omens, by occurrences of an unfamiliar character, such as storms, thunders, lightnings, comets, meteors, meteorites, and eclipses. Affairs of states and wars were guided by superstitions of fear. Whole armies used to throw away their weapons and run panic-stricken at the appearance of meteorites, meteors, and especially of comets. Even the ancient Athenians were influenced by strange, meteorological phenomena. On the appearance of a solar eclipse Pericles saved his ship by throwing his mantle round the helmsman, telling him that that was all that an eclipse was, and that there was no reason to be scared by the veiling of the sun from us. The father of pragmatic history, the great Thucydides, in his history of the Peloponnesian wars, puts the appearance of comets among national disasters.

The fear of the mysterious, the unknown, and the unfamiliar is a source of anxiety and distress in the young, or in the untrained and uncultured minds. Fear may become fixed and morbid when taking place in early childhood, when not inhibited by the course of further development, and, all the more so, when kept up by further events of life.

In most people the instinct of fear is controlled, regulated by education, and inhibited by the relatively secure life led in the herd, pack, group, and society generally. The instinct of fear, however, is but dormant and requires the opportune moment such as a social, mental epidemic, a "group-panic," to become manifested in its full intensity, giving rise to a morbid state of the "group-mind," or "herd-mind."

There are again cases when even under ordinary conditions fear becomes developed in the individual from early childhood either by lack of inhibitory training or by accidents in early child life. In all such cases the fear instinct becomes morbid, giving rise in later life to various forms of mental disease known as psychopathies, or recurrent morbid states.

We can, therefore, realize the full significance of the principle laid down by one of the greatest thinkers of humanity, Plato, that to learn "What to fear and what not to fear" is of the utmost consequence to the individual, both in his private and social activities.

Throughout the whole domain of the animal kingdom anything strange and unfamiliar is an occasion for the awakening of the fear instinct. The strange, the unfamiliar may be detrimental to the organism, and the animal recoils from meeting it directly. There must be exploration made before the reaction of approach can be effected. We find the same tendency in children and savages who run in terror of anything unusual.

On the whole escape is probably the safest course, since the unfamiliar may prove of great danger. The well known saying "Familiarity breeds contempt" has its significance in that the familiar does not arouse the fear instinct, and can be approached without risk. Reactions to a familiar object or known situation run in well established, habitual grooves.

In man the sense of familiarity may be acquired by the use of intelligence, by observations of various forms of unfamiliar situations and strange objects. Reason, leading to the understanding of the causes of things, turns the strange and unfamiliar into the familiar and the known, and thus dispels the terrors and horrors of the fear instinct.

The function of the intellect is to conquer the world by making man at home and familiar in this "wild universe." This is the course of human progress. "The aim of knowledge," says Hegel, "is to divest the objective world of its strangeness, and to make us more at home in it." In the words of the ancient poet:

Felix qui potuit rerum cognoscere causas,
Atque metus omnes, et inexorabile fatum,
Subject pedibus, strepitumque Acherontis avari.[2]

FOOTNOTES:

[1] See Chapter "Psychopathic Reflexes" in my volume "The Causation and Treatment of Psychopathic Diseases."

[2] Happy is he who knows the causes of things, who can trample on fear, inexorable fate, and the horrors of death.

CHAPTER IV

FEAR AND SUPERSTITION

An individual limited in intelligence, leading a narrow life, is specially subject to fear suggestions which can be easily aroused. Inhibitions of the personal self are produced by stimulation of the fear instinct with consequent easy access, by means of fear suggestions, to man's subconscious fear instinct, thus inducing various forms of morbid mental life.

When a person is limited in his interests, when he is ignorant and full of prejudices and superstitions, his critical, personal sense is embryonic, and the predisposition to fear suggestions is specially pronounced. He easily falls a victim to all kinds of bizarre beliefs and absurd superstitions, such as the mysticism which obsesses uncultured classes of all ages.

The optimistic, "metaphysical" beliefs, rampant in this country, are all due to the beggarly intelligence subconsciously obsessed by innumerable fear suggestions. Neurotic adherents cling to their irrational optimism in order to assuage the pangs, caused by the fear instinct, from which they are unable to free themselves.

In the embryonic personality of the child, as well as in the undeveloped or narrowed individuality of the adult, the sense of the strange, of the unknown, and of the mysterious, is apt to arouse the fear instinct. In fact, the unfamiliar arouses the fear instinct even in the more highly organized mind.

"Any new uncertainty," says Bain, "is especially the cause of terror. Such are the terrors caused by epidemics, the apprehensions from an unexperienced illness, the feeling of a recruit under fire. The mental system in infancy is highly susceptible, not merely to pain, but to shocks and surprises. Any great excitement has a perturbing effect allied to fear. After the child has contracted a familiarity with the persons and things around it, it manifests unequivocal fear on the occurrence of anything strange. The grasp of an unknown person often gives a fright. This early experience resembles the manifestations habitual to the inferior animals."

In another place Bain rightly says, "Our position in the world contains the sources of fear. The vast powers of nature dispose of our lives and happiness with irresistible might and awful aspect. Ages had elapsed ere the knowledge of law and uniformity prevailing among those powers was arrived at by the human intellect. The profound ignorance of the primitive man was the soil wherein his early conceptions and theories sprang up; and the fear inseparable from ignorance gave them their character. The essence of susperstition is expressed by the definition of fear."

Compayré, in speaking of the fear of the child, says, "In his limited experience of evil, by a natural generalization, he suspects danger everywhere like a sick person whose aching body dreads in advance every motion and every contact. He feels that there is a danger everywhere, behind the things that he cannot understand, because they do not fit in with his experience.

"The observations collected by Romanes in his interesting studies on the intelligence of animals throw much light on this question; they prove that dogs, for instance, do not fear this or that, except as they are ignorant of the cause. A dog was very much terrified one day when he heard a rumbling like thunder produced by throwing apples on the floor of the garret; he seemed to understand the cause of the noise as soon as he was taken to the garret, and became as quiet and happy as ever.

"Another dog had a habit of playing with dry bones. One day Romanes attached a fine thread which could hardly be seen, to one of the bones, and while the dog was playing with it, drew it slowly towards him; the dog recoiled in terror from the bone, which seemed to be moving of its own accord. So skittish horses show fright as long as the cause of the noise that frightens them remains unknown and invisible to them.

"It is the same with the child. When in the presence of all the things around him, of which he has no idea, these sounding objects, these forms, these movements, whose cause he does not divine, he is naturally a prey to vague fears. He is just what we should be, if chance should cast us suddenly into an unexplored country before strange objects and strange beings—suspicious, always on the *qui vive*, disposed to see imaginary enemies behind every bush, fearing a new danger at every turn in the road."

Similarly, Sully says, "The timidity of childhood is seen in the readiness with which experience invests objects and places with a fear-exciting aspect, in its tendency to look at all that is unknown as terrifying, and in the difficulty of the educator in controlling these tendencies."

Sully is right in thinking that education tends greatly to reduce the early intensity of fear. "This it does by substituting knowledge for ignorance, and so undermining that vague terror before the unknown to which the child and the superstitious savage are a prey, an effect aided by the growth of will power and the attitude of self-confidence which this brings with it." An uncultivated personality with a limited mental horizon, with a narrow range of interests, a personality trained in the fear of mysterious agencies, is a fit subject for obsessions.

In certain types of functional psychosis and neurosis the patient has an inkling of the fear instinct in his dread of objects, or of states of mind, lack of confidence, blushing, expectations of some coming misfortune and some mysterious evil, but he is not aware of the fear instinct as developed in him by the events and training of early childhood. *The fears of early childhood are subconscious.* At any rate, the patient does not connect them with his present mental affection.

In other types of psychopathic affections the patient is entirely unaware of the whole situation, he is engrossed by the symptoms which he regards as the sum and substance of his trouble; the fear is entirely subconscious. Frights, scares, dread of sickness, instructions associated with fear of the mysterious and unseen, injunctions with fear of punishment or failure in moral standards, enforcement of social customs with dread of failure and degradation,—all go to the cultivation of the fear instinct which in later life becomes manifested as *functional psychosis* or *neurosis*.

Functional psychosis or neurosis is an obsession, conscious and subconscious, of the fear instinct. Thus one of my patients became obsessed with fear of tuberculosis, manifesting most of the symptoms of "consumption," after a visit to a tubercular friend. Another patient was obsessed by the fear of death after visiting a sick relative of his in one of the city hospitals. Another became obsessed with the fear of syphilis after having been in contact with a friend who had been under antiluetic treatment. Still another of my patients, in addition to the fear of darkness, became obsessed with the fear of stars, and also with a fear of comets, regarded by some people as poisoning the air with noxious gases.

In all such cases anxiety and dread were present, but in none of the patients have I found an insight into the real state of the mind. In all of them the fear was traced to early childhood, to early experiences of the fear instinct, fostered and fortified by unfavorable conditions. In all of those fears there was a long history of a well-developed *subconscious fear instinct.*

I may assert without hesitation that in all my cases of functional psychosis, I find the presence of the fear instinct to be the sole cause of the malady. *Take away the fear and the psychosis or neurosis disappears.*

The fear instinct arises from the impulse of self-preservation without which animal life cannot exist. The fear instinct is one of the most primitive and most fundamental of all instincts. Neither hunger, nor sex, nor maternal instinct, nor social instinct can compare with the potency of the fear instinct, rooted as it is in self-preservation,—the condition of life primordial.

When the instinct of fear is at its height, it sweeps before it all other instincts. Nothing can withstand a panic. Functional psychosis in its full development is essentially a panic,—it is the emergence of the most powerful of all instincts, the fear instinct.

Functional psychosis or neurosis is a veiled form of the fear of death, of destruction, of loss of what is deemed as essential to life, of fear of some unknown, impending evil. How many times has it fallen to my share to soothe and counteract the fear instinct of panic-stricken psychopathic patients! A psychogenetic examination of every case of functional psychosis brings one invariably to the fundamental fear instinct.

Conflicts, repressions, imperfections, sex-complexes, sex-aberrations, and others do not produce psychopathic symptoms or neurotic states. It is only when mental states become associated with an exaggerated impulse of self-preservation and an intensified fear instinct that neurosis arises.

A close study of every neurotic case clearly discloses the *primary* action of those two important factors of life activity,—self-preservation and fear instinct.

CHAPTER V

THE POWER OF FEAR

The function of fear is quite clear. Fear is the guardian instinct of life. The intensity of the struggle for existence and the preservation of life of the animal are expressed in the instinct of fear. The fear instinct in its mild form, when connected with what is strange and unfamiliar, or with what is really dangerous to the animal, is of the utmost consequence to the life existence of the animal. What is strange and unfamiliar may be a menace to life, and it is a protection, if under such conditions the fear instinct is aroused.

Again, it is of the utmost importance in weak animals, such as hares or rabbits, to have the fear instinct easily aroused by the slightest, strange stimulus: the animal is defenseless, and its refuge, its safety, is in running. The unfamiliar stimulus may be a signal of danger, and it is safer to get away from it; the animal cannot take chances.

On the other hand, animals that are too timid, so that even the familiar becomes too suspicious, cannot get their food, and cannot leave a progeny,—they become eliminated by the process of natural selection. There is a certain amount of trust that nature demands even of its most defenseless and timid children.

Animals in whom the fear instinct can be aroused to a high degree become paralyzed and perish. Under such conditions the fear instinct not only ceases to be of protective value, but is the very one that brings about the destruction of the animal possessed by it. Intense fear paralyzes the animal.

"One of the most terrible effects of fear," says Mosso, "is the paralysis which allows neither of escape nor defense. Not all the phenomena of fear can be explained on the theory of natural selection. In their extreme degree they are morbid phenomena, indicating imperfection of the organism. One might almost say that nature had not been able to find a substance for brain and spinal cord which should be extremely sensitive, and yet should never, under the influence of exceptional or unusual stimuli, exceed in its reactions those physiological limits which are best adapted to the preservation of the animal." Mosso quotes Haller to the effect that "phenomena of fear common to animals are not aimed at the preservation of the timid, but at their destruction."

The fear instinct is no doubt one of the most fundamental and one of the most vital of animal instincts, but when it rises to an extreme degree, or when associated with familiar instead of strange and unfamiliar objects, then we may agree with Haller that the phenomena are not aimed at the preservation of the animal, but at its destruction; or, as Darwin puts it, are of "disservice to the animal." This is just what is found in the case of psychopathic or neurotic affections. The fear instinct, when aroused and cultivated in early childhood, becomes associated in later life with particular events, objects, and special states.

When the instinct of fear is aroused in connection with some future impending misfortune, the feeling of apprehension with all its physiological changes, muscular, respiratory, cardiac, epigastric, and intestinal, goes to form that complex feeling of anxiety so highly characteristic of the acute varieties of psychopathic maladies. When fear reaches its acme, the heart is specially affected; circulatory and respiratory changes become prominent, giving rise to that form of oppression which weighs like an incubus on the patient,—the feeling known as "precordial anxiety."

The fear instinct is the ultimate cause of functional psychosis,—it is the soil on which grow luxuriantly the infinite varieties of psychopathic disturbances. The body, sense, intellect, and will are all profoundly affected by the irresistible sweep of the fear instinct, as manifested in the overwhelming feeling of anxiety. The fear instinct and its offsprings—hesitation, anxiety, conflicts and repressions—weaken, dissociate, and paralyze the functions of the body and mind, producing the various symptoms of psychopathic diseases. The fear instinct keeps on gnawing at the very vitals of the psychopathic patient.

Even at his best the psychopathic patient is not free from the workings of the fear instinct, from the feeling of anxiety which, as the patients themselves put it, "hangs like a cloud on the margin or fringe of consciousness." From time to time he can hear the distant, threatening rumbling of the fear instinct. Even when the latter is apparently stilled, the pangs of anxiety torment the patient like a dull toothache.

Montaigne, writing of fear, says, "I am not so good a naturalist (as they call it) as to discern by what secret springs fear has its motion in us; but be this as it may, it is a strange passion, and such a one as the physicians say there is no other whatever that sooner dethrones our judgment from its proper seat; which is so true, that I myself have seen very many become frantic through fear; and even in those of the best settled temper, it is most certain that it begets a terrible confusion during the fit. Even among soldiers, a sort of men over whom, of all others, it ought to have the least power, how often has it converted flocks of sheep into armed squadrons, reeds and bullrushes into pikes and lances, and friends into enemies....

"The thing in the world I am most afraid of is fear. That passion alone, in the trouble of it, exceeding all other accidents. Such as have been well banged in some skirmish, may yet, all wounded and bloody as they are, be brought on again the next day to the charge; but such as have once conceived a good sound fear of the enemy will never be made so much as to look the enemy in the face. Such as are in immediate fear of losing their estates, of banishment or of slavery, live in perpetual anguish, and lose all appetite and repose. And the many people who, impatient of perpetual alarms of fear, have hanged or drowned themselves, or dashed themselves to pieces, give us sufficiently to understand that fear is more importunate and insupportable than death itself."

A well known writer, who is a psychopathic sufferer, writes: "Carlyle laid his finger upon the truth, when he said that the reason why the pictures of the past were always so golden in tone, so delicate in outline, was because the quality of fear was taken from them. It is the fear of what may be and what must be that overshadows present happiness; and if fear is taken from us, we are happy. The strange thing is that we can not learn not to be afraid, even though all the darkest and saddest of our experiences have left us unscathed; and if we could but find a reason for the mingling of fear with our lives, we should have gone towards the solving of the riddle of the world."

Anxiety states of neuroses and psychoses are essentially clue to the awakening of the fear instinct, normally present in every living being. The fear instinct is a fundamental one; it is only inhibited by the whole course of civilization and by the training and education of life. Like the jinn of the "Arabian Nights," it slumbers in the breast of every normal individual, and comes fully to life in the various neuroses and psychoses.

Kraepelin and his school lay special stress on the fact that "Fear is by far the most important persistent emotion in morbid conditions.... Fear is manifested by anxious excitement and by anxious tension." "Experience," says Kraepelin, "shows an intimate relationship between insistent psychosis and the so-called 'phobias,' the *anxiety states* which in such patients become associated with definite impressions, actions, and views." The states are associated with the thought of some unknown danger. Violent heart action, pallor, a feeling of anxiety, tremor, cold sweat, meteorisms, diarrhœa, polyuria, weakness in the legs, fainting spells, attack the patient, who may lose control of his limbs and occasionally suffer complete collapse.

"These states," says Kraepelin, with his usual insight into abnormal mental life, "remind one of the feeling of anxiety which in the case of healthy people may, in view of a painful situation or of a serious danger, deprive one of the calmness of judgment and confidence in his movements."

Thus, we find from different standpoints that the feeling of anxiety with its accompanying phenomena is one of the most potent manifestations of animal instincts, the fear instinct, which is at the basis of all psychopathic, neurotic maladies.

The fear instinct, as the subtle and basic instinct of life, is well described by Kipling:—

> Very softly down the glade runs a waiting, watching shade,
> And the whisper spreads and widens far and near;
> And the sweat is on thy brow, for he passes even now—
> He is Fear, O Little Hunter, he is Fear!

> Ere the moon has climbed the mountain, ere the rocks are ribbed with light,
> When the downward dipping trails are dank and drear,
> Comes a breathing hard behind thee—*snuffle—snuffle* through the night—
> It is Fear, O Little Hunter, it is Fear!
>
> On thy knees and draw the bow; bid the shrilling arrow go:
> In the empty, mocking thicket plunge the spear;
> But thy hands are loosed and weak, and the blood has left thy cheek—
> It is Fear, O Little Hunter, it is Fear!
>
> When the heat-cloud sucks the tempest, when the slivered pine trees fall,
> When the blinding, blaring rain-squalls lash and veer;
> Through the war gongs of the thunder rings a voice more loud than all—
> It is Fear, O Little Hunter, it is Fear!
>
> Now the spates are banked and deep; now the footless boulders leap—
> Now the lightning shows each littlest leaf-rib clear;
> But thy throat is shut and dried, and thy heart against thy side
> Hammers: Fear, O Little Hunter,—This is Fear!

It is interesting to learn what a practical and thoughtful surgeon, such as George Crile, has to say on the matter of fear. Dr. Crile lays stress on the facts that in his researches he finds evidence that the phenomena of fear have a physical basis similar to those morphological changes in the brain cells observed in certain stages of surgical shock and in fatigue.... That the brain is definitely damaged by fear may be proved by experiments.

"According to Sherrington the nervous system responds in action as a whole, and to but one stimulus at a time.... Under the influence of fear or (fear of) injury the integration of the common path is most nearly absolute.... Hence fear and injury (or fear of injury) drain the cup of energy to the dregs....

"We can understand why it is a patient consumed by fear suffers so many bodily impairments, (so many functional disturbances) and diseases even. We can understand the grave digestive and metabolic disturbances under strain of fear.... We can understand the variations in the gastric analyses in a timid patient alarmed over his condition and afraid of the hospital. The patient is integrated by fear, and since fear takes precedence over all other impulses, no organ can function normally (under the influence of fear)" ... Dr. Crile arrives at the conclusion that "Fear dominates the various organs and parts of the body...."

Dr. Crile lays special stress on the pathological character of the fear instinct: "That the brain is definitely influenced, damaged even, by fear has been proved by the following experiments: Rabbits were frightened by a dog, but were neither injured nor chased. After various periods of time the animals were killed and their brain cells compared with the brain cells of normal animals, widespread changes were seen (in the brain cells of the animals affected by fear). The principal clinical phenomena expressed by the rabbits were rapid heart, accelerated respiration, prostration, tremors, and a rise in temperature. The dog showed similar phenomena, excepting that, instead of such muscular relaxation as was shown by the rabbit, it exhibited aggressive muscular action."

Animals in which the fear instinct can be aroused to a high degree become paralyzed and perish. The animal mechanism is by no means perfect. A stab in the heart, a rip in the abdomen, a cut of the carotids, a prick in the medulla, a scratch of a needle infected with anthrax, or tetanus bacilli, a drop of hydrocyanic acid, an arrow tipped with curare, extinguish every spark of life. Organic material may be delicate and complex, but for that reason it is highly imperfect and vulnerable.

Living matter is the feeblest material in nature, and is as fragile as a delicate crystal vase. Protoplasm, or living matter, may be wonderful material, but it can be crushed with a pebble. The most beautiful colors may be displayed by a thin, delicate bubble, but it bursts at the least touch. Living matter is like a bubble, like foam on the ocean. Perhaps no better material is available for the functions of life.

Meanwhile it remains true that the flimsiness of living material makes it easily subject to decay and destruction. It is a profound error, having its root in prejudice, that nature always helps, and that the processes going on in the organism are always of benefit to the individual. Nature is as ready to destroy life as to protect it.

Preservation or destruction of a particular individual depends on the fact as to whether or no normal or pathological processes predominate in the total economy of the organism. This holds true of the fear instinct. The fear instinct is a delicate mechanism, and when its action is slightly intensified, the animal is on the way to destruction. For the cosmic forces are careless of the creatures which keep on pouring forth in generous profusion from the lap of nature.

Living matter, or protoplasm can only exist under special, restricted conditions,—the least variation means death. The more complicated, and more organized protoplasm is, the more restricted are the conditions of its existence. A rise of a couple of degrees of temperature or a fall means disease and death. The same holds true of the rise and fall of quantity and quality of bodily secretion of glands and of other organs. Protoplasm can only exist in an *optimum* environment. Any change spells disease and death.

The fear instinct, being at the heart of highly organized life activities, is delicately responsive to any changes and variations from the *optimum*, requisite for the proper functioning of the organism. Any deviation from the *optimum* environment, external or internal, produces corresponding changes in the fear instinct with consequent pathological changes in the organism.

The fear instinct like a delicate indicator is the first to get deranged, with harmful results to the organism as a whole. We can thus realize the importance of keeping the fear instinct in good condition. We can understand the significance of Plato's doctrine of rational guidance of the fear instinct. "What to fear and what not to fear" is at the basis of all organized life, individual and social.[3]

FOOTNOTE:

[3] See my work "The Source and Aim of Human Progress."

CHAPTER VI

FEAR AND DISEASE

If we examine closely the symptoms of fear, we invariably find the symptoms of functional psychosis or neurosis. Fear affects the muscular and sensory systems, the vasomotor system, the respiratory system, the sudorific glands, the viscera, the heart, the intestines, all organs and functions of the organism.

Bain, in describing the emotions of fear or terror, says, "Terror on the physical side shows both a loss and a transfer of nervous energy. The appearances may be distributed between the effects of relaxation and effects of tension. The relaxation is seen, as regards the muscles, in the dropping of the jaw, in the collapse overtaking all organs not specially excited, in trembling of the lips and other parts, and in the loosening of the sphincters. Next, as regards the organic processes and viscera. The digestion is everywhere weakened; the flow of saliva is checked, the gastric secretion arrested (appetite failing), the bowels deranged; the respiration is enfeebled. The heart and circulation are disturbed; there is either a flushing of the face or a deadly pallor. The skin shows symptoms—the cold sweat, the altered odor of the perspiration, the creeping action that lifts the hair. The kidneys are directly or indirectly affected. The sexual organs feel the depressing influence. The secretion of milk in the mother's breast is vitiated."

Darwin gives the following description of fear:—

"The frightened man at first stands like a statue, motionless and breathless, or crouches down as if to escape observation. The heart beats quickly and violently, but it is very doubtful if it then works more efficiently than usual so as to send a greater supply of blood to the body; for the skin instantly becomes pale, as during incipient faintness. The paleness of the surface, however, is probably in large part or is exclusively due to the vasomotor center being affected in such a manner as to cause the contraction of the small arteries of the skin. That the skin is much affected under the sense of great fear we see in the marvelous manner in which the perspiration immediately exudes from it. This exudation is all the more remarkable as the surface is then cold, and hence the term, a cold sweat; whereas the sudorofic glands are properly excited into action when the surface is heated. The hairs also on the skin stand erect, and the superficial muscles shiver. In connection with the disturbed action of the heart the breathing is hurried. The salivary glands act imperfectly; the mouth becomes dry and is often opened and shut. I have also noticed that under slight fear there is a slight tendency to yawn. One of the best symptoms is the trembling of all the muscles of the body. From this cause and from the dryness of the mouth, the voice becomes husky or indistinct, or may altogether fail."

If we turn now to the manifestations of psychopathic maladies, we meet with the same fear symptoms:—

(a) The attacks may be muscular, involving symptoms such as trembling, shaking, paresis, paralysis, or rigidity; there may be affection of locomotion or of muscular co-ordination.

(b) There may be sensory disturbances,—anesthesia, paresthesia, analgesia, or hyperalgesia as well as affection of muscular sense and kinesthesia.

(c) There may be skin disturbances, such as arrest of perspiration or profuse perspiration, especially under the influence of emotions, worry, and fatigue; such perspiration may also occur at night, and in some cases the fear of tuberculosis may be associated with such conditions.

(d) The lungs may become affected functionally, and there may occur respiratory disturbances; coughing, hawking, apnea, dyspnea, and asthmatic troubles.

(e) The heart becomes affected, bringing about precordial pain; palpitation of the heart, bradycardia, tachycardia, and cardiac arrhythmia.

(f) The stomach and intestines become affected, indigestion and vague fugitive soreness and pain may be experienced all over or in special regions of the abdomen; constipation or diarrhea may ensue.

(g) The renal apparatus may become affected and its activity arrested, or, as is more often the case in the milder forms of psychopathic troubles, there may be present an alteration in the amount or frequency of micturition, such as is found in the conditions of anuria and polyuria.

(h) Menstruation becomes disturbed, and we may meet with conditions of dysmenorrhea, amenorrhea, menorrhagia, and other disturbances of the tubes, ovaries, and uterus.

(i) There are disturbances of the nervous system, such as headache and a general dull sensation of fatigue and paresis of all mental functions, with dizziness and vertigo.

On the mental side we find in the psychopathies the following disturbances:—

(a) Affections of perceptual activity,—illusions and hallucinations.

(b) Affections of intellectual activity,—argumentativeness in regard to insignificant things.

(c) Affections of the moral sense,—scrupulousness, over-conscientiousness, not living up to ideal states.

(d) Affections of religious life,—fear of commission of sins and terror of punishment.

(e) Affections of social life,—timidity, blushing, etc.

(f) Affections in regard to objects, such as astrophobia, acmephobia, agoraphobia, claustrophobia, etc.

(g) Affections of conceptual life,—insistent ideas.

(h) Affections of the attention,—aprosexia.

(i) Affections of the will,—states of aboulia, indecision, discord, conflicts, and uncontrollable impulses.

(j) Affections of the memory,—amnesic and paramnesic states.

(k) General mental fatigue.

(l) Affections of sexual life,—impotence, perversion, and inversion.

(m) Affections in regard to marital relations.

(n) Affections in regard to personal life,—diffidence, self-condemnation, self-depreciation.

(o) Affections of apparent loss of personality,—feeling of self gone.

(p) Formation of new personalities,—dual and multiple personality.

In connection with all such neurotic affections we find invariably present a feeling of unrest, hesitation, doubt, conflict, discord, uneasiness, a feeling of anxiety, *conscious or subconscious*, feeling of some impending evil. In all such affections we find the brooding spirit of the most powerful of all animal instincts,—the fear instinct. *Neurosis is a disease of self-preservation and fear.*

CHAPTER VII

FORMS OF NEUROSIS

A brief outline of a classification of nervous and mental diseases, made by me in my various works, may be of help towards a clear understanding of neurotic disturbances.

The different forms of nervous and mental diseases may be classified into *Organic* and *Functional*.

By *organic* affections I mean to indicate pathological modifications of the neuron and its processes taking place in the very structure (probably the cytoreticulum) of the nerve cell. Under this category come such maladies as general paresis, dementia praecox, all mental and nervous affections of a degenerative and involutionary character. Such diseases are termed by me *Organopathies*, or *Necropathies*.

By *functional* affections I mean to indicate all neuron changes in which the functions of the neuron and its reactions to external and internal stimulations are involved in the pathological process without, however, affecting the anatomical structure of the nerve cell. The pathological changes are not permanent,—recovery of normal function is possible with the restitution of favorable conditions of nutrition and elimination.

Functional nervous and mental diseases are in turn subdivided into *Neuropathies* and *Psychopathies*.

Neuropathic diseases are disturbances of functioning activity, due to defective neuron matabolism, brought about by external stimuli, and more specially by harmful internal stimuli—glandular secretions, hormones, toxic and autotoxic agencies. The pathological, neuropathic process produces few, if any anatomical, changes in the structure of the neuron. The pathology of neuropathic diseases, (probably of the cytoplasm) is essentially *chemico-physiological* in nature.

Neuropathic diseases include maladies in which the neuron undergoes degenerative changes. At first there is an apparent increase, then an inhibition, and finally a complete suspension of neuron function, not terminating in the destruction of the neuron. Neuron restitution is possible.

Such affections are produced by mild poisons, organic, or inorganic, by autotoxic products, by hyposecretion or hypersecretion, or by absence of hormones in the economy of the organism. Here belong all the temporary, or recurrent maniacal, melancholic, delusional states, puerperal mania, epileptic insanity, the mental aberrations of adolescent and climacteric periods, periodic insanity, alternating insanities, and in general all the mental affections known under the description of manic-depressive insanity.

Where the disease depends on the *interrelation* of neurons in a complex group, on *association of systems* of neurons, the condition is *psychopathic* in nature.

In psychopathic troubles the neuron itself may remain unaffected, may be perfectly normal and healthy. The disorder is due to association with systems of neurons which are usually not called into action by the function of that particular neuron system.

By *Organopathies* or *Necropathies* I indicate a group of psychophysiological symptoms, accompanied by structural, necrotic changes of the neuron, terminating in the ultimate death of the neuron systems, involved in the pathological process.

By *Neuropathies* I indicate a group of psychophysiological manifestations due to pathological functional neuron modifications, capable of restitution through normal metabolism.

By *Psychopathies* I designate pathological phenomena of psychophysiological dissociation and disaggregation of neuron systems and their functions in clusters, the neuron itself and its special function remaining undamaged.

The psychopathies are further subdivided into *Somatopsychoses* and *Psychoneuroses* or *Neuropsychoses*.

The *Somatopsychoses are characterized by somatic symptoms*, by disturbances of bodily functions, such as paralysis, contractures, convulsions, anesthesia, analgesia, hyperalgesia, and other sensory disturbances, as well as by intestinal, cardiac, respiratory, and genito-urinary troubles.

The *psychoneuroses or Neuropsychoses are characterized by mental symptoms*. The patient's whole mind is occupied with mental troubles.

Such conditions are found in obsessions, fixed ideas, imperative impulses, emotional compulsions, and other allied mental and nervous maladies.

Somatopsychoses simulate physical and organic nervous troubles. Thus, many "hysterical" forms simulate tabes, or paralysis agitans, hemiplegia, paraplegia, or epilepsy, while many of the neurasthenic, hypochondriacal, and their allied states may simulate tumor, cancer, intestinal and glandular derangements, cardiac, laryngeal, pneumonic, hepatic, splanchnic ovarian, tubal, uterine, renal, and other bodily afflictions.

The neuropsychoses or psychoneuroses simulate all forms of mental disease, beginning with melancholia and mania, and ending with general paresis and dementia.

Psychoneurosis and *somatopsychosis* are diseases of the subconscious; in the former mental, in the latter physical symptoms predominate.

Psychopathic states should be rigidly differentiated from other disturbances, such as neuropathies and organopathies, or necropathies. The following diagram may be of help:

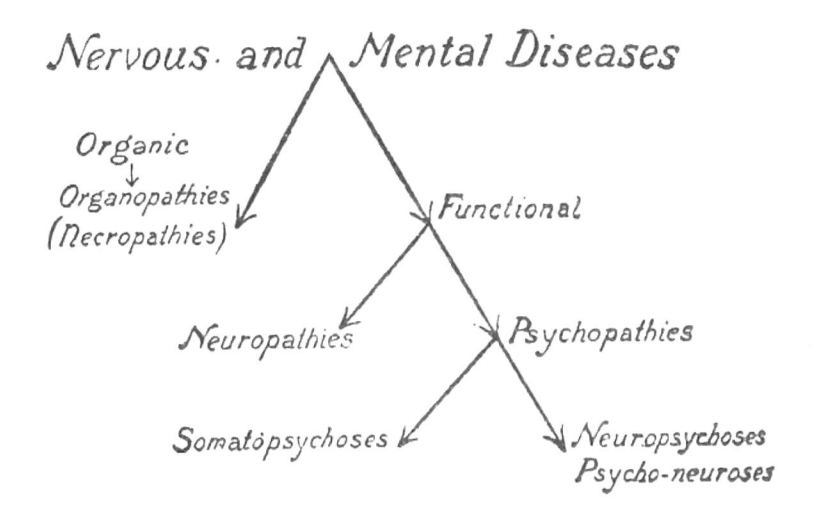

```
        Nervous and Mental Diseases
                  /\
                 /  \
       Organic  /    \
          ↓    /      \  Functional
   Organopathies       
   (Necropathies)       
                 \      /\
                  \    /  \
           Neuropathies   Psychopathies
                    \    /        \
                     \  /          \
              Somatopsychoses    Neuropsychoses
                                 Psycho-neuroses
```

Nervous and Mental Diseases
DIAGRAM I

CHAPTER VIII

FEAR AND THE HYPNOIDAL STATE

In my work on "Sleep" I report a series of interesting experiments carried out by me on guinea pigs, rabbits, cats, dogs, children, and adults.[4] I discovered one of the most important states of animal life, a state which I termed *hypnoidal*.

The study shows that in almost every animal, from the lowest to the highest, from frog to man, a somewhat sudden change of the usual environment deprives that animal of its activities and its functions. If the change is not too intense and prolonged, the animal merges into the hypnoidal state in which the lost functions are restored. During this hypnoidal state the functions are weakened, the animal may be regarded in a state of invalidism, its reactions being enfeebled, practically speaking, paretic.

Perhaps it is advisable to approach the phenomena from their more striking aspect. In seizing a triton, salamander, or frog, and stretching it on the table, one will observe with surprise that the animal remains in the same position given it. The most uncomfortable and bizarre position may be given to the limbs, and still the animal will not move. Testing the extremities one finds them rigid and resisting. Something similar we find in the hypnotic condition, when under the suggestion that the extremities are rigid, and they cannot be moved by the subject. The same can be done with a lobster and other animals of the same type.

Everyone has heard of the *experimentum mirabile* made by Kirchner in the seventeenth century. A rooster or hen is seized, the legs are tied with a string and the bird is put on the ground. A piece of chalk is passed over the beak,—the chalk tracing a line from beak to some distant point on the ground. When the bird is released, it remains in the same position. Some explain that the animal is kept prisoner, because it "imagines" that it is bound by the line of chalk. The chalk, however, is unnecessary. The animal may be seized, shouted in its ear, or kept down forcibly, and the same result will happen. This state has been termed by Preyer "cataplexy." The phenomenon can also be produced in insects, in mollusca.

Many investigators have been interested in this phenomenon. I have devoted a good deal of work to this condition which is also found in mammals in which it is induced by the fear instinct. In mammals, however, the state of cataplexy is not necessarily accompanied by rigidity, although it may be present, but there is a complete loss of voluntary activity. Horses tremble violently and become paralyzed at the sight of a beast of prey, such as a tiger or a lion. At the sight of a serpent, monkeys are known to be in such an intense state of fear that they are unable to move, and thus fall easy victims to the reptile.

Under similar conditions birds are so paralyzed by fear that they are unable to fly away from the source of danger, and fall a prey to the threatening serpent. The birds resemble very much the hypnotized subject in a state of catalepsy. Although the gibbons are the most agile of all the simians, they are easily taken by surprise, and captured without any resistance,—they are paralyzed by fear. Seals when pursued on land become so frightened that they are unable to offer any opposition to their pursuers, and let themselves easily be captured and killed.

In large cities one can often witness nervous people affected suddenly by the presence of danger; they remain immobile, in the middle of the street, becoming exposed to fatal accidents. The fear instinct paralyzes their activities, they are petrified with terror.

I was told by people who have experienced the effects of earthquakes, that during the time of the earthquakes they were unable to move, and the same condition was observed in animals, especially in young dogs. It is hard to move cattle and horses from a burning stable, on account of the fear of fire which obsesses the animals, so that they become paralyzed, suffocated and burnt to death. So vital is the fear instinct that the least deviation from the normal state is apt to play havoc with the safety of the individual.

The fear instinct is the most primitive, the most fundamental, and the most powerful of all instincts. When the fear instinct is let loose, the animal succumbs. We should not wonder, therefore, that with the aberration of the fear instinct, the life guardian of the individual, all orientation is lost, the animal becomes demoralized, and the organism goes to destruction. No other instinct can surpass the fear instinct in its fatal effects.

The more one studies the facts, the more one examines various psychopathic, functional maladies, without going into any speculations and without being blinded by foregone conclusions and pseudo-scientific hypotheses, the more one is driven to the conclusion that the fear instinct is at the bottom of all those nervous and mental aberrations, conscious and subconscious.

The infinite varieties of functional psychopathic diseases are the consequences of some abnormal association with the fear instinct which alone gives rise to the infirmities characteristic of functional mental maladies.

President Stanley Hall accepts my view of the subject. In a recent paper he writes: "If there be a vital principle, fear must be one of its close allies as one of the chief springs of the mind".... In spite of his former psychoanalytic inclinations President Hall asserts now that "Freud is wrong in interpreting this most generic form of fear as rooted in sex. *Sex anxieties themselves are rooted in the larger fundamental impulse of self-preservation with its concomitant instinct of fear.*" This is precisely the factor and the teaching which I have been expounding in all my works on Psychopathology.

So deeply convinced is Professor Stanley Hall of the primitive and fundamental character of the fear instinct, that he refers to the facts that "if the cerebrum is removed, animals, as Goltz and Bechterev have proved, manifest very intense symptoms of fear, and so do human monsters born without brains, of hemicephalic children, as Sternberg and Lotzko have demonstrated."

The fear instinct is of such vital importance that it is found in animals after decerebration, and persists in animals after spino-vago-sympathetic section. Sherrington found the fear instinct present in dogs after section of the spinal cord and also after complete section of the vago-sympathetic nerves, thus removing all sensations coming from the viscera, muscles, and skin, below the shoulder, leaving only the sensations from the front paws, head and cerebral activity. The dog was a sort of cerebral animal. The whole body below the shoulder, skin, muscle, viscera, were all anaesthetic, and yet the fear instinct remained intact.

On the other hand, after complete ablation of the cerebral hemispheres of the dog, so that the animal became spinal, all cerebral functions being totally wiped out, Goltz invariably found that the fear instinct remained unimpaired. *The fear instinct is inherent in animal life— existence. As long as there is life, there is fear.*

So potent, all embracing, and all pervading is the fear instinct, that the physician must reckon with it in his private office, in the hospital, and in the surgical operating room. In a number of my cases psychognosis, the study and examination of mental states, clearly reveals the fact that even where the neurosis has not originated in a surgical trauma, surgical operations reinforced, developed, and fixed psychopathic conditions.

The fear instinct is one of the most primitive and most fundamental of all instincts. Neither hunger, nor sex, nor maternal instinct, nor social instinct can compare with the potency of the fear instinct, rooted as it is in the conditions of life primordial.

When the instinct of fear is at its height it sweeps before it all other instincts. Nothing can withstand a panic. Functional psychosis in its full development is essentially a panic. A psychogenetic examination of every case of functional psychosis brings one invariably to the basic instinct of life, self preservation and the fear instinct.

As Whittier puts it:

Still behind the tread I hear
Of my life companion, Fear,
Still a shadow, deep and vast
From my westering feet is cast;
Wavering, doubtful, undefined,
Never shapen, nor outlined.
From myself the Fear has grown,
And the shadow is my own.

FOOTNOTE:

[4] The experimental work was carried on by me at the physiological laboratory, Harvard Medical School, and in my private laboratory, and published in my work on "Sleep."

CHAPTER IX

HEALTH AND MORBIDITY

While health cannot be separated from disease by a sharp line, the two are relative and fluctuating. Still, on the whole, the two can be differentiated by the criterion of hurt and dissolution. Any process or state conducive to hurt, and tending to dissolution of the organism may be regarded as pathological or abnormal. The same criterion should be applied, when differentiating the healthy, normal states of instincts and emotions from abnormal and morbid states of instinctive and emotional activities. Those states that further life activities are healthy, normal; those that hinder life are morbid.

The same holds true of the fear instinct. Every form of fear which, instead of helping or furthering vigor of life, instead of stimulating living energy, instead of being a protection, becomes a hindrance, a menace to the organism, is accompanied with suffering and distress, and ultimately leads to destruction, should be regarded as essentially morbid.

The following are the chief characteristics of morbid instinctive and emotional states:

I. When they are *disproportionate* to the cause.

II. When they are chronic.

III. When their feeling-tone is *painful, distressing*.

IV. When they are *non-adaptive* to the stimulations.

V. When the reactions are *not adjusted* to the external environment.

VI. When they are *uncontrollable*.

VII. When coming in *recurrent* or *periodic attacks*.

VIII. When the physical and mental reactions are of *great intensity*.

IX. When they are *dissociative*.

X. When they lead to *dissolution*.

Fear is not a matter of belief. To regard fear as a form of belief, is fallacious, dangerous, and suicidal. It is as dangerous as to consider smallpox and cholera the result of faith. We must never forget that fear is one of the most fundamental of animal instincts having its roots deep down in animal life existence. To ignore this fact is suicidal.

According to the great anthropologist, Galton: "Every antelope in South Africa has to run for its life every one or two days, and the antelope starts and gallops under the influence of a false alarm many times a day. Fear is a fundamental condition of animal existence."

The fear instinct in its healthy normal state is a protection and defense. As Ribot puts it: "The basis of fear exists in the organism, forms part of the constitution of animals and man, and helps them to live by a defensive adaptation:" In fact, we may even go to the point of affirming that the fear instinct, like all other healthy, normal instincts, is absolutely requisite in the total economy of animal and human life.

In man, however, fear should not be at the mercy of blind animal instincts and reflexes, but should be guided and controlled by reason, by reflection, by scientific, medical measures, by scientific sanitation, by physical and mental hygiene, and by the rational cultivation and development of all human functions and faculties.

One of the greatest Greek thinkers well puts it: "Imbeciles, fools, and the mad alone have no understanding of fear. True education, true reason, and true courage consist in the knowledge of what to fear and what not to fear."

Mysticism, occultism, and credulity act like virulent germs, fatal to man. "Metaphysical" cults anesthetize the intellect, put judgment into lethargic sleep from which there is no awaking. Mysticism kills the most precious essence of man's life,—the critical sense of human personality.

Occultism, mysticism, *et id genus omne* declare that "fear is a false belief, an error of the mortal mind." Mystics claim the "unreality" of the material fear instinct of which they are in "reality" in "mortal" terror. This zealous negation of fear is its strongest affirmation.

As a matter of fact, fear is one of the most stern realities of life. The neurotic in denying disease, evil, and fear is like the proverbial ostrich which on perceiving danger hides its head in the sand. *The "Love" of mysticism is the Fear of death.*

CHAPTER X

THE SUBCONSCIOUS[5]

Man's nerve cell organization may be classified into two main systems:

(I) The inferior, the reflex, the instinctive, the automatic centers.

(II) The superior, the controlling, selective, and inhibitory brain-centers of the cortex.

The double systems of nerve-centers have correspondingly a double mental activity, or double-consciousness as it is sometimes called, the inferior, the organic, the instinctive, the automatic, the reflex consciousness, or briefly termed the *subconsciousness*, consciousness below the threshold of self-consciousness; and the superior, the choosing, the willing, the critical, the *will-consciousness*. This controlling will-consciousness may also be characterized as the guardian-consciousness of the individual.

From an evolutionary standpoint, we can well realize the biological function or importance of this guardian-consciousness. The external world bombards the living organism with innumerable stimuli. From all sides thousands of impressions come crowding upon the senses of the individual. Each neuron system with its appropriate receptors has its corresponding system of reactions which, if not modified or counteracted, may end in some harmful or fatal result.

It is not of advantage to an individual of a complex organization to respond with reaction to all impressions coming from the external environment. Hence, that organism will succeed best in the struggle for existence that possesses some selective, critical, inhibitory "choice and will" centers. The more organized and the more sensitive and delicate those centers are, the better will the organism succeed in its life existence.

The guardian-consciousness wards off, so far as it is possible, the harmful blows given by the stimuli of the external environment. In man, this same guardian consciousness keeps on constructing, by a series of elimination and selection, a new environment, individual and social, which leads to an ever higher and more perfect development and realization of the inner powers of individuality and personality.

Under normal conditions man's superior and inferior centers with their corresponding upper, critical, controlling consciousness together with the inferior automatic, reflex centers and their concomitant subconscious consciousness, keep on functioning in full harmony. The upper and lower consciousness form one organic unity,—one conscious, active personality.

Under certain abnormal conditions, however, the two systems of nerve-centers with their corresponding mental activities may become dissociated. The superior nerve-centers with their critical, controlling consciousness may become inhibited, split off from the rest of the nervous system. The reflex, automatic, instinctive, subconscious centers with their mental functions are laid bare, thus becoming directly accessible to the stimuli of the outside world; they fall a prey to the influences of external surroundings, influences termed *suggestions*.

The critical, controlling, guardian-consciousness, being cut off and absent, the reduced individuality lacks the rational guidance and orientation given by the upper choice- and will-centers, and becomes the helpless plaything of all sorts of suggestions, sinking into the *trance states of the subconscious. It is this subconscious that forms the highway of suggestions.* Suggestibility is the essential characteristic of the subconscious.

The subconscious rises to the surface of consciousness, so to say, whenever there is a weakening, paralysis, or inhibition of the upper, controlling will and choice-centers. In other words, whenever there is a disaggregation of the superior from the inferior nerve-centers, there follows an increase of ideo-sensory, ideo-motor, sensori-secretory, reflex excitability; and ideationally, or rationally there is present an abnormal intensity of suggestibility.[6]

FOOTNOTES:

[5] The theory of the subconscious was first developed by me in my volume "The Psychology of Suggestion," 1898.

[6] I object to the term "Subliminal," because it is understood in a cosmic, or metaphysical sense. The term "co-conscious" is limited and refers to independently functioning, contemporaneous personalities, or mental systems. The term "Unconscious" is *misleading*, because it may refer to the metaphysics of Hartmann. At best it simply means nervous processes which, as such, belong to neurology, physiology, but not to the domain of abnormal psychology.

The term "subconscious," used by me in "The Psychology of Suggestion," means *tracts of mental states which may or may not function in the total mental reaction of the individual.*

CHAPTER XI

THE CONDITIONS AND LAWS OF SUGGESTION

In order to bring to the fore subconscious activities with their reflex, automatic psycho-motor reactions by removal of the upper consciousness I have found requisite, in my investigations, the following conditions:

Normal Suggestibility,—Suggestibility in the Normal, Waking State.

(1) Fixation of the Attention.

(2) Distraction of the Attention.

(3) Monotony.

(4) Limitation of Voluntary Activity.

(5) Limitation of the Field of Consciousness.

(6) Inhibition.

(7) Immediate Execution of the Suggestion.

Abnormal Suggestibility,—Suggestibility in Hypnotic and Trance States:

(1) Fixation of the Attention.

(2) Monotony.

(3) Limitation of Voluntary Activity.

(4) Limitation of the Field of Consciousness.

(5) Inhibition.

The nature of abnormal suggestibility, the result of my investigations, is a disaggregation of consciousness, a cleavage of the mind, a cleft that may become ever deeper and wider, ending in a total disjunction of the waking, guiding, controlling guardian-consciousness from the automatic, reflex, subconscious consciousness....

Normal suggestibility is of like nature,—it is a cleft in the mind. Only here the cleft is not so deep, not so lasting as in hypnosis or in the other subconscious trance states. The split is but momentary. The mental cleavage, or the psycho-physiological disaggregation of the superior from the inferior centers with their concomitant psychic activities is evanescent, fleeting, often disappearing at the moment of its appearance.

The following laws of suggestibility were formulated by me:

I. *Normal suggestibility varies as indirect suggestion and inversely as direct suggestion.*

II. *Abnormal suggestibility varies as direct suggestion and inversely as indirect suggestion.*

A comparison of the conditions of normal and abnormal suggestibility is valuable, since it reveals the nature of suggestibility, and discloses its fundamental law. An examination of the two sets of conditions shows that in abnormal suggestibility two conditions, distraction of attention and immediate execution are absent, otherwise the conditions are the same. This sameness of conditions clearly indicates the fact that both normal and abnormal suggestibility flow from some one common source, that they are of like nature, and due to similar causes.

Now a previous study led us to the conclusion that the nature of abnormal suggestibility is a disaggregation of consciousness, a slit produced in the mind, a crack that may become wider and deeper, ending in a total disjunction of the waking, guiding, controlling consciousness from the reflex consciousness. Normal suggestibility is of a like nature. It is a cleft in the mind. The cleft is not so deep, not so lasting as it is in hypnosis, or in the state of abnormal suggestibility. The split is but momentary, disappearing almost at the very moment of its appearance.

This fleeting, evanescent character of the split explains why suggestion in the normal state, why normal suggestibility requires immediate execution as one of its indispensable conditions. We must take the opportunity of the momentary ebb of the controlling consciousness and hastily plant our suggestion in the soil of reflex consciousness. We must watch for this favorable moment, not let it slip by, otherwise the suggestion is a failure. Furthermore, we must be careful to keep in abeyance, for the moment, the ever active waves of the controlling consciousness. We must find for them work in some other direction, we must divert, we must distract them. That is why normal suggestibility requires the additional conditions of distraction and immediate execution. For in the waking state the waking, controlling consciousness is always on its guard, and when enticed away, leaves its ground only for a moment.

In normal suggestibility the psychic split is but faint; the lesion, effected in the body consciousness, is superficial, transitory, fleeting. In abnormal suggestibility, on the contrary, the slit is deep and lasting,—it is a severe gash. In both cases, however, we have a removal, a dissociation of the waking from the subwaking, reflex consciousness, suggestion becoming effected only through the latter. For suggestibility is the attribute of the subwaking, reflex consciousness.

A comparison of the two laws discloses the same relation. The two laws are the reverse of each other, thus clearly indicating the presence of a controlling, inhibiting, conscious element in one case, and its absence in the other.

In the normal state we must guard against the inhibitory, waking consciousness, and we have to make our suggestion as indirect as possible. In the abnormal state, on the contrary, no circumspection is needed; the controlling, inhibitory, waking consciousness is more or less absent. The subwaking, reflex consciousness is exposed to external stimuli, and our suggestions are therefore the more effective, the more direct we make them.

Suggestibility is a function of disaggregation of consciousness, a disaggregation in which the subwaking, reflex consciousness enters into direct communication with the external world. The general law of suggestibility is:

Suggestibility varies as the amount of disaggregation, and inversely as the unification of consciousness.

CHAPTER XII

IS THE SUBCONSCIOUS A PERSONALITY?

The problem that interested me most was to come into close contact with the subwaking self. What is its fundamental nature? What are the main traits of its character? Since in hypnosis the subwaking self is freed from its chains, is untrammeled by the shackles of the upper, controlling self, since in hypnosis the underground self is more or less exposed to our view, it is plain that experimentation on the hypnotic self will introduce us into the secret life of the subwaking self. For, as we pointed out, the two are identical.

I have made all kinds of experiments, bringing subjects into catalepsy, somnambulism, giving illusions, hallucinations, post-hypnotic suggestions, etc. As a result of my work one central truth stands out clear, and that is the *extraordinary plasticity of the subwaking self.*

If you can only in some way or other succeed in separating the primary controlling consciousness from the lower one, the waking from the subwaking self, so that they should no longer keep company, you can do anything you please with the subwaking self. You can make its legs, its hands, any limb you like perfectly rigid; you can make it eat pepper for sugar; you can make it drink water for wine; feel cold or warm; hear delightful stories in the absence of all sounds; feel pain or pleasure, see oranges where there is nothing; you can make it eat them and enjoy their taste. In short, you can do with the subwaking self anything you like. The subwaking consciousness is in your power, like clay in the hands of the potter. The plasticity of the subconscious is revealed by its extreme suggestibility.

I wanted to get an insight into the very nature of the subwaking self; I wished to make a personal acquaintance with it. "What is its *personal* character?" I asked. How surprised I was when, after a close interrogation, the answer came to me that there cannot possibly be any personal acquaintance with it,—for *the subwaking self lacks personality*.

Under certain conditions a cleavage may occur between the two selves, and then the subwaking self may rapidly grow, develop, and attain, apparently, the plane of self-consciousness, get crystallized into a person, and give itself a name, imaginary, or borrowed from history. This accounts for the spiritualistic phenomena of personality, guides, controls, and communications by dead personalities, or spirits coming from another world, such as have been observed in the case of Mrs. Piper and other mediums of like types; it accounts for all the phenomena of multiple personality, simulating the dead or the living, or formed anew out of the matrix of the subconscious.

All such personality metamorphoses can be easily developed, under favorable conditions in any psychopathological laboratory. They can be easily formed, by suggestion in trance, hypnotic, and waking states. The newly crystallized personality is, as a rule, extremely unstable, ephemeral, shadowy in its outlines, spirit-like, ghost-like, tends to become amorphous, being formed again and again under the influence of favorable conditions and suggestions, rising to the surface of consciousness, then sinking into the subconsciousness, and disappearing, only to give rise to new personality-metamorphoses, bursting like so many bubbles on the surface of the upper stream of consciousness.

There are cases when the personality of the individual is changed, or more personalities are formed. This metamorphosis may be brought about *artificially*, by suggestion, either direct or indirect. This is often brought about in a state of hypnosis when any number of personalities may be formed at the will of the hypnotizer who may create them deliberately; or they may become formed by subtle indirect suggestion, coming from the hypnotizer, of which he himself is not fully conscious; or the personalities may be formed by auto-suggestions. Such phenomena may be regarded as the *artefacts of Psychopathology*.

There are again cases which are no play-personalities depending on hypnotic suggestion, or suggestion in waking life, but which are really due to pathological agencies. The former, due to suggestion, are *suggestion-personalities*, the latter, due to pathological agencies, are *pathological personalities*. The formation of multiple personality by means of suggestion does not belong to our present subject.

I have discussed these facts of suggestion personalities in my volume, "The Psychology of Suggestion," and other works. The pathological multiple personalities are of immense interest from many standpoints which we need not go into just at present, since our object is rather the causation, not the nature and character of the personalities themselves.[7]

The subwaking self is extremely credulous; it lacks all sense of the true and rational. "Two and two make five." "Yes." Anything is accepted, if sufficiently emphasized by the hypnotizer. The suggestibility and imitativeness of the subwaking self were discussed by me at great length. What I should like to point out here is the extreme *servility* and *cowardliness* of that self. Show hesitation, and it will show fight; command authoritatively, and it will obey slavishly.

The subwaking self is devoid of all morality. It will steal without the least scruple; it will poison; it will stab; it will assassinate its best friends unhesitatingly. When completely cut off from the waking person, it is precluded from conscience.

FOOTNOTE:

[7] The subject of pathological multiple personalities is discussed in my work, "Multiple Personality."

CHAPTER XIII

THE CHARACTER OF THE HYPNOIDAL STATE

In "The Psychology of Suggestion," I pointed out the conditions of normal and abnormal suggestibility. Among these conditions, monotony and the limitation of voluntary movements play an important rôle. Any arrangement of external circumstances, tending to produce monotony and limitation of voluntary movements, brings about a subconscious state of suggestibility in which the patient's mental life can be influenced with ease.

I find that in the subconscious hypnoidal state consciousness is vague and memory is diffused, so that experiences apparently forgotten come in bits and scraps to the foreground of consciousness. Emotional excitement is calmed, voluntary activity is somewhat passive, and suggestions meet with little resistance.

The induced subconscious hypnoidal state is a rest state, a state of physical and mental relaxation. It is a state of rest and relaxation that is specially amenable to psychotherapeutic influences. The important results obtained by me led to a closer study of what I then thought was a peculiar mental state designated by me as the *subwaking*, or the *hypnoidal* state.

The subwaking, or the hypnoidal state is essentially an intermediary state belonging apparently to the borderland of mental life. On the one hand, the hypnoidal state touches on the waking condition; on the other it merges into sleep and hypnosis. *A close study of the hypnoidal state shows that it differs from the hypnotic state proper and that it can by no means be identified with light hypnosis.*

In my years of work on patients and subjects, I have observed the presence of the hypnoidal state before the development of hypnosis and also before the onset of sleep. When again the hypnotic or sleep state passes into waking, the hypnoidal state reappears. The hypnoidal state then may be regarded as an intermediate and transitional state.

A somewhat related state has been long known in psychological literature as the hypnagogic state which precedes the oncome of sleep and is rich in hallucinations known under the term of *hypnagogic* hallucinations. In coming out of sleep, a closely related state may be observed, a state which I have termed *hypnapagogic*. In both states, hypnagogic and hypnapagogic, dream-hallucinations hold sway.

The hypnagogic and hypnapagogic states do not belong to light hypnosis, as it can hardly be claimed that men fall into light hypnosis twice, or possibly more than that, every day of their life. We do not go into light hypnosis with every nap we take. We do, however, go into the hypnoidal state when we pass into sleep or come out of sleep. Every drowsy state has the hypnoidal state as one of its constituents; every sleep state is preceded and followed by the hypnoidal state.

Hypnosis may be regarded as belonging to the abnormal mental states, while the hypnoidal state is more closely allied to waking and sleep, and belongs to the normal, physiological, mental states. At first, I regarded the hypnoidal state as peculiar, but as I proceeded with my observations and experiments I could not help coming to the conclusion that the hypnoidal state is found in all the representatives of animal life and is as normal as waking and sleep.

The hypnoidal state may be said to partake not only of the nature of waking and sleep, but also to possess some characteristics of hypnosis, namely, *suggestibility*. It is clear that, from the very nature of its mixed symptomatology, the hypnoidal state is variable and highly unstable. The hypnoidal state may be regarded in the light of an equivalent of sleep. Like sleep, the hypnoidal state has many levels of depth. It differs, however, from sleep in the rapidity of oscillation from level to level.

In the experiments of various investigators, the depth of sleep is found to be represented by a rapidly rising curve during the first couple of hours, and by a gradually descending curve during the rest of the hours of sleep. No such regularity of curve can be found in the hypnoidal state. The depth of the hypnoidal state changes very rapidly, and with it the passive condition and suggestibility of the patient.

For many years investigations of the hypnoidal state were carried out by me on subjects and patients, adults, and children. The work was entirely limited to the study of such states as found in man. Having found that during the hypnoidal state the condition of suggestibility is quite pronounced for therapeutic purposes, and having effected many cures of severe psychopathic maladies ranging throughout the whole domain of hysterical affections, neurasthenia, obsessions, drug habits, especially alcoholic ones, the hypnoidal state has become, in my practice, quite an important therapeutic agent. Other investigators have obtained some excellent results with the hypnoidal state in their treatment of various functional, psychopathic maladies.

Thus far, the work with the hypnoidal state has been confined entirely to observations and experiments on human subjects and patients, and also to the treatment of man's psychopathic ailments. I undertook a series of experiments on sleep, both from a phylogenetic and ontogenetic standpoint, following up the conditions and manifestations of sleep in the ascending scale of animal life, from the frog and the guinea pig, through the cat, the dog, to the infant and the adult.

My experiments clearly prove that the hypnoidal state is by no means confined to man, but is also present in animals. This is important since it indubitably shows how widely spread the hypnoidal state is throughout the domain of animal life. Moreover, the experiments clearly prove that the further down we descend in the scale of animal organization, the more prominent, the more essential, does the hypnoidal state become.

The conclusion is forced upon me that *the hypnoidal state is the primitive rest-state out of which sleep has arisen in the later stages of evolution. We may say that sleep and hypnosis take their origin in the hypnoidal state*.[8] Sleep and hypnosis are highly differentiated states; they have evolved out of the primitive, undifferentiated, hypnoidal state which is essentially a subwaking rest-state characteristic of early and lowly-organized animal life. *The hypnoidal state is the primordial sleep state.*

The development of the hypnoidal state into sleep has proven itself useful in the struggle for existence of the higher animals; it has, therefore, become fixed as the rest-state, characteristic of the higher representatives of animal life. Hypnosis and other trance-states, variations of the primitive hypnoidal rest-state, have become eliminated as useless and possibly harmful to the normal life adjustments of the higher animals and can only be induced under artificial conditions in but a fraction of the human race.

The hypnoidal state is the normal rest-state of the lower vertebrates and invertebrates. The rest or sleep state of the lower animals is a sort of passive waking state,—a subwaking state which has survived in man as the hypnoidal state. Of course, the state has been largely modified in man by the course of evolution, but it can still be clearly detected, just as the tail of the simian can be discerned in the human coccyx, or as the structure of the prehensile hand of the quadrumana can be still clearly traced in the foot of man. Waking, hypnoidal, and sleep-states may be termed *normal* states, while *hypnosis* and various other trance-states may be termed *sub-normal* states.

The relation of the hypnoidal state to waking, sleep, hypnosis, and other subconscious states may be represented by the diagram on following page.

The hypnoidal state is normal, it is present in all representatives of animal life.

Sleep, hypnosis, and trance-states are variations of the fundamental hypnoidal state. The sleep-state has proven useful and has become normal in the higher animals, while hypnosis like animal "cataplexy" and the various forms of trance-states, likewise variations of the fundamental hypnoidal state, characteristic of man, have not proven of vital value, and have fallen below the normal stream of consciousness with its concomitant adaptive reactions.

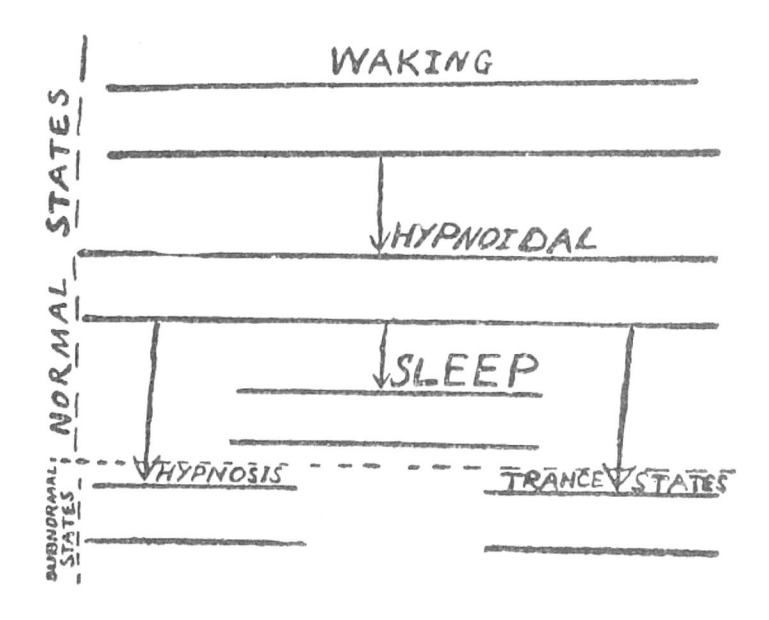

[Diagram: horizontal bands labeled WAKING, HYPNOIDAL, SLEEP, HYPNOSIS — — — TRANCE STATES; left-side labels: NORMAL STATES, SUBNORMAL STATES]

DIAGRAM II

The hypnoidal state is brief, variable, and unstable. They who have observed the rest-states of the lower metazoa can form a clear idea of the nature as well as of the biological significance of the hypnoidal state in the life of the lower animals. The animal is at rest for a brief period of time as long as it remains undisturbed by external conditions of its environment, or by internal conditions, such as hunger, sexual impulses, or other internal disturbances. Soon the animal begins to move, sluggishly at first, and then more quickly, and if there are no disturbing stimulations, comes to rest, to be again disturbed from its rest-equilibrium by the varying conditions of its environment.

The resting state is brief, irregular, differing from the waking state in but slight relaxation, in comparatively slow reactions to stimulations, and in a passive condition of the muscular system. Respiration is regular, and diminished in rate. The heart beat is slightly decreased, and general katabolic activity is somewhat reduced.

The animal, however, is quite alive to what is going on. *The animal rests, watching for danger.*

Resting and active states alternate periodically, if possible, but usually are irregular. The resting state is but a passive condition in which the animal may be considered to hover between waking and what we describe in the case of the higher animals as sleep. Sleep, in its proper sense, does not exist among the lower representatives of animal life.

This state of hovering between waking and sleeping, the characteristic of the hypnoidal state, is no doubt of paramount importance in the life-existence of the lower animals, considering the numerous dangers to which they are continually exposed. The animal must always be on the watch, either for food or for foe. It can only rest or "sleep" with its eyes wide open. The hypnoidal "sleep" can be best characterized as a *subwaking*, "twilight" rest-state.

I demonstrated in my experiments that the animal, while in the hypnoidal, subwaking rest-state, is apt to fall into a cataleptic state, especially when the movements are suddenly and forcibly inhibited. This cataleptic state, which reminds one of the hypnotic state, may be observed in the lower animals, such as the frog, the snake, the lobster, the bird, and, to a slighter degree, even in the higher animals, such as the guinea pig, the cat, the dog, especially in the young ones, such as the kitten, the puppy, and the infant.

There is little doubt that the cataleptic state into which animals fall during the hypnoidal rest-state is of some protective value in their life. The animal "freezes," "feigns death," and is thus either enabled to remain undetected by the animal on which it feeds or, what is still more important, is enabled to remain unnoticed by its enemy and thus escape certain death. The subwaking, hypnoidal state may be regarded as the fundamental rest-state of lower animals, and is characterized by a mixed symptomatology of waking, sleep, and hypnosis.

The hypnoidal state is a powerful instrument in the tracing of the past history of the growth and development of the symptoms of psychopathic or neurotic cases; and practically is of far greater value, inasmuch as the hypnoidal state has proven to be an easy agency in effecting a cure, and bringing about beneficial results in otherwise uncontrollable cases.

For the present, we can only say that the hypnoidal state is found in man but in a rudimentary condition. It is a vestige of man's primitive, animal ancestors. The hypnoidal state is brief, variable, forming the entrance and exit of repose,—the portals of sleep. The primordial rest-state has shrunk to a transitory, momentary stage in the alternation of waking and sleep. *The subwaking, hypnoidal rest-state shrinks with the increase of security of life.*

FOOTNOTE:

[8] Prof. Ed. Claperèdé of Geneva University, Switzerland, and Anastay seem to favor some similar view.

CHAPTER XIV

HYPNOIDAL PSYCHOTHERAPY

Once the hypnoidal state is induced by any of the various methods of hypnoidization, we can either attempt to follow up the history of the development of the malady, or we may chiefly work for therapeutic effects. It is, however, advisable, from a purely practical, therapeutic purpose to combine the two procedures; the cure is then effective and far more stable. When the history of the origin and development of the disease can not be traced, on account of the age or unintelligence of the patient, the therapeutic effects alone of the hypnoidal states have been utilized.

The getting access to subconscious experiences, lost to the patient's personal consciousness, makes the hypnoidal state a valuable instrument in the tracing of the origin and development of the symptoms of the psychopathic malady.

From a practical standpoint, however, the therapeutic value of the hypnoidal state is most important. Our experiments have revealed to us the significant fact that the hypnoidal state is the primordial rest-state; sleep is but a derivative form. In many conditions of disease it is advisable to have the patient revert to a simple and primitive mode of life. Similarly, in *psychopathic diseases a reversion to a simple, primitive state proves to be of material help to the patient.*

In plunging the patient into the hypnoidal state, we have him revert to a primitive rest-state with its consequent beneficial results. The suggestibility of the state, if skillfully handled, is apt to increase the therapeutic efficacy. Relaxation of nervous strain, rest from worry, abatement of emotional excitement are known to be of great help in the treatment of nervous troubles of the neurasthenic, or of the so-called "psychoasthenic" variety. That is what we precisely observe in the treatment of psychopathic or neurotic diseases by means of the agency of the hypnoidal state, the efficacy of which is all the greater on account of the presence of the important trait of suggestibility.

The most important fact, however, is *the access gained through the hypnoidal state to the patient's stores of subconscious reserve neuron energy, thus helping to bring about an association of disintegrated, dissociated mental-systems.*

Dr. John Donley in his article, "The Clinical Use of Hypnoidization" (*Journal of Abnormal Psychology for August-September, 1908), gives the following account of the method of hypnoidization:*

"The treatment of that large group of disorders, forgotten memories, and emotions is operative in the production of mental disaggregation, but also in those numerous instances where the experience causing the obsessive idea or emotion is well known to the upper consciousness.

"In hypnoidal states they were made to reproduce their obsessive thoughts and images and then to describe them in words. When this had been accomplished and they had received further assurance and persuasion from the experimenter, although the purely intellectual content of their obsessions remained known to them, the insistent automatic character and disturbing emotional factors had disappeared. In this metamorphosis of emotional reaction we may observe one of the most interesting and useful attributes of the hypnoidal state."

Dr. Donley gives a series of cases which he treated successfully from psychognostic and psychotherapeutic standpoints. The reader is referred to the original article.

"The value of hypnoidization," says Dr. T. W. Mitchell, "in the resurrection of dissociated memories is that which is perhaps best established. And this applies not only to the restoration of the forgotten experiences of ordinary amnesia, but to the recovery of dissociated memories that are of pathogenic significance.... Sidis himself has insistently taught that the reassociation of dissociated complexes effects a cure of psychopathic disease.... My own experience, so far as it goes, tends to corroborate in every respect the claims put forward by Sidis...."

While in the hypnoidal state the patient hovers between the conscious and the subconscious, somewhat in the same way as in the half-drowsy condition one hovers between wakefulness and sleep. The patient keeps on fluctuating from moment to moment, now falling more deeply into a subconscious condition in which outlived experiences are easily aroused, and again rising to the level of the waking state. Experiences long submerged and forgotten rise to the full light of consciousness. They come in bits, in chips, in fragments, which may gradually coalesce and form a connected series of interrelated systems of experiences apparently long dead and buried. The resurrected experiences then stand out clear and distinct in the patient's mind. The recognition is fresh, vivid, and instinct with life, as if the experiences had occurred the day before.

It cannot be insisted too much that the hypnoidal state is not a slight hypnosis. *The hypnoidal state is a light sleep state, a twilight state.* The hypnoidal state is the anabolic state of repose, characteristic of primitive life.

The hypnoidal state is an intermediary state between waking and sleep. *Subwaking* is an appropriate descriptive term of the character of the hypnoidal state.

The subwaking hypnoidal state, like sleep and hypnosis, may be of various depth and duration; it may range from the fully waking consciousness and again may closely approach and even merge into sleep or hypnosis. The same patient may at various times reach different levels, and hence subconscious experiences which are inaccessible at one time may become revealed at some subsequent time, when the patient happens to go into a deeper hypnoidal state.

On account of the instability of the hypnoidal state, and because of the continuous fluctuation and variation of its depth, the subconscious dissociated experiences come up in bits and scraps, and often may lack the sense of familiarity and recognition. The patient often loses the train of subconscious association. There is a constant struggle to maintain this highly unstable hypnoidal state.

One has again and again to return to the same subconscious train started into activity for a brief interval of time. One must pick his way among streams of disturbing associations before the dissociated subconscious experiences can be synthesized into a whole, reproducing the original experience that has given rise to the whole train of symptoms.

The hypnoidal state may sometimes reproduce the original experience which, at first struggling up in a broken, distorted form, and finally becoming synthesized, produces a full attack. The symptoms of the malady turn out to be portions, bits and chips of past experiences which have become dissociated, giving rise to a disaggregated subconsciousness.

The method of hypnoidization, and the hypnoidal states induced by it, enable us to trace the history and etiology of the symptoms, and also to effect a synthesis and a cure. The hypnoidal state may not be striking and sensational in its manifestations, but it is a powerful instrument in psychopathology and psychotherapeutics.

For many years my investigations of the hypnoidal state were carried out on subjects and patients, adults and children. Having found that during the hypnoidal state the condition of mental plasticity is quite pronounced for therapeutic purposes, and having effected many cures of severe psychopathic maladies, ranging throughout the whole domain of so-called hysterical affections, neurasthenia, obsessions, drug habits, especially alcoholic ones, the hypnoidal state has become in my practice quite an important therapeutic agent. Lately, others have obtained excellent results with the hypnoidal state in their treatment of various functional, psychopathic or neurotic maladies.

Perhaps it may be opportune here for the sake of further elucidation to give a few extracts from the Presidential address on "The Hypnoidal State of Sidis," given by Dr. T. W. Mitchell before the Psycho-Medical Society of Great Britain, January 26, 1911.

"The history of science," says Dr. Mitchell in his address, "affords us many instances in which the neglect of residual phenomena in experimental research has led to the overlooking of important facts, and prevented investigators from making discoveries which, had they paid attention to their residues, they could hardly have missed. The great chemist, Cavendish, probably missed the discovery of argon, because in his estimate of nitrogen of the air he neglected a residue which his experiments showed him could not be more than $1/_{120}$ part of the whole. More than a hundred years afterwards this residue was accounted for by the discovery of argon.

"Now in the history of Psychotherapeutics, from its earliest beginning down to our own time, we find many cases where the circumstances under which curative results have been obtained render it difficult for us to range these results under the category of the therapeutics of suggestion.

"Such cases as these may be regarded as the residual phenomena of the therapeutics of suggestion, and just as Cavendish and his successors too readily assumed that all the so-called nitrogen of the air was the same as the nitrogen of nitre, so we may be missing some important truth, if we too readily assume that all these therapeutic results are due solely to suggestion. The value of suggestion during hypnosis is well attested, and the possibility of effecting physiological and psychological changes by its means is supported by a large amount of experimental evidence. But evidence of this kind is lacking in regard to suggestion without hypnosis, and until it is forthcoming, we are justified in receiving with some suspicion the account of the therapeutic efficacy of suggestion in the waking state. We seem bound to consider whether some state of consciousness intermediate between waking and hypnosis may not be artificially induced and utilized for the purpose of giving therapeutic suggestion.

"The scientific investigation of states of consciousness intermediate between waking and hypnosis is a contribution to psychology and psychotherapy which we owe practically to one man—Dr. Sidis. A research into the nature of suggestibility led him to formulate certain laws and conditions of normal and abnormal suggestibility....

"By keeping the patient for a short time under the conditions of normal suggestibility we induce a peculiar mental state which Sidis named *Hypnoidal state*. The process by which it is induced is what Sidis calls, *hypnoidization*.

"By the use of various methods a state of consciousness is induced which differs from full waking, but is not hypnosis or ordinary sleep.

"The hypnoidal state is an intermediary territory, on the borderland of waking, sleep and hypnosis. In the course of a valuable experimental investigation of sleep in man and the lower animals, Sidis discovered that the hypnoidal state is a phase of consciousness which is passed through in every transition from one of these states to another. In passing from the waking state to ordinary sleep or hypnosis, there is always a longer or shorter hypnoidal stage. In the practice of hypnoidization the patient sometimes drops into hypnosis, or he may fall asleep without touching on hypnosis. And so also in awaking from sleep or from hypnosis, the hypnoidal state has to be passed through. Sidis found that the further we descend in the scale of animal life, the more important does the hypnoidal state become in relation to bodily rest and recuperation, and he concludes that it is the primitive rest-state out of which both sleep and hypnosis have been evolved.

"The relation to each other of waking, sleep, hypnosis and the hypnoidal state, may be represented in a diagram in which the primitive hypnoidal state is represented as a nucleus from which the segments of the larger circle, waking, sleep and hypnosis, have arisen. The transition from one of these segments to another can take place through the central territory with which they each have relations. (See diagram on page 110.)

"The spontaneous occurrence of the hypnoidal state in man is as a rule merely a transitory stage in the alternation of waking and sleep. From the point of view of evolution it is a vestige derived from a long race of ancestors, a rudimentary function which has been superseded by the more highly specialized rest-state, sleep. But it can be artificially induced and maintained by the methods which have been described, and it can be utilized with effect in the treatment of psychopathic disorders.

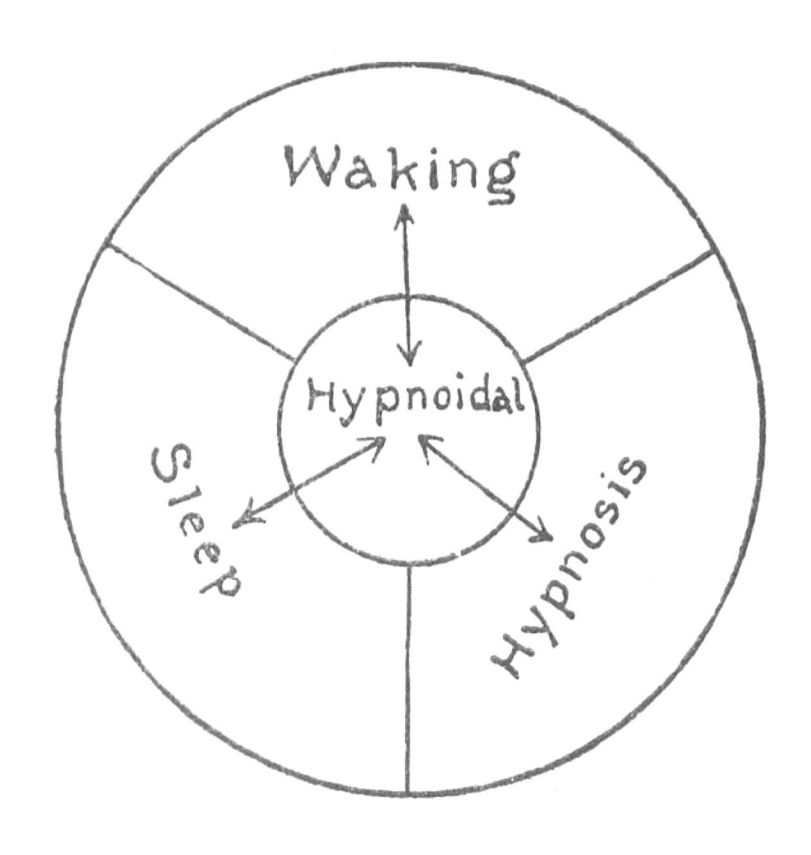

DIAGRAM III

"The therapeutic use of the hypnoidal state is a somewhat complex subject, for hypnoidization may be employed as an adjunct to other methods or as a curative measure in itself.

"The full record of hypnoidization is in the account of the well known Hanna case, given in his 'Multiple Personality.' This was a case of total amnesia, following a severe injury to the head. The patient, a cultured clergyman, was reduced to the mental condition of a newborn child. All his former acquisitions and memories had entirely disappeared, and he had to start learning everything again from the beginning. When he (the patient) was put into the hypnoidal state various fragmentary experiences of his past life emerged into consciousness, demonstrating to his observers that his lost memories were merely dissociated and not destroyed. This same method (hypnoidization) was made use of in other cases of amnesia, and it was found to be of great assistance in effecting the resurrection of dissociated mental material and its reintegration in consciousness.

"With the progress of his studies in Psychopathology, the reintegration of consciousness became, for Sidis, the aim of all therapeutic endeavor in connection with maladies that are associated with, or produced by, mental dissociation. The recurrent psycho-motor states of functional psychosis, insistent ideas, imperative concepts, persistent, or periodically appearing emotional states, so-called psychic epilepsy, and other states of dissociation all lent themselves to treatment by hypnoidization. By its means the dissociated complexes could be recovered, the psychogenesis of the malady could be traced, a synthesis of consciousness effected, and the patient thereby cured. As his confidence in his method increased, Sidis gradually extended its employment, until at the present time he seems to use it in every kind of disorder in which psychotherapy is indicated.

"I have no doubt that Dr. Bramwell induces in his patients a state of consciousness which is identical with the hypnoidal state of Sidis.

"My own experience, so far as it goes, tends to corroborate in every respect the therapeutic claims put forward by Sidis. I have observed the good effects of the hypnoidal state apart from any other measure.

"In his later writings Sidis insistently maintains that the use of hypnoidization alone is sufficient to cure certain morbid conditions. He bases this claim on the fact that he has found the hypnoidal state effective towards this end, and he interprets his results as being due to a release of reserve energy which has been locked up in the inhibited and dissociated systems or complexes.

"The *principle of reserve energy* is based upon a wide generalization of facts, namely, that far less energy is utilized by the individual than is actually at his disposal. In the struggle for existence, those forms of life which have accumulated a store of reserve energy that can be drawn upon in emergencies have the best chance for survival."

According to my experimental and clinical work the waking state, sleep, hypnosis, and the hypnoidal state, may be differentiated as follows:

(I) In the waking state the upper, controlling consciousness *predominates* over the subconscious. In other words, in the waking state the conscious is more responsive and more active than the subconscious which as a rule under such conditions may be regarded as partially dormant.

(II) In sleep *both* the conscious and the subconscious are *reduced* in activity, often even *inhibited* in function. Motor consciousness is *arrested*; motor control is paralyzed. The personality is *disintegrated*.

(III) In hypnosis the upper, controlling consciousness is *diminished* in activity, while the subconscious activities are *increased* in extensity and intensity. In hypnosis the relationship of the conscious and subconscious is interchanged,—the conscious becomes subconscious, and *vice versa*. The habitual type of character may become changed by suggestion, giving rise to double and multiple personality, according to the crystallization of various association systems, while the habitual, critical attitude is reduced in intensity.

(IV) In the hypnoidal state both conscious and subconscious functions are *lowered* in activity with no decrease in the intensity of critical attitude, and with *no change* of personality.

The hypnoidal state is therefore not a light hypnosis, but rather a *light sleeping state, a twilight state.* The hypnoidal state is a primitive rest-state out of which sleep and hypnosis have arisen in the course of animal evolution.

CHAPTER XV

EGOTISM AND FEAR

As we have pointed out, the fear instinct is the arousal of the impulse of self-preservation. Psychopathic conditions are at bottom fear states interrelated with hypnoidal states and with an abnormal, pathological condition of the impulse of self-preservation. This is manifested in the fundamental trait of extreme selfishness characteristic of psychopathic patients. The patient is entirely absorbed in himself, and is ready to sacrifice every one to his terrors.

For many years, day after day and night after night, I lived with patients who were under my care, observation, and treatment. One trait always revealed to me the predominant characteristic under the constantly changing psychopathic symptom-complex and that is *the extreme selfishness of the patients*. There is no greater egotism to be found than in the typical cases of psychopathic disorders. This egotism runs parallel to the condition of the psychopathic state. This does not mean that every egotist is necessarily psychopathic, but *every psychopathic case is essentially egotistic*.

The psychopathic patient does not hesitate a moment to sacrifice to his "affection" father, mother, brother, sister, husband, wife, lover, friend, and children. In severe cases the patient stops at nothing and only fear of suffering, sickness, evil consequences, and punishments can restrain the patient. In some extreme cases the patient is almost diabolical in his selfishness.

The constant sympathy which the patients crave from others, and which they demand, if it is not given to them immediately, is but an expression of their extreme obsession by the impulse of self-preservation. In their struggle for self-preservation they forget everything else, nothing is remembered but themselves. This condition becomes the ground character which is often expressed in a frank, brutal way. Even in the best of patients one can find glimpses into the depths of the psychopathic soul which is nothing but the immense egotism of the beast, worsted in the struggle for existence, tortured by the agonizing pangs of the fear instinct.

In the vanity, conceit, arrogance, and overbearing attitude towards others, friend or stranger, as well as in the total indifference to the suffering of his intimate friends and acquaintances, we once more find the expression of that terrible selfishness which obsesses the psychopathic patient. In order to get rid of some small inconvenience, or to obtain some slight pleasure, the patient will put others as well as his "near and dear ones" not only to inconvenience, but to permanent pain, and even torture.

The patient lacks confidence, at least that is what he complains of, but he does not hesitate to demand of his best friends and even of total strangers all the services possible, if they are given to him, thinking that he is fully entitled to them. The patient has the conceit and vanity of his great worth in comparison with other people. The world and especially his family, physicians, attendants, friends, acquaintances, lovers, should offer their happiness and life for his comfort.

Even when the psychopathic patient does some altruistic act, it is only in so far as he himself can benefit by that deed. He is ready to drop it as soon as the work does not answer his selfish purposes. Himself first and last, that is the essence of psychopathic life.

The patient is convinced of his goodness and kindness, and of his human affections which are far superior to those of the common run. He adores himself and he is always ready to dwell in the glory of his delicacy and extraordinary sensitivity. This trait he is specially anxious to impress on his friends, on his family, and even on those whom he apparently loves. "I am the delicate being of whom you all, unappreciative, gross, insensible people should take care." That is the principle on which the psychopathic patient lives. The patient will do anything to attract attention to this side of his personality. He will emphasize his sickness, exaggerate his symptoms, and even manufacture them for the benefit of those who dare to ignore him or who pay little attention to his condition, to his wants, needs, caprices, passing whims, and especially his fears, which underlie all his wishes and desires. *There is nothing so tyrannical and merciless as the autocratic, fear-obsessed "weak" will of a psychopathic or neurotic patient.*

The patient's whole attention is concentrated on himself, or more specially on the symptoms of his psychopathic malady, symptoms which obsess him for the time being. Whatever the symptoms be, permanent or changing, the patient's demand is to have others sympathize with the illness from which he suffers, to have them realize the "fearful" agonies which he undergoes. The selfishness of the patient is exacting and knows no bounds. The whole world is to serve him, and be at his command. The psychopathic patient is driven by the impulse of self-preservation and by the furies of the fear instinct.

Many of my psychopathic patients tell me that they feel sensitive as long as they witness the sufferings of other people, otherwise they do not care to know anything about them. They are anxious to have such things away from them as a nuisance. They insist on being surrounded only with pleasant things or with persons and objects that contribute to their health and happiness. Everything is absorbed by the worship of Moloch Health to whom the patients sacrifice everything. Pain, suffering, and distress of other people are looked at only from the standpoint of the possible effect they may have on the patient's "precarious health." Like Nero, who was probably a psychopathic character, the psychopathic patient is ready to burn others for his health; if necessary, to torture "health and happiness" out of his best friends.

One of my patients, who is highly intelligent, tells me frankly that he uses others to squeeze out of them strength for himself. As soon as he can no longer get it, or has obtained all he can, he is anxious to part with them, gets tired of them, and even begins to be resentful because they are in the way of his health. Another of my patients was ready to burn parks, stables, and destroy everything, if he knew that it was good for his health. Other patients of mine do not hesitate to wake up the whole house to help them in insomnia or indigestion. Many of my patients take pleasure in forming acquaintances and even friendship with people, ask for their sympathy, require their help and assistance, come to them early in the morning and late at night, disturb their sleep in the small hours of the morning, display all their symptoms of indigestion, nausea, eructation, and vomiting. The patients then turn round, abuse the person who helps them, telling him disagreeable things, because he is no longer useful. A few hours later the patients may turn again for help to the same person, because they find that they could still make use of him.

Psychopathic patients do not hesitate, for the alleviation of their pains, of depression, of insomnia, to take a bath in the early morning and wake up all the other patients. They are entirely absorbed in themselves. Self is the only object of their regard. A clever lawyer, aptly characterized one of my most severe and typical psychopathic cases as "egomaniac." "When you talk of gravity, 'I am gravity,' she claims. Talk of the Trinity: 'I am the Trinity.'" As a matter of fact every psychopathic patient is an egomaniac.

Bacon's aphorisms about self-lovers may well apply to psychopathic patients: "And certainly it is in the nature of extreme self-lovers, as they will set a house on fire, and it were but to roast their eggs.... That which is specially to bc noted is, that those which are *sui amantes sine rivali*, are many times unfortunate."

Driven by the impulse of self-preservation and by the anguish of extreme fear, the psychopathic patient may be pitied as a most unfortunate, miserable wretch.

In the psychognosis of the particular condition, mental or nervous, be it object, idea, or action from which the patient suffers, the impulse of self-preservation with its instinctive emotion of fear can always be found in the background of consciousness or in the subconsciousness.

An insight into a series of cases will help best to understand the fundamental psychopathological processes that give rise to the different forms of psychoneuroses and somatopsychoses.

The inhibition of the patient's activities, produced by the most primitive impulse of self-preservation with its instinct of fear, limits the patient's life to such an extent that the interests and the activities are reduced to automatic repetition of reactions of a stereotyped character. The stimuli must be the same, otherwise the patient does not care to respond. He loses interest in his business, in reading, in his work, and games. The attention keeps on wandering. Games, pleasures, and hobbies in which he formerly used to take an interest lose their attraction for him. The life he is disposed to lead is of a vegetative existence. He is afraid of anything new. Things are done in an automatic way. *Routine and automatisms are characteristic of his activities.*

The psychopathic or neurotic patient talks about his humanitarian ideals, about his great abilities superior to the common run of humanity, and how with his talents he is willing and has been willing to confer benefits on poor suffering humanity in spite of the fact that he has to struggle with his poor health, physical, nervous and mental. In spite of the overwhelming fatigue due to ill health, and in spite of the fearful ideas and impulses that have beset him day and night he still has succeeded in fighting his way through.

The patient hankers for notoriety, for praise, for appreciation by other people. He is apt to complain that the family, neighbors, acquaintances, friends cannot appreciate his good points, his good will, and his high ideals to which he conforms his life, tortured as it is with pains and suffering of poor health. The *egocentric* character of the psychopathic patient is bound up in his abnormally developed impulse of self-preservation and in his pathological state of the fear instinct.

Thus one patient opens his account with the phrase: "From boyhood I had a sensitive conscience."

Another patient writes: "As a child I had a keener instinct as to the real unexpressed attitude of those about me toward each other than the average child."

One of my patients, a puny being of mediocre intelligence, writes: "I have always, from the earliest childhood, felt that I was different from those about me; and I must acknowledge that it was not alone a feeling of inferiority on account of poor control, but a feeling that I understood more than they. I was, however, of a delicate constitution and suffered from ill health."

Psychopathic patients subscribe to the "cheerful" effusions of "New Thought," and plaster the walls of their rooms with elevating "Rules for Health and Happiness." Psychoanalysis and Christian Science are the rage. The victims hide behind the veil of sickly, psychopathic "Love."

The writings and accounts of the patients are full of introspection about health, and about the minutiae of their feelings in the various parts of their body. Some of the patients with a literary turn keep on writing volumes about the most minute symptoms of their troubles to which they happen at any moment to be subject. I have numbers of manuscripts, biographies, autobiographies, all telling the same old story of "blighted lives" due to ill health, drugs, and treatment, all describing with the over-scrupulous exactness of microscopic anatomy the different symptoms that plague them by night and by day. The patients tell of their talents and remarkable abilities, superior to the average run, of their ill luck and failures, due to their unfortunate state of ill health.

In quoting from some of the accounts given to me by the patients themselves I wish to attract attention to this side of the patient's mental condition, the expression of the impulse of self-preservation, manifested in the general panic of health, or fear of disease, whether nervous or physical.

A patient of mine, a clerk of mediocre intelligence, with hardly any ability, but with plenty of selfishness, introspection, and immeasurable conceit, writes about his ideals in life:

"I would ask that this manuscript be considered in connection with my other two writings. I have already partially covered this ground in my autobiography. I should be glad to have my general outlook on life considered, and to receive suggestions relative to vocations and avocations, since my anxieties regarding these are inseparably intermingled with my thoughts of physical and mental health.

"Of course since childhood my ideals have undergone a gradual modification. First, there was the religious motive of life: I wanted to be a soldier of the cross and assist in the regeneration of souls and their preparation for the life beyond.... I began to meditate upon ethical theories.... It appears that in doing the world's work the tendency is to specialize.... In the matter of choosing my employment my own interest is identical with the interest of society. At different times of my life I have fancied I had a liking for one calling or another.... My lines of thought have gradually drifted into the philosophical (patient means the various occult scribblings about 'health metaphysics'). I now ask myself why I should be a lawyer, a physician, a minister, a philanthropist or any other special thing? I conceive that a man's life is largely what circumstances make it, and it may be, therefore, that I shall always be a clerk in an office, trying to be useful in a small way; but now we are talking of influencing such matters as far as we can by choice. I imagine that perhaps my field is in the line of ethics, philosophy, or whatever words may be used to signify the *general principles* governing human affairs. My reasons for thinking so are as follows: First, I feel a strong interest in those principles comparing to no other interest in my life. Second, I find very few people who seem to feel any such interest in such matters. Third, I believe such principles to be of supreme importance. The question is,—Is my position in regard to general truths so peculiar that I should regard it my mission to give those subjects more attention in study and expression than do other men?

"The question I want to settle is,—Do other men feel this same philosophical interest, realize the broad field of human obligation, and come down to special occupations, not because they are more interesting to them than the general field, but because they realize they must specialize in order to properly assist in carrying on the world's work? If this be so then I am mistaken in thinking I should give particular attention to general principles. But my observations have gone to show that the average physician, lawyer, merchant or politician is not interested in the broad questions of life, but only in medicine, law, business, or politics, caring little for the relation of his vocation to other vocations except as he makes his bread by it. Why then if the various departments of human activity must be correlated, and if the individuals making up those respective departments have no disposition to do the correlating,—should it not be done by those who are interested in the general field?"

It means that such work could be and should be done by the patient, by the philosophical clerk, interested in the general "metaphysics" of health.

Such confessions can be easily elicited from psychopathic patients even in their best states of apparent diffidence, humility. *This paranoidal aspect of self-aggrandizement is present in all psychopathic cases.* In some this trait stands out more clearly and distinctly than in others. It is, however, present in all psychopathic patients, if one observes them closely and attentively. It is the expression of an intensified state of the impulse of self-preservation and fear instinct. In other words, it is a state of an exaggerated, hypertrophied egotism.

"We must appeal to a law higher than the material law," a patient writes in his account. "I worried much over it. Since that time the relation of mind and matter greatly interested me.... My health at this time failed, I lost appetite and strength, had hysterical symptoms. I was treated for general neurasthenia." ... Psychopathic, philosophical and ethical speculations and interests have their sole source in fear of sickness and self-preservation.

"One of my anxieties," another patient writes, "of my present life is connected with my business and my relationship to my partners. I am naturally conscientious and inclined to be not only earnest and sincere, but serious. My nature, instincts, and desires are not superficial. Yet my relation to the business is a superficial one. I am neither fitted by natural tastes nor by training for the indoor, rather mechanical, conventional, and routine processes upon which business and commercial success depends....

"Without the common motives of an ordinary merchant (greed) I am placed in the position of the one who lives not by the usual and conventional standards of right and wrong, but rather by a more exalted and more rigid one of his own making which, unsupported by habit, and institutions, requires a greater loyalty, a higher resolve, and a firmer will than is required of the conventional and conforming citizen. Emerson says it demands something Godlike in one who would essay such a task, not placing the same values on money, trade, commerce, and profits as the natural money maker and money lover, and not the opportunity to substitute and supplement the usual motives by and with the larger, and to me more compelling, of community betterment and employee welfare...." This man had abandoned his wife and three children.

Another patient writes of himself, "The hypersensitive nervous system with the initial shock has inhibited the development of my highest potentialities and my highest endeavors." He summarizes his symptoms: "Dread and anxiety about being away from home and friends, self-consciousness, mental sluggishness, quick fatigue, inability for deep thought, general state of irritability."

A neurotic patient tells me that he suffers from fatigue, insomnia, dullness, inability of concentration of attention, failure in studies, slowness of comprehension, and so on; and yet he gives his opinion with papal infallibility on every conceivable subject, and hints at being an undeveloped, unappreciated genius. The psychopathic, neurotic patient rarely, if ever, suffers from a complaint of inferiority. His real fear is that his superiority may be humbled.

Obsessed by the impulse of self-preservation and fear instinct, and with utter disregard of others, the patients are convinced of their extraordinary kindness, gentleness, sympathy, martyrdom, and even saintliness. It is from this class that neurotic philanthropists are recruited. Psychopathic patients are always ready "to sacrifice themselves for the good of humanity." They talk endlessly about goodness, and may even devote themselves to charity and instruction of the "poor and degraded." A patient of mine worked for three years for the "good of the poor," had "high ideals and a sensitive conscience," according to his accounts, but abandoned readily his wife and children.

Another young woman, a typical psychopathic, full of high ideals, ran away with a married man, had a child that died of exposure. This patient was interested in modern education and improvement of humanity. In reality she never cared to do anything for anybody, and without any hesitation took advantage of others in order to satisfy the least whim that might have crossed her mind, especially those whims that relate to health. She had all kinds of directions, prescriptions, exercises, requisite for the strength and health of the body and the nerves.

One of my patients used to be anxious about my going and coming. Was it love or devotion? I found out that he was afraid that I might be killed. This fear was developed in him by an actual accident in which his brother had died, but the same fear associated with me was due to the fact that the patient was sure that my treatment was requisite for his health and welfare. He was in fear lest I might be killed, he would be unable to get his treatments, and thus lose time in getting back his health.

For the sake of his "health" the patient will not stop at anything. Neurotics may well name their troubles "Health and Science." *The psychopathic, neurotic patient makes of health his science and religion, because self-preservation and fear are at the bottom of the psychopathic, neurotic constitution.*

CHAPTER XVI

NEUROTIC PARASITISM

The psychopathic patient may be regarded as a case of parasitism. The parasite, living on his host, gradually loses all active functions, a condition followed by atrophy of organs no longer necessary to the life existence of the organism.

According to Demoor, "Atrophy begins with function when an organ has become useless. This uselessness may arise from two causes: the function may be no longer useful to the individual or to the species, or it may be assumed by another organ." When an organism turns parasite it is an economy of nutrition and energy to save as much as possible. The tendency of parasitism is to dispense with unnecessary functions in the struggle for existence.

The loss of function is from the less useful, to the more useful, to the functions absolutely indispensable to survival; from the less essential, to the more essential, to functions absolutely essential to the life existence of the individual. The life activity of the parasite becomes more and more narrowed, circumscribed, and dwindles down to a few functions requisite to its life existence, namely self-preservation, nutrition, and reproduction.

With the further increase of parasitism even the digestive and reproductive functions become simplified, the parasitic individual becomes reduced to the most fundamental of all impulses, the impulse of self-preservation and reproduction.

The penalty of parasitic life is the *simplification* of organic activities, the atrophy of all higher and complex life processes. This is what takes place in the case of the psychopathic individual. All higher activities, all higher interests cease.

In many neurotic cases of the severe type even *the sexual instinct becomes gradually atrophied. The patient's life is narrowed down to the impulse which is absolutely requisite for individual life existence, namely the impulse of self-preservation with its concomitant fear instinct.*

The growth of the impulse of self-preservation with its fear instinct brings about their hypertrophy which in turn hastens the degenerative processes or atrophy of all higher and more complex activities. The psychopathic patient in the process of degeneration and atrophy falls so low that not only moral, social, intellectual, but simpler psychomotor reactions become gradually diminished and atrophied. *In severe cases even the instinct of sex, requisite for the preservation of the species, is made subservient to the impulse of self-preservation and the fear instinct.*

In psychopathic life all activities are narrowed down to the pettiness of individual existence. It is not sex, it is not species-interests, nor conflicts, nor self-repressions that trouble the neurotic patient. An abnormal impulse of self-preservation and fear instinct are at the bottom of all psychopathic miseries. *All psychopathic, neurotic interests are reduced to the sorry life of self and fear.*

Lacking interest in anything but himself, terrorized by the fear of existence, the psychopathic patient lives a dreary, monotonous life out of which he seeks to escape. Monotony, *ennui*, indifference form the curse of his life. The patient is in a frantic condition, constantly in quest of interests which he cannot enjoy. Nothing can interest him, because he has no other interest but himself, and that is so narrow, that it can hardly fill existence.

As a matter of fact he is afraid to meet his fears, he is afraid of himself. He is afraid to come to a decision, never at peace, ever at war with himself. He is bored with himself, wearied with everything and with everybody. He is constantly eager to find new pastures and new excitements, so as to fill with some living interest his poor, narrow, mean, short existence obsessed by fear, misery, wretchedness, and brutish selfishness.

The patient is afraid to work, because it may "fatigue and exhaust" him, and may bring about a state of disease, while he looks for health. He has no interest, because he only thinks of his little self, reduced to digestion, evacuation, and sleeping. The psychopathic patient leads an inactive existence of a sluggard, a lazy, idle existence of a parasite, and still he is driven to life and activity which, from the very nature of his narrow, parasitic individuality, he can no longer enjoy. He has the ideals of a hero and lives the life of a coward. This puts the patient in a state of dissatisfaction, discontent, and ceaseless contest with himself and others. Fear and self never leave him at peace. He is ever in a state of agitation, restlessness, and anxiety.

Obsessed with the anxious fears of self-impulse, the patient avoids the terrors of life, and drags the grey, monotonous existence of a worm. Hence there is a tendency in the psychopathic patient to be on the lookout for ever new energetic personalities, lean on them, suck out all the energies he possibly can, then reject his new friends unhesitatingly and brutally, and be again in search for new personalities who can disperse, for ever so brief a time, the fearful monotony and dread of his miserable, psychopathic, neurotic existence.

The neurotic patient may be characterized as a psychopathic leech, or truer still, a psychopathic vampire. For it is on the life and blood of other people that the psychopathic ogre is enabled to carry on his bewitched, accursed, narrow, selfish existence, full of terror and anguish of life.

"When the attack is on," exclaimed a psychopathic patient, affected with cardiac palpitation and intense fear, "I am too d——d scared about myself to think about her!" referring to the woman with whom he was in love. The psychopathic patient is a parasitic ogre with an hypertrophied ego.

Patients who claim to love children when the latter are well and healthy, avoid them, like a pest, when the children happen to fall sick, for fear of disease and for fear that the sick children may produce an evil influence on the patient's "sensitive" nerves. The patient is afraid to come near sickness, or even afraid to hear of evil things, such as description of misfortunes, ailments, accidents, and sufferings, because they may upset him and arouse his fears of himself.

All the patient wants is to be surrounded with cheer, joy, merriment, excitement, and happiness which he is unable to enjoy. The psychopathic patient is in constant search after happiness. Not that he is interested in the problem of happiness from a moral, philosophical, or even purely religious standpoint. His interest is of the crudest, the meanest, the most selfish kind. It is happiness for self,— for a low, mean, short, and brutish self. Psychopathic search for happiness is the anguish of the beast, cornered by terror. The patient is tortured by an unsuccessful search for happiness, ever tantalized by self and fear. Egotism, fear, ennui, restlessness, anxiety, discord are the harpies of psychopathic, neurotic life.

The love of the psychopathic patient is at bottom self-love; it is like the love of the wolf for the lamb. Lover, husband, child, friend, father, mother, brother, sister, are all victims to the patient's greedy self.

The fear instinct has a positive and negative aspect. There is the fear of life, fear of putting forth energy in meeting the exigencies of life. The patient is afraid to participate in the struggle of life. Struggle spells to him danger, peril,—fear of the external world. Struggle means to him fear, suffering, and misery. The patient avoids society, avoids not only strangers, but even his acquaintances, friends, and sometimes his own family.

While he constantly craves for ever new stimulations to his depleted nerves, he is at the same time in terror of everything that is *new*. The patient is afraid of life, he shirks duties, responsibilities, efforts, and joys of life struggle. Hence his love of automatism, routine, and fear-fatigue.

The fear manifests itself more often in the form of the negative side of life, such as fear of sickness, weakness, incapacity, degradation, loss of vitality, and generally the fear of death. *Neurotic states are due to fear of life and fear of death.*

CHAPTER XVII

FUNDAMENTAL PRINCIPLES

The following principles may be regarded as fundamental in the development of psychopathic or nervous ills:

I. *The Principle of Embryonic Psychogenesis*

The mental states of psychopathic or nervous ills are of an infantile, child type. In this respect the mental states simulate cancerous and other malignant growths of an embryonic character. The psychopathic mental states are not only of a childish character, but they are often associated with child experiences of early life. The psychopathic condition points to some early fear-producing experience, or fear awakening shock.

II. *The Principle of Recurrence*

Fear experiences tend to repeat themselves in consciousness, and especially in the subconscious states of the child. This repetition or recurrence keeps alive the psychopathic fear nucleus, and *fixes* it in the mind. Fixed fear systems become further developed by the subsequent experiences of life. The aroused fear instinct may either become weakened or strengthened. When the conditions of life are unfavorable and adverse, tending to further cultivation of the impulse of self-preservation and the fear instinct, the outcome is a psychopathic disposition, ending in a nervous state with typical symptoms of some definite nervous trouble, formed by the *latest* or *ultimate* fear experiences.

III. *The Principle of Proliferation and Complication*

With the growth of the child the fear experiences increase and multiply. These experiences become associated with the original child nucleus of fear and thus a complexity of fear systems is built up. Worries, depressions, and anxieties help to increase and develop the psychopathic system of groups of fear experiences. The morbid state grows like an avalanche in its progress downwards.

IV. *The Principle of Fusion or of Synthesis*

All the fear experiences become associated and grouped gradually around the original child fear experience which is often of a subconscious character. The long series of fear experiences becomes fused and synthesized by the central fear instinct and impulse of self-preservation, which are fundamental in every being, but which have been specially cultivated by the course of events and experiences in the neurotic patient. The experiences become fused, synthesized, and systematized, forming one complex network of closely interrelated fear obsessions with the fear instinct and impulse of self preservation in the background.

V. *The Principle of Contrast*

Feelings and emotions follow by contrast. Excitement is followed by depression, enjoyment by disgust, exhilaration by disappointment. This is well brought out in the changes observed in the psychopathic self and fear states.

Fear may be followed by *anger*, especially against those who are sure to show no opposition, or may even manifest fear. The excitement of fear in others is a way which diminishes fear in the patient and helps him to have confidence in himself, strengthening his impulse of self preservation.

The fear of the psychopathic may even resort to love so as to gain safety and protection from the tantalizing agonies of the fear instinct. *That is why some physicians are deceived, and ascribe psychopathic troubles to love instead of to the real fundamental cause of all psychopathic disorders, namely self-preservation and the fear instinct.*

Similarly mysticism, a psychopathic malady of a social character, has its origin in the impulse of self-preservation and the fear instinct, and takes refuge in "love" or in "union" with the Infinite which serves as a rock of protection, security, and salvation from all terrors of life. *Psychopathic love is a neurotic fear delusion.* There is nothing more deceptive and delusive than psychopathic love,—for it takes its origin in self and fear.

VI. *The Principle of Recession*

Experiences are blotted out from memory in the course of time. A very small percentage of impressions is registered by the brain, a still smaller percentage can be reproduced, and out of them a very small percentage carries *recognition* as memory, that is, of impressions experienced before. *Forgetfulness is therefore a normal physiological function characteristic of the brain and mind.*

Forgetfulness depends on at least three conditions, lack of registration, lack of reproduction, and lack of recognition.

There will correspondingly be at least three forms of amnesia or forgetfulness, *amnesia of registration, amnesia of reproduction, and amnesia of recognition.* The real problem of Psychology is not so much the lapses of memory, but the *why* and *how* of memory, and especially of recognitive memory.

This, however, we may establish as a law that when memory in regard to definite experiences weakens in the course of time, the lapse follows *from recognition to reproduction, and finally to registration.* Recognition fails first, then comes the failure of memory reproduction, and finally memory registration of the special experience becomes blurred and wiped out. This may be termed *the law of memory decay, or of memory regression.* This is the principle of memory recession.

Some, though by no means all, child memories or infantile experiences follow this law of regression or recession. Child experiences, like all old experiences, tend to recede in their course of decay or of regression below the threshold of consciousness. The experiences are not recognized on reproduction, or are reproduced with great difficulty, or have even lost the function of being reproduced. When under such conditions, the experiences are said to have become subconscious, or have receded into the subconscious.

On the other hand some of those subconscious experiences, or subconscious memories may, under favorable conditions, once more regain their functions of reproduction and recognition, and become fully conscious. This may occur in various trance states, subconscious states, and in various psychopathic conditions.

Such states, however, rarely fix the experiences in memory, because the states are instable, temporary, and the memories lapse with the disappearance of the states. This principle of recession may be regarded as one of the fundamental facts of the Psychopathology of the Subconscious. In fact, *subconscious states may also be termed Recessive States.*

VII. *The Principle of Dissociation*

Recessive states, becoming marginal and subconscious, lapse from voluntary control, they cannot be recalled deliberately and consciously by the activities of voluntary, recognitive, associative memories, constituting the mental life of personality, and hence may be regarded as mental systems in a state of *dissociation*. The lapsed states are present subconsciously when not completely blurred and obliterated by the process of decay or regression.

Dissociated, subconscious states, when affected by the impulse of self-preservation and the fear instinct, tend to become parasitic, and like malignant growths may suck the life energy of the affected individual. Under such conditions we have psychopathic, subconscious, dissociated states.

VIII. *The Principle of Irradiation and Diffusion*

In the dormant, subconscious states the fear instinct gradually extends to other subconscious states. The fear instinct acts like a malignant growth, like a fermenting enzyme. The subconscious fear instinct gradually infiltrates, diffuses, irradiates its affective state throughout the subconscious life of the patient, finally giving rise to a psychopathic disposition with its selfishness, apparent repressions, apprehension, anxiety, anguish, terror, and panic. This may also give rise to the general psychopathic character of doubt, indecision, and *conflicting* states, all being determined by the underlying fear instinct.

IX. *The Principle of Differentiation*

With the growth of the impulse of self preservation and with the development of an exaggerated fear instinct, the individual becomes more and more neurotic and psychopathic. This general, neurotic, mental state attaches itself to various events in the life of the individual. The psychopathic disposition keeps on progressing from one event to another. Each one may be regarded as a separate fear state, or phobia. Finally the disposition may settle on the last event in the patient's life experience. This last event may often become the nucleus, or rather the apparent nucleus of the neurosis.

The last experience appears to be central. *As a matter of fact there is a great number of fear states or of phobias in the neurotic patient.* A few only appear to predominate in the network of fear events. The network of fears is woven into an incongruous whole by the impulse of self-preservation and the fear instinct. This network becomes differentiated into a tangle of numerous fear states.

X. *The Principle of Dominance*

The last fear states or *Ultimate Fear States* which stand out clearly and distinctly in the patient's mind become the leading, the dominant abnormal, pathological states. The patient thinks that they are the real source of all his troubles, and if they were removed he would be cured. As a matter of fact the ultimate states are not *causes*, but *occasions. The real causes of the psychopathic constitution are the exaggerated impulse of self-preservation and the intensified fear instinct.*

XI. *The Principle of Dynamogenesis*

Recessive, and especially dissociated systems, being dormant subconsciously, may become envigorated, may accumulate emotion, and when the opportunity comes, may react to external stimuli with vigor and energy. The attacks may occur like epileptic fits. They often so well simulate epileptic maladies that even good clinicians have classed such attacks under the term of larval epilepsy, psychic epilepsy, hystero-epilepsy, or psychic equivalent of epilepsy. This subconscious energy manifestation may be termed *Dynamogenesis.*

XII. *The Principle of Inhibition*

Self-preservation and the fear instinct inhibit associated mental systems, producing morbid states. *Morbid mental states, however, are not produced by inhibitions, or repressions.* It is only when the inhibitive factors are self and fear that a true morbid mental state, or neurosis arises. To regard self repression as a bad condition and leading to diseases is to misapprehend the nature of man, to falsify psychology, and to misrepresent the development of humanity. The self should not become hypertrophied. Self-preservation should not become overgrown. The self must be kept within limits. The self impulse should be kept under control by the individual. For true happiness is to be a law unto oneself. As the great Greek thinkers put it: Happiness is in self rule. The unruly are miserable. In fact, self-control is absolutely requisite to mental health, to sanity. *Self-repression is requisite for happiness. Self-repression never leads to disease.* It is only when self-repression is produced and dominated by selfishness and fear that morbid states of a psychopathic, neurotic character are sure to arise. It is not inhibitions that produce fear, but *it is fear that produces inhibitions.* To ascribe neurosis to self-repression and to conflict is like attributing malaria or tuberculosis to air and light.

XIII. *The Principle of Mental Contest and Discord*

Mental states associated with intense emotions tend to take a dominant lead in consciousness. This, however, may be totally opposed by the general character of the individual. In such cases the whole mental set, being in opposition to the total individuality, is in contest with the character of the person who is then in state of discord. A mental set in contest with the make-up of the person is usually inhibited, becomes subconscious, and as a rule fades away from the mind, often leaving no trace even in memory, conscious or subconscious. In some cases where a compromise is possible, a reconciliation is effected. The mental set is assimilated, and disappears from consciousness as an independent, functioning state.

When, however, the opposing or contesting mental set is based on a fundamental impulse and accompanying instinct, such as the impulse of self-preservation and the fear instinct, a total inhibition is not always possible, even a compromise may not be successful, because the mental set is in association with the core of the individual,— namely self-preservation. The contesting mental set remains, in what Galton terms, "the antechamber of consciousness." The mind is in a state of tension, in a state of anxiety, in restless, uneasy discord, due to the fear instinct, the companion of the impulse of self-preservation. The contesting mental set, charged with intense fear emotion, presses into the foreground of consciousness, and a contest, a discord, ensues in the mind of the individual, a contest, a discord, a conflict which keeps the person in a state of indecision and lack of will power.

The partly inhibited, contesting mental set, when not fading away, may thus remain in the mind, and act like a splinter in the flesh, giving rise to a state of discomfort. This is just what happens when the individual has not been trained to assimilate fear states, and is unable to adjust fear reactions to the welfare of total psycho-physiological life activity.

In cases where the impulse of self-preservation and the fear instinct have become aroused, the contesting fear set of mental states presses again and again to the foreground of consciousness. When no compromise of the contesting states can be brought about, when the fear set cannot be assimilated, the mind is in a state of restless discord. *It is not, however, the discord that produces the neurosis, it is the impulse of self-preservation and the fear instinct that constitute the cause of the psychopathic, neurotic condition.*

XIV. The Principle of Diminishing Resistance

In proportion as the neurotic attacks keep on recurring the formed pathological system is gaining in energy and in ease of manifestation. The psychopathic attacks with their symptoms emerge at an ever diminishing intensity of stimulation. The resistance of healthy normal associations is ever on the decrease until a point is reached when all power of resistance is lost. The conscious and subconscious groups which enter into the psychopathic system, forming the neurosis, get control over the patient's life, and become an uncontrollable, psychopathic obsession.

XV. The Principle of Modification

The patient attempts to control or alleviate his fear state by a totally different fear state. In the long run this is a losing game. For the general fear disposition becomes ultimately reinforced. Finally he may land in the mystic regions of love or of an Infinite Love in which he expects to find safety, protection, and salvation from the miseries of exaggerated self impulse and intensified fear instinct. Such a course, however, leads to a swamp in which the patient's individuality becomes engulfed and obliterated. The end is mental suicide.

These fundamental principles of neurosis-development should be kept in mind in the examination and study of psychopathic cases. The cases adduced in this volume will help one to understand the mechanism of the main factors and principles of neurosis.

CHAPTER XVIII

ILLUSTRATIONS, NEUROTIC HISTORIES

The psychopathic character appears to be full of contradictions, "a house divided against itself." Neurotics are like "the troubled ocean which never rests." Some of my patients complain of fatigue, physical and especially intellectual, inability of concentration of attention, and yet they hint at being undeveloped, unappreciated geniuses. The patient may be said to suffer from a paradoxical state of "humble superiority."

A few of my cases may help one to form some faint idea of the intensity of the impulse of self-preservation and fear instinct which obsess the psychopathic sufferer.

M. A. Age 43, female, married; sister and brother died of tuberculosis. When young, she herself had an attack of tuberculosis from which, however, she entirely recovered. This made her, from her very childhood, think of herself and of the fear of death. She suffers from headaches, backaches, indigestion, and intestinal pains. Her mind is entirely engrossed with herself. The whole world is for her sake, and she does not scruple to utilize anyone who is willing to serve her. She takes advantage of everybody and does not care what the feeling of others might be about her extreme selfishness. If she were sure that no fine or punishment would follow, she would not hesitate to take anything that belongs to others, no matter whether it be a friend or enemy, provided it does her good, drives away some of her discomforts, fear of disease, or gives pleasure to her, even at the expense of other people's agonies. If there were a prize for selfishness, she would be sure to get it. She is sure to take advantage of people who do not know her and who practice the ordinary activities and amenities of life in regard to her. She does not get offended when people refuse her demands. She goes to look for other victims who have as yet no knowledge of her temperament and "sickness." Everything is legitimate to her in order to get well and healthy.

The patient talks of high ideals and of service to humanity, and yet she has not hesitated to lure away a man who had a wife and three children. She made him divorce his wife who was her bosom friend, and marry herself. She spends all his money on her "artistic dresses," while his former wife and his little family are allowed just enough to keep them from starvation. The patient goes around travelling, visits physicians, cures herself, keeps on being sick in various health resorts, learning all kinds of fads, modes of "healthy living."

The patient is in terror of disease and of old age. She fears even to think of such things. She carries around with her all kinds of prescriptions and directions as to how to preserve youth. I was especially instructed by her husband not to inquire for her age. Everything must be subservient to her impulse of self-preservation and instinct of fear. She has dwindled to a parasitic existence, obsessed with the lowest instincts of life. She avoids all responsibilities. She wants to get as much as she can in order to obtain for herself the highest possible benefit. When she meets people who do not know her, she is quick in taking advantage of them. Life to her has no duties but rights. Patient is a typical Nero, a Caligula. She would cheerfully sacrifice a nation to get out a mite of pleasure, comfort, and health.

V. S. Age 49, female. Married; no children. She has three sisters and two brothers who are all well. As a child she lived in great poverty. She was neglected and met with accidents and scares; suffered from sickness until her little body was emaciated from privation. She managed, however, to go through school and become a clerk in a small store; she was very careful of her appearance which meant to her a good marriage, comfortable life. She also took care of her health which was rather precarious, on account of the many colds accompanied by severe headaches. At the same time on account of the poor life led, she also suffered from some obscure troubles. After years of precarious health and quests for happiness, for marriage, she succeeded in capturing a well-to-do merchant in whose store she had worked as a clerk. Immediately after marriage she rigged up a beautiful home with "rich mahogany furniture" which the husband regarded with a gasp, settled down to a life of leisure, to complete idleness, and began to attend to her health....

The patient began to find more and more troubles with her organs, from the top of her head to the pelvis and intestines. Nothing was quite right. Things could be improved. The impulse of self-preservation gained more and more control over her. Along with this impulse the fear instinct gained in strength, became more and more extensive.

The patient became full of fear which, by the principle of proliferation and diffusion, kept on growing and diffusing in ever new directions, and spreading to ever new associations and systems. The central fear was poverty. The patient was afraid she might become poor. This was naturally a fear from her early childhood,—the fear of suffering in poverty, a fear which persisted throughout her life. The fear became accentuated and developed with time. She was afraid to spend money, especially sums above a five dollar bill. No matter how much she tried to reason with herself this fear persisted. She was afraid to buy new things which she regarded more or less expensive. She was afraid to put on new dresses, to buy new furniture, to spend money in any way. In fact, quite often the fear was so uncontrollable that even when she had no thought of threatening poverty she was in a panic of being confronted with expensive purchases.

The fears then began to spread to other things,—such as giving away small articles or loaning books, or presenting any things or objects that might be regarded as expensive and valuable. The fears spread to other objects of importance and value.

Along with it she had fears of indigestion and nutrition, nausea, vomiting, intestinal pains, discomfort, and especially an inordinate amount of distress when in a state of nervous excitement.

The patient was as obstinate as a mule, though claiming that she was doing her best and trying everything in her power to co-operate. She was doing everything in her power to frustrate the physician's directions, claiming at the same time that she was doing her best to follow scrupulously the doctor's orders. She claimed she was nice to people when she was nasty and offensive to everybody who in any way happened not to fall in with her whims and caprices. In fact, even those who went out of their way to please her and did everything in attending to her, and helping her in every way day and night, even those she treated with lack of consideration, even positive disdain and contempt. She was the incarnation of demoniacal obsession of psychopathic meanness and egotism.

She abused and dominated her husband by her sickness, trouble, fainting and crying spells, headaches, moans and weeping. She made him do everything she pleased. In fact, she tyrannized over her husband, and kept on claiming she loved him. She could not for a moment be without him, and complained that on account of her extreme devotion to him, "her will was broken."

She was a regular termagant, a demon incarnate. She knew how to make a scene and put the blame on her "dear ones." It was enough for her to suspect what her friends wanted her to do, she was sure out of sheer malice, to act the contrary. She was distrustful, spying on others, sneaky and lying without any scruples; and yet "no one was so mild, so ideal, so kind, so affectionate, so considerate, so calm as she was." She went around reciting poetry about ideals, health, and happiness. She persuaded herself that she was highly educated, that she was the best business woman, the best critic, appreciative of poetry and of art in general. She was a veritable Nero, an "egomaniac" devoid of all love and human sympathy. She suffered so much, because she was so unusually altruistic. A coyote in her fear, a tigress in her rage, she claimed the gentleness of the dove and the innocence of the babe.

Not for a moment could she fix her attention on anything but herself, eating, drinking, sleeping, and feeling. Nothing interested her but herself. She avoided work, however short and easy. She could, however, talk of herself, of her achievements, of her moral, intellectual qualities by the hour and by the day. Even games did not interest her, nothing but herself, and self. This was so evident that one of the attendants noticed this characteristic psychopathic trait, and described her as "egomaniac." She was the "Great I am." "The Ego-person is the reflection of the Ego-god." ...

Whenever one spoke of a great man, she was sure to have her opinion of him. She was at any rate superior to him. She could give her opinion on any conceivable subject in literature, economics, and politics.

She was as cunning as a savage, and as treacherous as a wild brute, and yet she was to all appearances a veritable saint, full of suffering for the sins of humanity, and for the faults of her husband who was "boyish and foolish, whom she had to manage," and whom she did control and handle with an iron rod.

There is no doubt, however, that she herself was driven by her intense, uncontrollable impulse of self-preservation and by the instinct of fear. What especially terrorized her was the slow but sure *extension of the fear instinct to more and more objects and acts*. The fear instinct kept on creeping on her, slowly choking the life sources of her being. To call the patient "egocentric" is a mild descriptive term,—"tigress," "satan," "fiend," would be more appropriate appellations. In her terror of self-preservation she tormented herself and others. She was a firebrand from hell, a firebrand fanned by the furies of self and fear.

F. W. Age 47; female, married; has no children. The patient claims to have been an invalid from childhood; that she was of extremely delicate health; she always had to take care of her health, and had to go through all kinds of diseases, especially gastro-intestinal troubles. At the age of eighteen she got married and then her family felicity began. She began to complain of all kinds of infirmities. The gynecologist humored her with operations and treatments. The fear disease became strengthened, and finally she cultivated a typical pathophobia; she was in terror of some fearful malady that might possibly take possession of her.

The patient always wanted to have someone near her. This fear of remaining alone dated from childhood, when at the least discomfort, she asked and screamed in terror for help. A companion, or nurse had to be with her day and night, so as to protect her from any impending evil.

Occasionally, to relieve her feelings, in the middle of a conversation, whether for the sake of impressing her family, her husband or her physicians with the gravity of her disease, or as a vent for the rising instinct of fear, she emitted a scream, wild and weird, reminding one of the howling of a timber wolf, or of a wild whoop of an Indian. This was a habit she kept up from childhood. It was a reaction of her fears, and a protection, it was a call for help which was sure to attract attention. The family could not refuse help at hearing such an unearthly call. Later on, it was consciously and unconsciously utilized by the patient as a rod to rule the family and especially her husband, when the latter happened to become refractory. The fear reaction was thus used as a protection and as a weapon of defense.

Things had to run according to her pleasure, or else she was put in a state of nervous excitement and fear with its awful yell of which the family and the husband were in perfect terror; they yielded unconditionally. The patient literally subjugated her husband by her spells of fear, especially by the fearful acoustic performance, the aura, the harbinger of a psychopathic attack.

The patient was always discontented and grumpy. Nothing could satisfy her, nothing was good enough for her. Everybody was criticized. No matter how one tried to please her, she always found fault with the person. In fact, the fault-finding was in proportion to the eagerness one tried to serve and oblige her. The nurses are not good, the servants intolerable, and people in general are bad, mean, stupid, and vulgar. She claims she comes from an "old New England family, from good stock." Her grandfather was a fisherman, and her father a petty tradesman. The patient makes pretensions to education, poetry, art, and drawing. In reality, she is quite dull and ignorant.

G. A. Female, age 63; the patient was obsessed with pathophobia for over thirty-five years. She has been to a number of physicians, and to many sanitariums, looking for health everywhere, not finding it anywhere. The fears date to her early childhood. She was regarded as a delicate child, the fear of disease was strongly impressed on her. She went through a number of children's diseases. Although she had several sisters and brothers, the child's supposed delicate constitution was the fear and worry of the parents. This fear was communicated to the child, who for the rest of her life became a psychopathic patient with the characteristic developed impulse of self-preservation and intense fear of disease. She could not think of anybody but herself, everything had to be arranged for her,—for her food, for her sleep, and for her rest. She kept on complaining at the slightest change either in herself, in others, about the arrangements of the house, or about the weather. Everything had to be arranged just as she demanded, otherwise she was sick, or was going to become dangerously ill.

When about the age of thirty, she married a widower with two children. She trained the children to obey her commands implicitly, otherwise she resorted to the rod of sickness. The pathophobia, consciously or unconsciously, became a power which she wielded in the most tyrannical way. The children had to sacrifice themselves for the pleasure of the sick step-mother. They had to stay with her, and minister to all her whims and fears. The very individuality of the children became almost obliterated by the persistent, egotistic tyranny of the sick, old step-mother. She was like a regular vampire, sucking the life blood of her family.

It goes without saying that the same fear of disease tamed her husband over whom she ruled with an iron hand. The least opposition to her whims, or to her fears of possible disease made her so sick with all kinds of pains that the family and the husband were driven into submission.

The woman was obese as a hippopotamus, well nourished, with a florid complexion, and with an appetite that would shame a Gargantua. The rarest, the best, and the most appetizing dainties had to be on her table. She made of her meals a form of worship, requisite to propitiate the goddess of maladies. She did not hesitate to take the best morsels from the plates of her daughter and son in order to satisfy her appetite which was supposed to be "delicate and small."

The patient was conscious of every square inch in her body; she was afraid that some form of malady may lurk there. She was a typical case of pathophobia. Fear of disease and quest of health were ever in her mind. She could not talk, or think of anything else, but herself and her symptoms. She made of her step-daughter a poor, colorless being, a day and night nurse, tyrannized over by pitiful, neurotic whimpering.

When the patient happened to wake during the night for ever so short a period of time, she did not hesitate to wake her step-daughter, tired as the latter was by constant attendance on this psychopathic shrew. The daughter had to wake up everybody who could in any way bring comfort to that "poor, old, suffering invalid." After much groaning, moaning, and bewailing her bitter lot the invalid took some medicine to appease the fear of disease, partook of some nourishing food to keep up her strength and health, and went to sleep for the rest of the night.

Years ago, the patient was under the care of Weir Mitchell who sent her to me as a last resort. Dr. Weir Mitchell characterized the patient as an "American humbug." As a matter of fact, the patient herself was convinced that she was on the verge of death, and was in terrible agony of her fears of disease, fears which made her quest for health a matter of life and death. The patient was obsessed by *parasitic egotism*, the *quintessence of psychopathic affections*.

Many times during the day she paced the room reciting elevating passages from the Bible, from "great poets,"— Emerson being her favorite writer.

I have heard neurotics with their "Mortal Mind," "Sin and Error," "Disease and Nothing," recite edifying phrases such as: "The decaying flower, the blighted bud, the gnarled oak, the ferocious beast, like the discords of disease, sin, and death are unnatural" ... "Fear is inflammation, error" ... "*Adam, a-dam, a-dam, dam, dam*"....

A man, thirty-eight years old, married, highly sensitive, suffers from migraine; he is irritable and restless. When about eight years old, he wandered in the woods near his house. An Italian ran after him, flourishing a big knife. The boy ran away in terror. When he reached home he dropped from exhaustion and fear. Once or twice, on account of the fear of sharp objects, he actually hurt himself while handling knives. This increased his terror and fixed his fear. The instinct of fear was still further developed and stimulated by a series of events, such as falling into a river, from which he was saved. He does not like to take baths, he is afraid to enter a river, and he is in terror of sharp objects, such as knives and razors.

The patient is extremely selfish. He insists on playing games which he likes much, irrespective of the pleasure of his friends and acquaintances. All he cares for is to have a good time, to neglect his duties to his family. In his business he is exacting of others, although he himself is rather slovenly in his work, and slow in the performance of his obligations. He always insists on having his own way. Other people's rights do not trouble him, provided his rights are carefully and scrupulously observed. He always demands services from others, especially from his friends.

The patient's mind is occupied with his health, his fears, and his ailments. The interest he takes in his friends and acquaintances is how far they may serve his purposes of pleasure, game, health, and avoidance of fear of disease. His wife and child are regarded from a personal standpoint of his own good, otherwise they are totally ignored. When they interfere with him, or arouse his fears, he becomes impatient, angry, and furious. He claims to be the most considerate and kindest of men, brimful of humanitarian ideals. He thinks that he can accomplish more than anyone else in his circumstances. Nothing is too good for him, nobody is superior to him. As a rule things are badly conducted, he finds fault with everybody and with everything. He is driven by psychopathic furies,—discord, fear, and maddening egotism.

CHAPTER XIX 1
CHAPTER XX 1
[9] 134
[9] 134

HYPNOIDAL TREATMENT

Psychopathic or neurotic maladies do not depend on the abnormal action of some one organ or function, but on a general condition common to all bodily and mental functions,—the fundamental primitive fear instinct which relates to life in general.

The deranged functions, cardiac, respiratory, or sexual,—fatigue, conflict, shock, repression and others are only the *occasions*. To regard any of these occasions as the sources of psychopathic maladies is like regarding the weather-cock as the cause of the wind. *Self-preservation and the fear instinct alone form the source of all psychopathic maladies.*

I adduce here a few cases which may be taken as typical:

Mrs. M. C., aged thirty-two years. Family history good; well developed physically and mentally. A year before the present trouble set in, patient suffered from a severe attack of grippe. Menstruation, which was before painless and normal in amount, became painful and scanty, accompanied by headaches, indisposition, irritability, crying spells and backache which lasted long after the menstrual period was over. The family physician ascribed the symptoms to endometritis, mainly cervical and treated her with absolute rest, fomentations, injections, scarification and dilatation of the cervix, and finally curetted the uterus. As the patient grew worse under the treatment, she was taken to a gynecologist, who after an examination suggested an operation. The operation was duly performed, with the result that the nervous symptoms became intensified, and the attacks increased in violence and duration. The turn of the nerve specialist came next. Hysteria, neurasthenia, and the more fashionable "psychasthenia" have been diagnosed by various neurologists. A year of psychoanalysis made of the patient a complete wreck, with depression, introspection and morbid self-analysis. Patient was put by neurologist under Weir Mitchell's treatment.

When the patient came under my care, she was in mental agonies, a complete wreck. I gave up the Weir Mitchell rest treatment, sent away the nurse, released the patient from solitary bed confinement, told her to leave the sick room, to give up dieting and medicines, and to return to a normal, active life. I kept on treating her by the hypnoidal state. The patient began to improve rapidly, and finally all her physical and mental symptoms disappeared; she has continued for over six years in excellent condition of health.

A study of the case traced the fear instinct to experiences of early childhood, fears accentuated and developed into morbid states by the deleterious tendencies of the treatment, giving rise to a *somatopsychosis*, the physical symptoms mainly predominating.

A lady, aged fifty-nine years, suffered from kynophobia. When about the age of twenty-nine years she was bitten by a dog; since then she was afraid of hydrophobia. She kept on reading in the papers about cases of hydrophobia until the fear became developed to an extraordinary degree and became fixed and uncontrollable. According to the principles of evolution of psychopathic states, the fear kept on extending. The fear psychosis included all objects that might possibly carry the germ of hydrophobia. The neurosis became a mysophobia.

As in all other cases of psychopathic states the psychosis was traced to the fear instinct, the germ of which was laid in the patient's early history. The patient was a timid child, and was afraid of strange animals. In the village where she lived there were a few cases of hydrophobia which impressed her when a child. This germ was in later life developed by thirty years' cultivation.

Psychopathic or neurotic symptom complexes I observed in children whose early training was favorable to the awakening and development of the fear instinct. In children affected with fear of animals I traced the fear psychosis to the parents who were afraid of animals, on account of actual traumas in their life history, *the child being influenced by imitation, by suggestion, often subconscious, by the behavior of the parents in the presence of animals.* Such children are predisposed to recurrent psychopathic states.

In all such cases the etiology is easy to find, if the patient is carefully examined. In many cases the fear instinct with its symptom complex is associated with external objects, giving rise to the so-called phobias. Instead, however, of being associated with external objects, the fear instinct is frequently associated with somatic functions (pathophobia), or with mental activities (phrenophobia).

Man, aged forty-seven years; actor; family neurotic. Patient suffered from anorexia, indigestion, choking, vomiting, gagging, eructation, gastralgia, and occasional pains in the limbs. He led a rather gay and irregular life up to the age of thirty-two years, when he had syphilis, for which he was under treatment for two years. This scared him because he had the opportunity to see the consequences of syphilis in many of his friends. He had been under continual fear of the possibility of development of parasyphilitic diseases.

Seven years ago, at the age of forty years, he had to watch at the bedside of an intimate friend, who had been suffering from severe gastric crises of tabes dorsalis. After one specially exhausting night of vigil, worry and fear, he went to bed for a short nap and woke up with the idea of general paresis and intense fear. From that time he began to suffer from symptoms of tabes with fear of general paresis.

The patient had been an imaginative child; he had his fear instinct cultivated from early childhood by stories of frights, scares, and horrible accidents. When ten years old, his grandfather gave *Faust* to him to read. Since then the patient was troubled with the fear of selling his soul to Satan. The patient was religious in his childhood, prayed much, and was possessed by the fear of committing sins. "It has now all come back," he complained. A great number of fears could be traced to his early childhood. The somatic symptoms were the manifestations of association of experiences of parasyphilitic diseases, based on the pathological state of the fear instinct, a case of pathophobia, a somatopsychosis.

A few hypnoidal treatments effected a cure. The patient returned to his occupation, free from any distressing symptoms.

H. M. aged twenty-seven years, male, Canadian. Family history good; looked pale, anemic, and frail; very intelligent, sensitive, restless, and had a tendency to worry. About a year ago, he began to feel depressed, to worry about his health; thought he suffered from tuberculosis. His physician assured him that nothing was the matter, but he had an uncontrollable fear of consumption; and the idea kept on recurring. Up to the age of nineteen years he was perfectly well. He was then laid up with a sore knee for a few weeks. He had time enough to brood over the knee, and read some literature on the subject. He thought it was tuberculosis and worried much. The knee, however, got well, and gradually he forgot all about it, although the idea of tuberculosis often made him feel uncomfortable, and the idea of "water in the knee" used to flash through his mind, to pass away the next moment.

A year ago, however, he happened to lose his work, became despondent, began to worry and to brood over his financial troubles, slept restlessly, suffered from anorexia, and began to lose flesh. The idea of the knee and the fear of tuberculosis got possession of him. He could not rid himself of the idea of tuberculosis. If in the clinic the physician assured him that he was all right, he felt better for a couple of hours; but often it did not last even as long as that. The least pain, cough, heart beat, a feeling of chill or heat, and the like, brought the idea and fear of tuberculosis back to his mind with renewed energy. He was obsessed by the fear of tuberculosis and felt he was doomed to certain death, a psychosomatic pathophobia.

Hypnoidal states did good service. The patient's mental condition began to improve rapidly. He was no longer troubled with depression, insomnia, and fears; began to gain in weight, appetite improved, felt energy flowing in; began to look for work in real earnest, finally found it, and kept at it.

Man, aged forty-three years, suffered from palpitation of the heart, fainted easily, especially on physical examination by physician, or at the beginning of medical treatment. He suffered from indigestion for which he had been under treatment for a number of years by physicians who gave him medicine for his bowels and also from time to time kept on washing his stomach. He had a great fear of becoming a victim of cardiac troubles, especially of some unknown, terrible, valvular affection. When under my care he kept on asking to be taken to heart and stomach specialists, to be examined, and have some radical operation performed. Frequently under the influence of the fear states and obsession of heart and stomach trouble, especially the heart, he would collapse suddenly, be unable to walk, and be afraid that he suffered from some paralysis.

On examination the patient revealed a history full of various traumas which, from his very childhood until he came under my care, helped to bring about his psychopathic condition, and developed the fear instinct to an extraordinary degree.

Physicians had the lion's share in this special case by their rearing of the fear instinct, and by their favoring the patient's phobias by their examinations, by their prescriptions, and by the diet and treatment. The patient was in such a panic that he kept on taking his pulse on the least occasion, was feeling his heart, stomach, and intestines at every opportunity. The hypertrophied growth of his morbid self and fear instinct had invaded and dominated the patient's whole personality, developed a typical psychosomatic pathophobia with its recurrent states. The patient was cured by hypnoidal states.

In the *Trudi for 1913 of the University of Moscow, Russia, Doctor Ribakov made an extensive study of a series of cases of psychopathic or psychoneurotic asthma, and arrived at a conclusion similar to my own, although he was no doubt unaware of my work and publications on the same subject. He came to the same conclusion as I that the etiology of neurosis is to be found in fear, which alone forms the basis of psychopathic neurosis. All other factors, social, professional, sexual, religious, repressions, conflicts are only occasions of the disease. It is fear, and fear alone that forms the pathology of the psychopathic neurotic symptom complex.*

A young lady was afflicted with ornithophobia, fear of birds, fear of chickens. The sight of a chicken set her into a panic. The patient is very timid, and this timidity can be traced to her early childhood. When at the age of six, a play-mate threw a live chicken at her in the dark. The child was terribly frightened, screamed, and fainted. The mother used to tell her fairy stories full of adventure, of ghosts, of dragons, and of monsters. This prepared the patient to react so violently to the sudden attack made by the flight, struggling, and feel of the chicken in the dark. Since that time, patient has formed an uncontrollable fear of live birds.

Another patient of mine, a lady of forty-nine years, single, suffered from potamophobia, a fear of going into rivers, or into the ocean. When about seven years old she was thrown into water by one of her elder sisters. She was nearly drowned and was half dead with fear when rescued. Since then she has been in terror of water, or rather of rivers and oceans. Several times she made conscious efforts to get rid of the fear, but the attempts were unsuccessful. In fact, the more she was forced or forced herself consciously to get into the water, the greater was the fear. This fear became all the more intensified, when some of her intimate friends were drowned in a boat. This fixed the fear which became uncontrollable.

A patient of mine, a man of thirty-five years, was afraid of going out in the dark. This was traced to early associations of fears of the dark, to superstitious beliefs in ghosts and spirits cultivated in the patient's early childhood. He was afraid to remain alone in the dark or to go down at night into cellars or other secluded places. This fear was unfortunately still more intensified by an accident. At the age of twenty-seven, one night when returning late from a visit, he was assaulted from behind by foot-pads. This accident fixed the fear of darkness.

A lady of sixty-seven years, with pronounced arteriosclerosis, had an attack of hemiplegia of the left side. She suffered from motor aphasia, but did not lose consciousness. The paralysis cleared up in a few days, but the sudden attack demoralized her. Since that time she is in terror of another attack. She watches for symptoms, and the least sensation of faintness throws her into a panic. The patient is the wife of a general and was in China during the Boxer riots, in the Spanish American war, in the

Philippines, and other military engagements. The fear instinct was cultivated in her by all such conditions.

In her early childhood there were fears and frights of child character, enough to arouse the fear instinct, which was gradually developed and cultivated by the circumstances of life and by worries in the course of the various wars, of which she was a witness. Finally the fear culminated by the stroke of paralysis.

Similarly, I had patients who suffered from tuberculosis, from asthma, from heart trouble, and from all kinds of intestinal affections which specially abound in psychopathic cases. All such cases can be clearly traced to various somatic symptoms based on the fear instinct. The etiology is fear, the arousal and development of the fear instinct in respect to the special symptom complex.

A patient, aged twenty-six years, suffered from agoraphobia at various intervals. As a child of nine years, he was attacked by rough boys. He freed himself and ran in great terror. The boys threatened him with another "licking" when he appeared again on the street. He was afraid to go out for several weeks. The parents forced him to go and buy some things. Living in a rough neighborhood, on account of his father's circumstances, he had been many times subjected to knocks, blows, and assaults by rough boys, until the fear of the open street became fixed into the well known form of agoraphobia.

Another case, that of a lady of thirty-eight years, married, suffers from ailurophobia, or fear of cats. This can be traced to the patient's early childhood. When she was a child her brothers and sisters went through attacks of diphtheria, which was ascribed to infection caused or transmitted by cats. The patient was specially impressed with the danger from cats. Under such training and suggestion given in early childhood, the patient gradually formed a fear of cats. This fear was still more intensified and became a panic when she was put into a dark room and a cat was let loose on the poor victim by her mischievous companions, who knew of the patient's fear. When the patient had children of her own, she was still more affected by the fear of cats, on account of the subconscious and conscious fear of the possibility of infection transmitted by cats to her children.

All those cases were investigated and cured by hypnoidal states.

Mr. D., a young man of twenty-five years, was born in Poland. As far as can be ascertained, the parents as well as the brothers and sisters are well. A physical examination of the patient reveals nothing abnormal. There are no sensory, no motor disturbances. He complains of severe headaches, preceded by a feeling of indisposition, depression, vertigo and distress. During the attack there is hyperesthesia to touch, pressure, temperature, and to visual and auditory stimulations. *The patient shivers and looks pale.* The cold experienced during the attack is so intense that the patient has to wrap himself in many blankets, as if suffering from a malarial paroxysm.

Fears have strong possession of the patient's mind. He is afraid to remain in a closed place in the daytime and especially at night. When he has to remain alone at night, he is in an agony of fear, and cannot go to sleep. Every passer-by is regarded as a robber or murderer, and he quakes at the least noise. When walking in the house in the dark, he has the feeling as if someone were after him, and occasionally even experiences the hallucination of some one tugging at his coat. He is mortally afraid of the dead and shuns a funeral. The patient has also a fear of dogs, a kynophobia. The fear is irresistible, and is as involuntary as a reflex.

An investigation, by means of the hypnoidal states, brought out of the patient's subconscious life the following data: When a child of three years, the patient lived with his family in a small village near a large forest infested with wolves. In one of the intermediary states a faint memory, rather to say a vision, struggled up, a vision of wolves and dogs. Some one cried out: "Run, wolves are coming!" Crazed with fear, he ran into the hut and fell fainting on the floor. It turned out to be dogs instead of a pack of wolves. It is that fright in early childhood which has persisted in the subconscious mind, and, having become associated with subsequent experiences of attacks of dogs, has found expression in the patient's consciousness as an instinctive fear of dogs.

But why was the patient in such abject terror of dead people? This found its answer in the experiences and training of his early life. When a young child, the patient heard all kinds of ghost stories, and tales of wandering lost souls and of spirits of dead people hovering about the churchyard and burial grounds; he heard tales of ghouls and of evil spirits inhabiting deserted places, dwelling in the graves of sinners and the wicked. He listened to stories of haunted houses and of apparitions stalking about in the dark. His social and religious environment has been saturated with the belief in the supernatural, as is usually the case among the superstitious populations of Eastern Europe. We cannot wonder, then, that an impressionable child brought up under such conditions should stand in mortal fear of the supernatural, especially of the dead.

When the patient was about nine years old, his parents noticed some prominences on his right chest. It was suggested to them that the hand of a dead person possessed the property of blighting life and arresting all growth, and would, therefore, prove a "powerful medicine" for undesirable growths. It happened that an old woman in the neighborhood died. The little boy was taken into the room where the dead body was lying, and the cold hand of the corpse was put on the child's naked chest. The little fellow fainted away in terror. The fear of dead people became subconsciously fixed, and manifested itself as an insistent fear of the dead, and, in fact, of anything connected with the dead and the world of spirits.

The patient had hardly recovered from the shock of the "dead hand," when he had to pass through a still more severe experience. A party of drunken soldiers, stationed in the little town, invaded his house and beat his father unmercifully, almost crippled him: they knocked down his mother, killed a little brother of his, and he himself, in the very depth of a winter night, dressed in a little shirt and coat, made his escape to a deserted barn, where he passed the whole night. He was nearly frozen when found in the morning, crouching in a corner of the barn, shivering with fear and cold.

From that time on the headaches manifested themselves in full severity, with hyperesthesia and death-like paleness and intense cold of the body. The early cultivation of the fear instinct resulted in a *neurosis* with its recurrent states.

Another patient is a man of thirty years; his family history is good. He is physically well developed, a well known professor of physics in one of the foremost institutions in this country. He suffers from attacks of loss of personality. The attack is of a periodical character, coming on at intervals of two weeks, occasionally disappearing for a few months, then reasserting itself with renewed energy and vigor. During the attack the patient experiences a void, a panic, which is sudden in its onset, like *petit mal*. The trouble was diagnosed as larval or psychic epilepsy; the man was referred to me by Dr. Morton Prince as an extremely interesting, but puzzling neurological case.

Patient feels that his "self" is gone. He can carry on a conversation or a lecture during the attack, so that no outsider can notice any change in him, but his self is gone, and all that he does and says, even the demonstration of a highly complex problem in integral calculus is gone through in an automatic way. The fury of the attack lasts a few moments, but to him it appears of long duration. He is "beside himself," as he puts it. He seems to stand beside himself and watch his body, "the other fellow," as he describes it, carry on the conversation or the lecture. He is "knocked out of his body, which carries on all those complicated mental processes." For days after he must keep on thinking of the attack, feels scared and miserable, thinking insistently, in great agony, over his awful attack, *a recurrent psychoneurotic phrenophobia.*

At first the patient could trace this attack only as far back as his seventh year. Later on, earlier experiences of childhood came to light, and then it became clear that the *attack developed out of the primitive instinctive fear of early childhood,* fear of the unfamiliar, fear of the dark, of the unknown, of the mysterious, fears to which he had been subjected in his tender years.

This state was further reinforced by the early death of his parents, it was hammered in and fixed by hard conditions of life, full of apprehension and anxiety. Life became to the child one big mysterious fear of the unknown. The fear instinct formed the pathological focus of the attack. As the patient puts it: "It is the mystical fear of the attacks which overpowers me."

With the disintegration of the focus the symptom complex of the attacks disappeared. The patient is in excellent condition, he is doing brilliant work in physics and chemistry and is professor in one of the largest universities in Canada.

I present another case apparently "paranoidal," a case interesting from our standpoint. The patient is a man of twenty-seven years; his parents are neurotic, religious revivalists. As far back as the age of eight he suffered from agonizing fears of perdition and scares of tortures in hell, impressed on his sensitive, young mind during the revivals. He is very religious, obsessed with the fear of having committed an unpardonable sin. He thinks he is damned to suffer tortures in hell for all eternity. He keeps on testing any chance combinations, and if his guesses turn out correct, he is wrought up to a pitch of excitement and panic. For to him it means a communication coming from an unseen world of unknown mysterious powers. With his condition diagnosed as "paranoidal dementia praecox," the patient was committed to an insane asylum, from which he was subsequently released.

The attack comes in pulses of brief duration, followed by long periods of brooding, depression, and worry. The primitive fear of pain, of danger and death, and the sense of the mysterious cultivated by his religious training, reached here an extraordinary degree of development. Among the earliest memories that have come up in the hypnoidal state was the memory of a Sunday school teacher, who cultivated in the patient, then but five years of age, those virulent germs which, grown on the soil of the primitive instinctive fear and the highly developed sense of the unknown and the mysterious, have brought forth poisonous fruits which now form the curse of his life. The case is a typical *psychoneurotic phrenophobia* with its characteristic recurrent states.

"It is difficult," the patient writes, "to place the beginning of my abnormal fear. It certainly originated from doctrines of hell which I heard in early childhood, particularly from a rather ignorant teacher who taught Sunday school. My early religious thought was chiefly concerned with the direful eternity of torture that might be awaiting me, if I was not good enough to be saved."

After a couple of years of persistent treatment by means of the hypnoidal state and by methods of association and disintegration of the active subconscious systems, the patient recovered. He entered a well known medical school and took the foremost rank among the medical students.

In the investigation or psychognosis of psychopathic cases I invariably find the psychopathology to be a morbid condition of the fear instinct, rooted in the primordial impulse of self-preservation. The psychognosis of this underlying pathological state and disintegration of the latter are of the utmost consequence in the domain of psychopathology and psychotherapeutics.

FOOTNOTE:

A full account of the cases is published in my volume "The Causation and Treatment of Psychopathic Diseases."

FEAR CONFESSIONS

A few "Confessions" made by psychopathic sufferers will help us best to understand the character, the mechanism, the factors, and principles of neurosis:

I

"As you are desirous of knowing more about my life and environment, I state concerning them as follows:

"You will remember that I told you that my step-father was a liquor dealer. Throughout all the time that he was in business we either lived over the bar-room or else right in the place where the liquor was sold. My step-father was a very heavy drinker, a man of violent nature, and decidedly pugnacious. As a child I have been scared to death by drunken brawls, and many nights have been dragged out of bed by my mother who would flee with me to the house of a neighbor for safety.

"I might say that until I was seventeen years old, I lived in continual terror of something going to happen. If he was arrested by the police, as often happened, our home would be a scene of turmoil until the case was settled.

"I remember one incident very plainly, when he came home one night completely covered with blood as the result of being held up by thugs, and another time when he left the house to subdue some quarreling drunks with a pistol and returned after an exchange of shots with his hand shot through.

"As a child, I was inclined to study, and associated very little with other children. My mother tells me that I talked early, but when about three years old I began to stammer. This trouble bothered me a great deal, and I used to worry about it all the time, especially in school when I would try to recite. I might add that even now, when excited, I am troubled in the same way.

"My step-father has been subject to nightmares nearly all his life; when asleep he would cry and moan and would be unable to move until some one would shake him out of it. He was terribly afraid of them, and I remember he used to say that he expected to die in one of them. I used to be left alone with him quite frequently, and I stood in constant fear of his dying; and if he fell asleep, as he frequently did in the day time, I would wake him or watch his respiration to see if he was alive.

"At other times I have been awakened in the night by his cries and would assist my mother in bringing him to consciousness. It was during one of these times that I became aware of my heart palpitating, and whenever he had such a spell, I would be in a state of fear and excitement for some time after. He would have these nightmares nearly every night and some times four or five times in one night, and I might add that he has them even now.

"I began to have attacks of dizziness in the streets, and finally one day, I had one, and all symptoms and fears of the attack came on in school, and from that time on I have watched my respiration and suffered from dizziness, mental depression, and sadness.

"You have asked me to tell you more in detail about the attacks or nightmares to which my step-father was subject, and which always frightened me greatly, especially when a child.

"My step-father had the habit of falling asleep quite often, even in the day time, and I have never known him to go to sleep without having an attack in some form. If one watched him asleep, as I often did, one could tell by his respiration when an attack was coming. His breathing would become slower and hardly perceptible, and finally he would begin to moan, and cry out; then, when shaken vigorously and spoken to, he would awaken in great fear and apparent suffering. If he had an attack, and we did not respond soon enough, he would be very angry and say that we cared not if he should die. We were so afraid of these attacks that we had trained ourselves to be ever on the look-out for his cries, even at night.

"It really seemed as if his life rested in our hands. I might say that sometimes these attacks lasted several minutes, before he could be awakened. He used to say that at such times he always dreamed someone was choking, beating, or otherwise torturing him. He had been told by some physician that he would ultimately die in such an attack.

"These attacks were sufficient to precipitate a small panic in the house. I know not a single hour of the day or night, but that I have either been called or awakened by my mother in her efforts to awaken him. With the attack over, I would be trembling all over, and my heart would be beating madly. I can remember these attacks from my earliest childhood, and it seems to me that on one occasion, at your office, I was startled just as these attacks used to make me."

While in the hypnoidal state, patient exclaimed: "I am afraid. All my life I lived under terror.... This is just my disease,—fear."

II

"I lived from infancy in a state of apprehension and fear. In my home there seemed to be always a tension. I don't know that I ever relaxed there during my waking hours. I was never at peace mentally. This was largely brought about by my mother's chronic condition of fear. I should not have had such a large development of the fear habit had there been any neutralizing influence. But my father was a weak character, living under fear, being afraid of responsibility, so that my character was closely molded on his. He gave me no moral fiber to resist fears of mother, and so did not help me to build any character of my own. I still carry with me the state of apprehension and fear that I contracted in my early life. I had only one serious illness in my life outside of my nervous troubles. Had an attack of bowel trouble somewhere near the age of six. I was once struck in the face by a dog's teeth. I have had various cancer experiences.

"My father, when I was very young, had some irritation of the throat. A physician told him he was in danger of cancer. I can recall him anxiously looking at his throat. Later a neighbor went to a 'plaster specialist' to have a supposed cancer of the tongue removed. His wife was often at our home talking of his sufferings.

"While attending dental school I contracted some trouble. I went to a physician near where I lived. He talked to me of a possibility of syphilis. I became much frightened, and read all I could find on syphilis. The books scared me still more. At last on the advice of friends, I went to another physician who reassured me, and I lost part of my fear.

"After this I returned home for a summer vacation. This was in 1904. That summer my tongue felt sore, I looked at it, and found it peculiar. This aroused my fears of syphilis.

Upon returning to Chicago in the fall (1904) I asked my physician to recommend a specialist. He sent me to a syphilographer, who told me I had no syphilis, but that the condition of my tongue was caused by gall bladder trouble. He wished me to have the gall bladder operated which I refused to do. I thought no more about my tongue until I studied cancer in oral surgery. I would then occasionally worry over my condition. About this time an actor whom I knew died of cancer of the tongue. I worried over my tongue, being afraid of cancer, for several days after this. I then went along for seven or eight years without much thought of my tongue.

"One day in February 1913, after some pain in my side which brought the thoughts of gall bladder and then of the tongue, I asked advice of a physician. He looked at my tongue and said: 'I don't wish to frighten you, but you should have that tongue attended to. You might some day have a cancer there.' He sent me to a throat specialist who said the condition of my tongue was due to a back tooth. I had the tooth removed. I afterwards consulted Dr. L., a surgeon at Eau Claire, Wis., with the idea of having the gall bladder operated upon. He laughed at the gall bladder trouble, but sent me to Battle Creek Sanitarium with the idea, I think, that the change would relieve me of my fears. At Battle Creek I was told I had a mild case of colitis, and was put under treatment for it.

"While at Battle Creek my fears grew less. I remained at Battle Creek about two months. Shortly before leaving there I was given a Wasserman test. This they told me was faintly positive. I was then given three injections of Neo-Salvarsan. I then left Battle Creek and stopped at Chicago to see Dr. P. Dr. P. said any Wasserman would be positive, taken with no more care than mine had been. That there was no reason to think there was any syphilis anyway. He then sent me to Dr. W., an internist, who said I had hyperacidity of the stomach.

"I did not feel very badly at this time, although my fears of cancer persisted. I was carrying on the work in my office. Later in the summer I went to the Mayo Clinic at Rochester, Minn., where I was given a local application for my tongue. In the fall of 1913, while in Milwaukee I consulted an oral surgeon, Dr. B. He said 'I will send you to Dr. F., a dermatologist who knows more about diseases of the tongue than any man I know.' I consulted Dr. F. who said: 'Geographical tongue, do not worry about it.' My fears were instantly relieved. I seldom thought of my tongue in the next two years.

"In the fall of 1916 I had some trouble with my stomach. This seemed to bring my fears to mind and one day my fear of cancer returned. There was a connection between my fears and the stomach and gall bladder trouble diagnosed in regard to my tongue. At least the stomach trouble would bring thoughts of the tongue condition.

"I tried to help myself out of my mental condition by reading articles on cancer. This made me worse. I went to Chicago where I was told by Dr. S., a dermatologist, that radium might remedy the condition of my tongue. I had several applications of radium. After this I still worried a great deal. I went through the spring and summer under a nervous strain, but still able to carry on my work. That fall (1917) I had such intense fear that I was attacked by acute insomnia. I was unable to sleep without Veronal. The day after my insomnia began I found myself very weak. I was pale, and my heart would pound on the least exertion. I had also a great deal of pain in my bowels. I went to Chicago and consulted Dr. E., Dean of Northwestern University Medical School. He told me such conditions usually traveled in a circle, that my nervous condition might leave me in a few months. I went through the winter in this condition.

"I began to have a great fear of the fact that it was necessary to use hypnotics. This fear of drugs was strong, and overshadowed my other fears. I read an article on hypnotics as a habit; this added to my fear of them.

"Before using hypnotics I noticed my sexual power was less, or rather there was no pleasure in it. This did not trouble me as I thought it a part of my nervous condition.

"In April, 1918, I went again to Battle Creek. I did very well there for a week, but then got into a deep depression, became weak, and was frightened to think I was no better. I remained in Battle Creek for three weeks, and then went home. A month later I went to St. Paul and consulted a neurologist. He did not know what to do for me.

"I went to Milwaukee and consulted another neurologist. I was becoming more despondent all the time. I decided to go to a sanitarium to see if I could not get rid of my drug habit. I went to Wauwatosa, Wis., and remained there three weeks, but I could see they did not know what to do for me.

"In August I entered the Rest Hospital at Minneapolis and remained there for a while under the care of Dr. J. I managed to drag along, terrorized by my condition and by the fact that I could get no relief.

"The drug habit was my greatest obsession at this time. I used bromides and chloral hydrate,—changed hypnotics frequently.

"In January, 1919, I saw Dr. P. of Chicago, who sent me to a sanitarium where I received no help. I then hunted through magazines for articles on nervous diseases. I read of Dr. S. and his work and came under his care at Portsmouth in May, 1919. While there I learned to control my fears. I left Portsmouth in August feeling sure of myself. I would occasionally have a depression which would not frighten me and did not remain with me long. I was looking forward to a happy future.

"During the summer of 1921 I felt tired most of the time. However, I was still sure of being able to handle myself. One day after feeling very tired my fear of cancer returned. I got into a panic and started East to see Dr. S. On arriving in Boston I found he was in the West. I went to Dr. P.'s office; was sent to Dr. W. and by him to a psycho-analyst. The psycho-analyst said I had a 'mother complex, without usual sexual features.' Psycho-analysis proved a failure, and I abandoned the treatment with disgust, as useless and silly."

The patient was under my care for five months. He is now back to his dental work. He writes to me that he is gaining rapidly in weight, and is in excellent condition.

III

"I am a married woman of fifty-two. All my life I have been imprisoned in the dungeon keep of fear. Fear paralyzes me in every effort. If I could once overcome my enemy, I would rejoice forever more.

"In childhood everything cowered me. I was bred in fear. At five or six my mother died, and I feared and distrusted a God who would so intimidate me and bereave me. I heard tales of burglars being discovered hiding under beds, and a terrified child retired nightly for years. I was in agony of fears. My fears I never told. Later I heard of the doctrines of God's foreknowledge, and, as a little rebel, I would place dishes on the pantry shelves, changing from place to place, and then giving up in despair, knowing that if foreknowledge were true, God knew that I would go through with all that performance.

"Through childhood I feared suicide. It was a world of escape that appealed to me and yet appalled me. I also heard of somnambulism, and I never saw a keen bladed knife, but I dreaded that in my sleep I might do damage to myself or to my friends in a state of unconsciousness.

"In my twenties I did attempt suicide a number of times, but somehow they proved unsuccessful. I always aimed to have it appear an accident. I dreaded to have my death appear as a stain and disgrace to my family which I loved.

"I always fear to walk at any height, on a trestle over running walls, or even to walk on a bridge without side railings.

"As a child I was afraid of the dark, I was afraid of going out on the street in a dark night. In fact, even a moonlight night terrified me when I remained alone. I was afraid to go into dark places, such as cellars, or into lonely places even in the daytime.

"As a child I was always shy, fearful, timid, and self-conscious to a painful degree. Even as a grown-up woman I am often a sufferer from the same cause, although I have sufficient self-control to conceal it.

"I have to be careful of my state of health, as the latter is very delicate. I am a chronic sufferer from indigestion and constipation, although I somehow manage to regulate these troubles.

"When I need my nerves in good control so frequently, they are in a state of utter collapse. My brain is in a state of confusion, in a state of whirl just when I need to think the clearest. My poor brain feels as if a tight band encircled and contracted it. It seems to me as if the brain has shrunken from the temples.

"My memory is unreliable. Often I read quite carefully, but I am unable to recall what I have read. Especially is this so, if called upon without previous warning. My brain goes into a panic of an extremely alarming kind.

"I was told that I was a woman of a good brain and of great talent, that all I needed was to exercise my will and determination, and that I would succeed. I lack concentration and I lack confidence.

"In my childhood hell fire was preached. Fore-ordination and an arbitrary God were held up to my childish comprehension. I was bred in fear, and self destruction resulted."

IV

The following valuable account given by an eminent physician brings out well the factors and principles of neurosis expounded in this volume:

"You ask me to write about my fears. I give you a brief account.

"As a child, as far as memory carries, I had a fear of ghosts, of giants, of monsters, and of all kinds of mysterious and diabolical agencies and witchcraft of which I had heard a number of tales and stories in my early childhood. I was afraid of thieves, of robbers, and of all forms of evil agencies. The fears were stronger at daytime, but more so at night. Strange noises, unexpected voices and sounds made a cold shiver run down my back.

"I was afraid to remain alone in a closed room, or in the dark, or in a strange place. It seemed to me as if I was left and abandoned by everybody, and that something awful was going to happen to me. When I happened to be left alone under such conditions I was often in a state of helplessness, paralyzing terror. Such states of fear sweep occasionally over me even at present. I find, however, that they are far more complicated with associations of a more developed personal life. I know that in some form or other the fears are present, but are inhibited by counteracting impulses and associations. I still feel a cold shiver running down my back, when I happen to go into a dark cellar in the dead of night, or happen to remain alone in a dark, empty house. Such fears date back to my fourth year, and possibly to an earlier time of my childhood.

"As a matter of contrast-inhibitions of such fears I may either brace myself and put myself in a state of courage and exaltation, or when this does not succeed, I let my mind dwell on other fears and troubles. I find that the last method is often far more effective in the inhibition of fear states which at the moment are present with me. All I need is to press the button, so to say, and awaken some other fears, the present fears diminish in intensity, and fade away for the time being. I actually favor, and welcome, and even look for disagreeable and painful experiences so as to overcome some of my present fears. The new fears are then treated in the same way.

"As I became older, about the age of eight, I began to fear disease and death. This may be due to the infectious diseases that attacked many members of our family, about this time. In fact, I have been present at the death bed of some of them, and the impression was one of terror, mysterious horror. I was afraid I might get diseases from which I might die. After my witnessing the last agonizing moment of death, my elders thought of removing me to a safer place; their fears and precautions still more impressed the fear of danger of disease and death. I may say that I really never freed myself from the fear of disease and death. The latter fear is always present with me in a vague form, always ready to crop up at any favorable opportunity. This fear, in so far as it is extending its tentacles in various directions, is often the bane of my life. Even at my best there is always a kind of vague fear of possible danger, lurking in various objects which may be infected or possibly poisonous.

"This fear has been spreading and has become quite extensive, involving my family, my children, my friends, my acquaintances, and my patients. Usually I ignore these fears, or get control over them by an effort of will. When, however, I happen to be fatigued, or worried over small things in the course of my work, or happen to be in low spirits by petty reversals of life, these fears may become aroused. Under such conditions I may become afraid, for instance, of drinking milk, because it may be tuberculous.

"This fear may spread and involve fear for my children and my patients; or again I may be afraid of eating oysters and other shell fish, because they may be infected with typhoid fever germs. I may refuse to eat mushrooms, because they may be poisonous. The other day I was actually taken sick with nausea and with disposition to vomiting after eating of otherwise good mushrooms. The fear seized on me that they all might be poisonous 'toadstools.' Such fears may extend to ever new reactions and to ever new associations, and are possibly the worst feature of the trouble.

"I have a fear of coming in contact with strangers, lest I get infected by them, giving me tuberculosis, influenza, scarlet fever, and so on. This mysophobia involves my children and my friends, inasmuch that I am afraid that strangers may communicate some contagious diseases. A similar fear I have in regard to animals, that they may possibly be infected with rabies, or with glanders, or with some other deadly, pathogenic micro-organism. I am afraid of mosquito bites, lest they give me malaria, or yellow fever. The fears, in the course of their extension, may become ever more intense and more insidious than the original states.

"As a child I had some bad experiences with dogs; I was attacked by dogs and badly bitten. Although this fear is no longer so intense as it was in my childhood, still I know it is present. My heart sometimes comes to a sudden standstill, when I happen to come on a strange dog. When the strange dog growls and barks, all my courage is lost, and I beat an inglorious retreat. It is only in the presence of other people that I can rise to the effort of walking along and apparently paying no attention to the dog. This is because I fear the opinion of others more even than I fear the growls of dogs. My social and moral fears are far greater than my purely physical fears.

"When I became older, about the age of eighteen to twenty, a new form of fear appeared, like a new sprout added to the main trunk, or possibly growing out of the main fear of disease and death, that is the fear of some vague, impending evil. The fear of some terrible accident to myself and more so to my family, or to any of the people of whom I happen to take care, is constantly present in the margin of my consciousness, or as you would put it, in my subconsciousness. Sometimes the fears leave me for a while, sometimes they are very mild, and sometimes again they flare up with an intensity that is truly alarming and uncontrollable. The energy with which those fears become insistent in consciousness, and the motor excitement to which they give rise are really extraordinary. The fear comes like a sudden flood. The energy with which those fears rise into consciousness is often overwhelming.

"Fear gets possession of me under circumstances in which my suspicions are, for some reason or other, aroused to activity, all the more so if the suspicions of possible impending evil are awakened suddenly. In other words, the fears arise with stimulations of associations of threatening danger to myself and to my family. I am afraid that something may happen to my children; I fear that they may fall sick suddenly; I fear that some terrible accident may happen to them; I fear that they may fall down from some place, and be maimed or be killed. I fear that my children and other members of my family may be poisoned by people who are not well disposed towards them. I am afraid that they may pick up some food that was infected, or that they may be infected in school by children who happen to suffer from some infectious maladies. I am afraid that my children may be overrun by some vehicles, by automobiles, or that they may be killed in an accident, that they may be killed by a street car, or even that the house may collapse. This latter event has actually taken place when I was a child. In fact, many, if not all of those fears have actually their origin in my experience.

"As I write you these lines, memories of such events come crowding upon my mind. Are they the noxious seeds that have been planted on the soil of fear? I am afraid sometimes that even the food I and my children as well as other people eat may give rise to toxic products and thus produce disease. Often in the dead of night, I may come to see my children in order to convince myself that they have no fever, and that they are not threatened by any terrible disease. The very words 'sickness,' 'disease,' 'not feeling well,' 'death,' arouse my feeling and sometimes throw me into a panic. I am afraid to use such words in connection with any of my children. I am afraid that the evil mentioned may actually happen.

"When a child I learned about testing and omens. If a test comes through in a certain way, it is an omen of good luck, otherwise it means bad luck. This superstitious testing and omens have remained with me, and that in spite of my liberal training and knowledge of the absurdity of such superstitions. I may test by opening the Bible at any page, or I may test by anything that might occur, according to my guesses. All of these fears I know have no meaning for me, they are senseless and absurd, but they are so rooted in my early childhood, they have been so often repeated, they have accumulated round them so much emotion of fear that they come to my mind with a force which is truly irresistible. Many of the fears have multiplied to such an extent that I cannot touch anything without rousing some slumbering fear.

"To continue with my fears; I am often afraid that the doors are not well locked, and I must try them over and over again; I go away and come back again, and try and try again, and once more. It is tiresome, but as the fear is constantly with me, and is born again and again, I cannot be satisfied, and must repeat the whole process over and over until I get tired, and give up the whole affair in sheer despair. In such cases a contrary and different fear comes in handy. One devil banishes another. I am afraid that the gas jet is left open, and I must try it over and over, and test the jets with matches. This process of testing may go on endlessly. The fear remains and the process must begin again until it is stopped by sheer effort of will as something meaningless, automatic, and absurd. The performance must be stopped and substituted by something else.

"Colds, or attacks of influenza of the mildest character have given rise to fears of pneumonia. Pain in the abdomen, or a little intestinal distress has awakened fears of possible appendicitis, or of tumor, or intestinal obstruction. The least suspicion of blood in the stools awakens the fear of possible cancer. Vomiting or even nausea brings fears of cancer of the stomach. There is no disease from which I have not suffered.

"The same fears have naturally been extended to my children, and to all those who are under my care. The least symptom is sufficient to arouse in me fears of possible terror and horrible consequences.

"I am afraid that suits may be brought against me, or that some of my own people, patients and even employees whom I discharged, may bring legal action against me in court, or blackmail me. When I leave home, I am afraid that something terrible has happened. The fear of impending evil is always with me. The fears have invaded every part of my being. It seems as if there is no resistance in my mind to those terrible fear states.

"Perhaps it may interest you to know that, although I am quite liberal, and even regarded as irreligious, still I am afraid to express any word against God, Christ, saints, martyrs of any church and denomination, be they Christian, Mohammedan, Buddhist, or pagan. I am afraid lest they may hear me and do me harm; I fear to say a word even against the devil or Satan. I am obsessed by fears. Fears pursue me as long as I am awake, and do not leave me alone in my sleep and dreams. Fears are the curse of my life, and yet I have control of them, none but you has any suspicion of them. I go about my work in a seemingly cheerful and happy way. The fears, however, are the bane of my life, and torture me by their continued presence.

"I tried to find whether or not those fears had any relation to my wishes or to my sexual experiences. I must say that I find they bear no relation whatever to wish or sex. My mental states grow on fear, take their origin in fear, and feed on fear. Fear is the seed and the soil of all those infinite individual phobias that keep on torturing me unless opposed by a supreme effort of my will.

"Truly the Biblical curse well applies to my life.

"'The Lord will make thy plagues wonderful, and the plagues of thy seed, even great plagues, and of long continuance, and sore sickness, and of long continuance. Moreover, he will bring upon thee all the diseases of Egypt, which thou wast afraid of, and they shall cleave unto thee. And every sickness and every plague, which is not written in the book of this law, them will the law bring upon thee, until thou be destroyed. Thou shalt find no ease, neither shall the sole of thy foot have rest; but the Lord shall give thee a trembling heart, and failing of eyes, and sorrow of mind. And thy life shall hang in doubt before thee, and thou shalt fear day and night and shall have none assurance of thy life. In the morning thou shalt say, Would God it were even! and at even thou shalt say, Would God it were morning! for the fear of thine heart wherewith thou shalt fear....'

"I laid bare my soul before you. I permit you to do with this document whatever you may think fit."

V

"I was born of healthy parents; grand-parents were also healthy. All lived to a ripe old age, and died of natural causes. Father is still living; I was a healthy normal child with little sickness up to the age of 16. A few years prior I belonged to a gymnasium and enjoyed superb physical strength and health, though I was from childhood somewhat of a coward. I then became associated with some youngsters who liked night life. This association influenced me to join them in their nightly escapades.

"Between overtaxing myself in my work and trying to keep up with the boys socially my system was drained. This was kept up for about five years. I was working for a dry cleaning establishment the owner of which did not appreciate my hard work. I gave ten hours a day service, but he required even more, so that I spent as many as fifteen and eighteen hours a day, and kept that up for about five years.

"It was in January, 1911, at the age of twenty while sitting in a restaurant eating my lunch, I felt a strange sensation coming over me, such as blood rushing to my head, followed by weakness, trembling, and fainting spells. I summoned up what will power I had left, shook my head in effort to brace up, and tried to finish my meal, but without success. I left the restaurant and coming outside felt the same sensation. I leaned against a building, and my knees gave way from under me until I was compelled to lie down. I made an attempt to get up, boarded a street car, and started for my father's store which was about a mile down the street. As I stepped on the platform I felt the same spell coming over me. Some of the men standing on the back platform saw my condition, and helped me. I arrived at the store where I collapsed.

"An ambulance was called, and I was taken to the city hospital. The interne diagnosed the case as acute indigestion. He prescribed some soda tablets, and told me to be careful with my diet. I felt relieved at what he told me, because I thought it was not so serious as I had expected. For I thought the end was near. My brother who accompanied me spoke kind and encouraging words which soothed my nerves.

"On the street car my thoughts started to go over the whole of what had occurred. I could not control myself and gave way again. When I got home I could not eat. I lay down and tried to get some sleep, but sleep was out of the question. My thoughts always wandered back to these spells, and that would bring back another spell. I took the tablets prescribed by the physician, but they did not help me any.

"The next day I tried to go to work, but could not on account of these spells. I then decided to call our family physician. He told me it was a nervous breakdown, and prescribed bromides. I kept on having these spells in spite of the bromides. I was at a loss what to do. From then on I became afraid to venture anywhere, to go to any place, for fear of these spells. My real trouble began. I was afraid to live, and afraid to die, afraid to go out, afraid to lie down, always afraid of these spells.

"I remained at home for a couple of weeks, but the spells continued. I then decided to try another doctor. This time a stomach specialist, and as might be expected he claimed my stomach was the cause of my disturbances. The news was gratifying to me. I knew that stomach troubles could be cured, and the thought helped to quiet some of the fears. I went back to work after a few weeks. The belief in the efficacy of the drug enabled me to get down town to work, but I kept on having spells, losing weight, and feeling miserable.

"I decided to try another physician. This time a nerve specialist. After examination he diagnosed the case as nervous prostration. He gave me what he called a good nerve tonic. In addition to it he used to stripe my back with red hot instruments. I was under this doctor's care for about a year. I kept on going to work whenever I could, but the spells continued right along, at home in the night, or at work in the daytime. After a year of treatment I felt no better.

"I decided to try another nerve specialist,—his diagnosis was depletion of the nerves. He advised me to come in a couple of times a week for electric treatment. I followed instructions for a couple of months, but the spells continued just the same.

"One April day there was an electric storm. The lightning caused in me a great dread and fear. The wind broke some of the windows in our house. I had then the worst spell. I lost consciousness. When I awoke I was worse than ever. I was just choked up with tear of everything and everybody.

"I found I could no longer live in C., for the last bit of life was ebbing right out of me. I started on the train for Los Angeles. No one can realize the suffering I had to endure on my trip out West.

"Everybody on the train talked about accidents, wrecks, and robberies. After arriving in Los Angeles I felt somewhat relieved, but the spells kept on just the same. I consulted a great nerve specialist in Los Angeles. He claimed I had neurasthenia, and that I was much run down. His method of therapy was different from the rest. He suggested renting a cottage along the ocean front, and he would furnish a trainer whose wife was to take care of the cottage. The trainer was supposed to have some knowledge of physical culture and massage. After being in this camp for three months I saw no improvement in my condition.

"I went to another doctor who employed a different method. He would inject pig serum into my arm three times a week. After a thorough trial I found no relief.

"I then decided to try Christian Science for a while, but I had no relief from all my woe and misery. (When asked why he went to Christian Science while he was of Jewish faith, he replied that he was in such a state of fear that had he been ordered to be a cockroach he would have tried to become one).

"I tried another nerve doctor. After a while it was the same old story. I then tried chiropractice. After three months' trial I found out that I had to give it up, because the manipulator aggravated my condition. Towards the end I felt such pains in my back and spine that I was compelled to lie in bed for a week before I could recover enough strength to sit up. I then tried Osteopathy. I felt no better, so I had to abandon that.

"In search for health I could not stop here, so I went to another nerve specialist who after examination claimed to have discovered something different from any other physician. He discovered I had a pair of tonsils in my mouth which did not look well to him. He ordered them removed; that meant an operation under an anesthetic. Can you imagine my feeling when he told me the news? I had a terrible time in making up my mind what to do. Bad as I felt I made up my mind that I might as well die under ether as in any other way. I consented to the operation. It is needless to go into details here of what took place after the operation. Words cannot express it. All the tortures of hell would have been paradise towards what I went through after this operation.

"I have been going since from physician to physician, each one claiming that I haven't been to the right one, and that he was the proper physician who understood my case and could cure me. No one has been able to effect a cure."

As an example of the patient's state of extreme fear the following instance may be given. One day he came to me, a picture of misery and depression. He told me he had suffered agonies for the last couple of days, on account of an "ingrowing hair." It turned out that the patient overheard a conversation among his gossips, that some one died of an "ingrowing hair." This news strongly impressed him, and aroused his fear instinct, since he discovered an "ingrowing hair" on his throat. I found his throat was wrapped around with cotton, and covered with adhesive plaster. On unwrapping the mess I found just an ordinary little pimple. I threw away the wrappings, and gave the patient a scolding, and ridiculed him for his silliness. He felt as he said in "paradise." A competent observer will find this trait of trivial fears, characteristic, in various degrees, of every psychopathic patient.

By a series of trance states the patient was freed from his psycholeptic fear attacks; he is now in good health, and attending successfully to his business.

CHAPTER XXI

FEAR TRANCE APPARITIONS

The following study of a psychopathic case brings out the character of the fear trance dream.

Mrs. A. is twenty-two years old; Russian; married. She suffers periodically from attacks of violent headaches, lasting several days. Family history is good. The patient was brought up in the fear of ghosts, evil spirits, magical influences, and diabolical agencies. Mrs. A. is easily frightened, and has suffered from headaches and pressure on the head for quite a long time, but the pain became exacerbated some five years ago. The attack is sudden, without any premonitory feelings, and lasts from eight hours to two days. The headache often sets in at night, when she is asleep, and she wakes up with frightful pain.

At the time of the first attack she was much run down. Otherwise the patient is in good condition, but complains that her memory is getting bad. Patellar reflex is exaggerated. Field of vision is normal. The eyes show slight strabismus and astigmatism, corrected by glasses which did not in the least diminish the intensity as well as the frequency of the headaches.

Mrs. A. suffers from bad dreams and distressing nightmares, the content of which she cannot recall in her waking state. She also often has hallucinations, visions of two women wrapped in white, pointing their fingers at her and running after her. She never had any fall, nor any special worry or anxiety, never suffered from any infectious diseases.

After a persistent inquiry, however, she gave an account of an accident she met with when a child of eight. Opposite her house there lived an insane woman of whom she was mortally afraid. Once when the parents happened to be away, the insane woman entered the house, caught the child, and greatly frightened her. Another time she was sent out by her parents to buy something in a grocery store. It was night and very dark. She bought the things and on the way back she saw two women in white with hands stretched out running after her. She screamed from great fright and ran home.

Mrs. A. is afraid to remain alone, and especially in the dark. She is not so much afraid in the street as in the house. The two women appear to her now and then, and she is mortally afraid of them.

The patient was put into hypnotic state. There was marked catalepsy; the eyes were firmly closed, and she could not open them when challenged. Suggestion of general well-being was given and she was awakened. On awakening, she could not remember what had taken place in the hypnotic state.

Next day she was again put into hypnosis and went into a deeper state than the day before. She was asked whether she thought of the crazy woman occasionally, she replied in the negative. The patient spoke in a low, suppressed voice, the words coming out slowly, as if with effort and with fear. It was then insisted that she should tell one of her recent dreams. After some pause, she said: "Last night I had a bad dream; I dreamt that I stood near a window and a cat came up to the same window. I saw it was crazy. I ran away, the cat ran after me and scratched me. Then I knew that I was crazy. My friends said there was no help for me.

"I dropped the baby, ran, and jumped down stairs. I remember now that when I fell asleep I saw a woman, maybe the crazy woman. I covered myself; I knew I was only afraid, and that she was not real. Six weeks ago I saw the same woman, when falling asleep or when asleep. I ran away, and she ran after me."

Mrs. A. in relating these dreams, shivered all over and was afraid, as if actually living the dream experience over again. "It was this woman who caught me in her arms, kissed me, and embraced me, and did not let me go, until my screams brought friends and my father; they took me away from her by force."

Gradually some more dreams emerged. "I dreamt some time ago that the woman came to me and spilled hot water on me. Another time I dreamed that I was in the insane asylum; she came out, told me she was well; I was greatly frightened and ran away."

Mrs. A. then became quiet. After a while she began to relate a series of dreams. Some time ago she dreamed that the woman entered the room where her father was and ran up to him, evidently with the intention of hurting him. Her father ran away, and she hid herself in a closet in the next room. "I also dreamt that the woman was shadowing me in an alley. She wanted to get hold of me, while I was trying to get away from her. I turned round, and she gave me such a fierce look. I ran and she could not catch me. I should die, if she catches me. In one of my dreams about her, I saw people putting cold water on her, and I could hear her scream. It was awful. I dreamt I went upstairs, opened the door and met her. I was badly frightened. I jumped out of the window."

This is an extract from a letter sent to me by the patient's husband: "... She had another attack. It did not last long, and it was not severe. She dreamt several times a week. I shall try to relate them as accurately as possible. She dreamt that I left the room for a while. Our baby was asleep in the next room. All of a sudden she heard baby cry out: 'Mamma, I am afraid.' She told the baby to come to her as she herself was afraid to leave the bed. Baby came to her. The child looked frightened, her face pale with fear, exclaiming 'Mamma, a devil.' As the child cried out, my wife heard a noise in the room, something moved close by. She became scared. It seemed to her that something terrible and unknown was after her. She wanted to scream for help, but could not. A hand was stretched out after her to catch her. She woke up in great terror. Another time she dreamt that she was in a hall way. She saw a woman and became frightened. It was the same crazy woman. My wife is exceedingly nervous, and is in fear that something awful is going to happen to her or to the family."

A rich, subconscious dream-life of agonizing fears was thus revealed, a life of terrors of which the patient was unaware in her waking state. The dreams referred to the same central nucleus, the shock and fears of her early childhood. Worries about self and family kept up and intensified the present fear states.

Her selfishness has no bounds, her fears have no limits. The symptoms of the "fear set," as in all other psychopathic cases, took their origin in the impulse of self-preservation with its accompanying fundamental fear instinct.

This patient was cured after a long course of hypnotic treatment.

CHAPTER XXII

RECURRENT FEAR STATES,—PSYCHOLEPSY

There are cases in which the nature of the psychopathic states stands out more clearly and distinctly than in others. They occur periodically, appearing like epileptic states, in a sort of an explosive form, so that some authorities have mistaken them for epilepsy, and termed them psychic epilepsy. My researches have shown them to be recurrent explosions of subconscious states, which I termed *psycholepsy*. They really do not differ from general psychopathic states, but they may be regarded as classic *pseudo-epileptic*, or *psycholeptic* states; they are classic *fear-states—states of panic*.

M. L. is nineteen years of age, of a rather limited intelligence. He works as a shopboy amidst surroundings of poverty, and leads a hard life, full of privations. He is undersized and underfed, and looks as if he has never had enough to eat. Born in New York, of parents belonging to the lowest social stratum, he was treated with severity and even brutality. The patient has never been to any elementary school and can neither read nor write. His mathematical knowledge did not extend beyond hundreds; he can hardly accomplish a simple addition and subtraction, and has no idea of the multiplication table. The names of the President and a few Tammany politicians constitute all his knowledge of the history of the United States.

Family history is not known; his parents died when the patient was very young, and he was left without kith and kin, so that no data could be obtained.

Physical examination is negative. Field of vision is normal. There are no sensory disturbances. The process of perception is normal, and so also is recognition. Memory for past and present events is good. His power of reasoning is quite limited, and the whole of his mental life is undeveloped, embryonic. His sleep is sound; dreams little. Digestion is excellent; he can digest anything in the way of eatables. He is of an easy-going, gay disposition, a New York "street-Arab."

The patient complains of "shaking spells." The attack sets in with tremor of all the extremities, and then spreads to the whole body. The tremor becomes general, and the patient is seized by a convulsion of shivering, trembling, and chattering of teeth. Sometimes he falls down, shivering, trembling, and shaking all òver, in an intense state of fear, a state of panic. The seizure seems to be epileptiform, only it lasts sometimes for more than three hours. The attack may come any time during the day, but is more frequent at night.

During the attack the patient does not lose consciousness; he knows everything that is taking place around him, can feel everything pretty well; his teeth chatter violently, he trembles and shivers all over, and is unable to do anything.

The fear instinct has complete possession of him. He is in agony of terror. There is also a feeling of chilliness, as if he is possessed by an attack of "fear ague." The seizure does not start with any numbness of the extremities, nor is there any anaesthesia or paraesthesia during the whole course of the attack. With the exception of the shivers and chills the patient claims he feels "all right."

The patient was put into a condition close to the hypnotic state. There was some catalepsy of a transient character, but no suggestibility of the hypnotic type. In this state it came to light that the patient "many years ago" was forced to sleep in a dark, damp cellar where it was bitter cold. The few nights passed in that dark, cold cellar he had to leave his bed, and shaking, trembling, and shivering with cold and fear he had to go about his work in expectation of a severe punishment in case of non-performance of his duties.

While in the intermediary, subwaking, hypnoidal state, the patient was told to think of that dark, damp, cold cellar. Suddenly the attack set in,—the patient began to shake, shiver, and tremble all over, his teeth chattering as if suffering from intense fear. The attack was thus reproduced in the hypnoidal state. "This is the way I have been," he said. During this attack no numbness, no sensory disturbance, was present. The patient was quieted, and after a little while the attack of shivering and fear disappeared.

The room in which the patient was put into the subconscious state was quite dark, and accidentally the remark was dropped that the room was too dark to see anything; immediately the attack reappeared in all its violence. It was found later that it was sufficient to mention the words, "dark, damp, and cold" to bring on an attack even in the fully waking state. We could thus reproduce the attacks at will,—those magic words had the power to release the pent-up subconscious forces and throw the patient into convulsions of shakings and shiverings, with chattering of the teeth and intense fear.

Thus the apparent epileptiform seizures, the insistent psychomotor states of seemingly unaccountable origin, were traced to subconscious fear obsessions.

The following case is of similar nature. The study clearly shows the subconscious nature of such psycholeptic attacks:[10]

Mr. M., aged twenty-one years, was born in Russia, and came to this country four years previously. His family history, as far as can be ascertained, is good. There is no nervous trouble of any sort in the immediate or remote members of his family.

The patient himself has always enjoyed good health. He is a young man of good habits.

He was referred to me for epileptiform attacks and anaesthesia of the right half of his body. The attack is preceded by an aura consisting of headache and a general feeling of malaise. The aura lasts a few days and terminates in the attack which sets in about midnight, *when the patient is fully awake*. The attack consists of a series of spasms, rhythmic in character, and lasting about one or two minutes. After an interval of not more than thirty seconds the spasms set in again.

This condition continues uninterruptedly for a period of five or six days (a sort of status epilepticus), persisting during the time the patient is awake, and ceasing only during the short intervals, or rather moments, of sleep. Throughout the whole period of the attacks the patient is troubled with insomnia. He sleeps restlessly for only ten or fifteen minutes at a time. On one occasion he was observed to be in a state of delirium as found in post-epileptic insanity and the so-called Dämmerzustände of epilepsy. This delirium was observed but once in the course of five years.

The regular attack is not accompanied by any delirious states or Dämmerzustände. On the contrary, during the whole course of the attack the patient's *mind remains perfectly clear.*

During the period of the attack the whole right side becomes anaesthetic to all forms of sensations, kinaesthesis included, so that he is not even aware of the spasms unless he actually observes the affected limbs.

The affected limbs, previously normal, also become paretic. After the attack has subsided, the paresis and anaesthesia persist (as sometimes happens in true idiopathic epilepsy) for a few days, after which the patient's condition remains normal until the next attack. After his last attack, however, the anaesthesia and paresis continued for about three weeks.

He has had every year one attack which, curiously, sets in about the same time, namely, about the month of January or February. The attacks have of late increased in frequency, so that the patient has had four, at intervals of about three or four months. On different occasions he was in the Boston City Hospital for the attacks.

There was a profound right hemianaesthesia including the right half of the tongue, with a marked hypoaesthesia of the right side of the pharynx. All the senses of the right side were involved. The field of vision of the right eye was much limited. The ticking of a watch could not be heard more than three inches away from the right ear. Taste and smell were likewise involved on the right side. The muscular and kinaesthetic sensations on the right side were much impaired.

The patient's mental condition was good. He states that he has few dreams and these are insignificant, concerned as they are with the ordinary matters of daily life. Occasionally he dreams that he is falling, but there is no definite content to the dream.

These findings were indicative of functional rather than organic disease. The *previous history* of the case was significant. The first attack came on after peculiar circumstances, when the patient was sixteen years of age and living in Russia. After returning from a ball one night, he was sent back to look for a ring which the lady, whom he escorted, had lost on the way. It was after midnight, and his way lay on a lonely road which led by a cemetery. When near the cemetery he was suddenly overcome by a great fright, thinking that somebody was running after him. He fell, *struck his right side*, and lost consciousness. The patient did not remember this last event. It was told by him when in a hypnotic state.

The patient was a Polish Jew, densely ignorant, terrorized by superstitious fears of evil powers working in the dead of night.

By the time he was brought home he regained consciousness, but there existed a spasmodic shaking of the right side, involving the arm, leg, and head. The spasm persisted for one week. During this time he could not voluntarily move his right arm or leg, and the right half of his body felt numb. There was also apparently a loss of muscular sense, for he stated that he was unaware of the shaking of his arm or leg, unless he looked and saw the movements. In other words, there was right hemiplegia, anaesthesia, and spasms.

For one week after the cessation of the spasms his right arm and leg remained weak, but he was soon able to resume his work, and he felt as well as ever. Since then every year, as already stated, about the same month the patient has an attack similar in every respect to the original attack, with the only exception that there is no loss of consciousness. Otherwise the subsequent yearly attacks are *photographic pictures, close repetitions, recurrences of the original attack.*

A series of experiments accordingly was undertaken. First, as to the anaesthesia. If the anaesthesia were functional, sensory impressions ought to be felt, even though the patient was unconscious of them, and we ought to be able to get sensory reactions.

Experiments made to determine the nature of the anaesthesia produced interesting results. These experiments show that the anaesthesia is not a true one, but that impressions from the anaesthetic parts which seem not to be felt are really perceived subconsciously.

Different tests showed that the subconscious reactions to impressions from the anaesthetic hand were more delicately plastic and responsive than the conscious reactions to impressions from the normal hand. We have the so-called "psychopathic paradox" that *functional anaesthesia is a subconscious hyperaesthesia.*

It is evident then that there could be no inhibition of the sensory centres, or suppression of their activity, or whatever else it may be called. In spite of the apparent, profound anaesthesia, the pin pricks were felt and perceived. Stimulations gave rise to perception, cognition, to a sort of pseudo-hallucinations that showed the pin pricks were counted and localized in the hand. The results of these tests demonstrate that in psychopathic patients all sensory impressions received from anaesthetic parts, while they do not reach the *personal* consciousness are perceived *subconsciously*.

Inasmuch as the sensations are perceived, the failure of the subject to be conscious of them must be due to a *failure in association*. The perception of the sensation is dissociated from the personal consciousness. More than this, these *dissociated* sensations are capable of a certain amount of independent functioning; hence the pseudo-hallucinations, and hence the failure of psychopathic patients to be incommoded by their anaesthesia. This condition of dissociation underlies psychopathic states.

For the purpose of studying the attacks, the patient was hypnotized. He went into a deep somnambulic condition, in which, however, the *anaesthesia still persisted*. This showed that the dissociation of the sensory impressions was unchanged.

In hypnosis he related again the history of the onset of the trouble. His memory became broader, and he was able to give the additional information, which he could not do in his waking state, that at the time he was badly frightened, he fell on his right side. Moreover, he recalled what he did not remember when awake, that throughout the period of his attacks when he fell asleep, he had vivid dreams of an intense hallucinatory character, all relating to terror and fall.

In these dreams he lived over and over again the experience which was the beginning of his trouble. He again finds himself in his little native town, on a lonely road; he thinks some one is running after him; he becomes frightened, calls for help, falls, and then wakes up with a start, and the whole dream is forgotten. After he wakes he knows nothing of all this; there is no more fear or any emotional disturbance; he is then simply distressed by the spasms.

While testing the anaesthesia during hypnosis, an attack developed, his right arm and leg began to shake, first mildly and then with increasing intensity and frequency. His head also spasmodically turned to the right side. The movements soon became rhythmic. Arm and leg were abducted and adducted in a slow rhythmic way at the rate of about thirty-six times per minute. With the same rate and rhythm, the head turned to the right side, with chin pointing upward. The right side of the face was distorted by spasm, as if in great pain. The left side of the face was unaffected. Pressure over his right side (where he struck when he fell) elicited evidences of great pain. Respiration became deep and labored, and was synchronous with each spasm. The whole symptom-complex simulated Jacksonian epilepsy.

Consciousness persisted unimpaired, but showed a curious and unexpected alteration. When asked what was the matter, he replied in his native dialect, "I do not understand what you say." It was found that he had lost all understanding of English, so that it was necessary to speak to him in his native dialect. His answers to our questions made it apparent that during the attack, as in his dreams, he was living through the experience which had originally excited his trouble.

The attack was *hypnoidic, a fear attack*, hallucinatory in character. He said that he was sixteen years old, that he was in Rovno (Russia), that he had just fallen, because he was *frightened*, that he was lying on the roadside near the cemetery, which in the popular superstitious fear is inhabited by ghosts. At that hour of the night the dead arise from their graves and attack the living who happen to be near.

The hypnoidic state developed further, the patient living through, as in a dream, the whole experience that had taken place at that period. He was in a carriage, though he did not know who put him there. Then in a few moments he was again home, in his house, with his parents attending on him as in the onset of his first epileptiform seizures.

The attack terminated at this point, and thereupon he became perfectly passive, and when spoken to answered again in English. Now he was again twenty-one years old, was conscious of where he was, and was in absolute ignorance of what had just taken place.

It was found that an attack could regularly and artificially be induced, if the patient in hypnosis was taken back by suggestion to the period when the accident happened.

The experiment was now tried of taking him back to a period antedating the first attack. He was told that he was fifteen years old, that is, a year before the accident occurred. He could no longer speak or understand English, he was again in Rovno, engaged as a salesman in a little store, had never been in America, and did not know who we were. Testing sensation, it was found that it had spontaneously returned to the hand. *There was not a trace of the anaesthesia left.* The hands which did not feel deep pin pricks before now reacted to the slightest stimulation. *Spontaneous synthesis of the dissociated sensory impressions had occurred.* Just as formerly before the accident, sensation was in normal association with the rest of his mental processes, so now this association was re-established with the memories of that period to which the patient was artificially reduced.

The patient was now (while still believing himself to be fifteen years old) taken a year forward to the day on which the accident occurred. He says he is going to the ball tonight. He is now at the ball; he returned home; he is sent back to look for a ring. Like a magic formula, it calls forth an attack in which again he lives through the accident,— the terror and the spasms.

It was thus possible to reproduce an attack at any time with clock-like precision by taking him back to the period of the accident, and reproducing all its details in a hypnoidic state. Each time the fear and the physical manifestations of the attack (spasms, paresis, and anaesthesia) developed. These induced attacks were identical with the spontaneous attacks, one of which we had occasion to observe later.

At periodic intervals, as under the stress of fear, the dormant activity is awakened and, though still unknown to the patient, gives rise to the same sensori-motor disturbances which characterized the original experience. These subconscious dissociated states are so much more intense in their manifestations by the very fact of their dissociaton from the inhibitory influences of the normal mental life.

The psychognosis of such cases reveals on the one hand a dissociation of mental processes, and on the other hand an independent and automatic activity of subconscious psychic states, under the disaggregating, paralyzing influence of the fear instinct.

A patient under my treatment for four months during the year of 1922 presents interesting traits. I regard the case as classic as far as the fundamental factors of neurosis are concerned.

Patient, male, age 32, married, has two children. He lives in an atmosphere of fear and apprehension about himself. He comes from a large, but healthy family. The patient is of a rather cowardly disposition especially in regard to his health. He worked hard in a store during the day, and led a life of dissipation at night. One day, after a night of unusual dissipation, or orgy, when on his way to his work, he felt weak, he was dizzy, he became frightened about himself; he thought he had an attack of apoplexy, and that he was going to die. His heart was affected, it began to beat violently, and he trembled and shivered in an "ague" of intense fear. The palpitation of the heart was so great, the trembling was so violent, and the terror was so overwhelming that he collapsed in a heap. He was taken to his father's store in a state of "fainting spell." A physician was called in who treated the patient for an attack of acute indigestion.

For a short time he felt better, but the attacks of terror, trembling, shivering, weakness, pallor, fainting, palpitation of the heart and general collapse kept on recurring. He then began to suffer from insomnia, from fatigue, and is specially obsessed by fear fatigue. He is in terror over the fact that his energy is exhausted; physical, mental, nervous, sexual impotence. This was largely developed by physicians who treated him for epilepsy, putting him on a bromide treatment; others treated and diagnosed the case as cardiac affection, kidney trouble, dementia praecox, and one physician operated on the poor fellow for tonsillitis. The patient was terrorized. He was on a diet for toxaemia, he was starved. He took all sorts of medicine for his insomnia.

The patient became a chronic invalid for ten years. He was in terror, scared with the horrors of sleepless nights. He has been to neurologists, to psychoanalysts, and he tried Christian Science, New Thought, Naturopathy, and Osteopathy, but of no avail. The condition persisted. The attacks came on from time to time like thunder storms. There were trembling, shivering, chattering of teeth, palpitation of the heart, weakness, fainting, and overwhelming, uncontrollable terror.

The first time I tried to put the patient into a hypnoidal state was nine at night. I put out the electric light, lighted a candle, and proceeded to put him into a hypnoidal condition. The patient began to shiver, to tremble, to breathe fast and heavily, the pulse rose to over 125, while the heart began to thump violently, as if it were going to jump out. He was like one paralyzed, the muscles of the chest labored hard, and under my pressure the muscle fibers hardened, crackled, became rigid, and he could not reply when spoken to. It took me some time to quieten him. He was clearly in a state of great panic. I opened his eyelids and found the eye ball turned up. The whole body was easily put in a state of catalepsy. Clearly the patient was not in a hypnoidal state, he was in a state of hypnosis. Night after night he fell into states of hypnosis with all the symptoms of intense fear attacks. When the fear attacks subsided the depths of the hypnotic state proportionately diminished.

In my various clinical and laboratory experimental work, covering a period of a quarter of a century, I have gradually come to the conclusion that fear and hypnosis are interrelated. In fact I am disposed to think that the hypnotic state is an ancient state, a state of fear cataplexy, or rather trance obedience. While the hypnoidal state is a primitive sleep state, the hypnotic condition is a primitive, fear condition, still present in lowly formed organisms.

After some time the general fear instinct becomes alleviated. The patient goes by habit into a trance hypnotic state under the influence of the hypnotizer in whom he gains more confidence. The patient gets into a state of trance obedience to the hypnotizer of whom he is in awe, and who can control the patient's fear instinct.

Man obeys the commands, "the suggestions" of the hypnotizer, of the master whom he subconsciously fears, and who inspires him with awe, with "confidence-fear". The crowd, the community, "public opinion," the mob, the leader, the priest, the magician, the medicine man, are just such forces, such authorities to procure the slavish obedience of the subconscious described as hypnosis. Soldiers and slaves fall most easily into such states.

Man has been trained in fear for milleniums, in fear of society, custom, fashion, belief, and the authority of crowd and mob. He fears to stand alone, he must go with the crowd.

Man is a social being, a hypnotized, somnambulic creature. He walks and acts like a hypnotized slave. Man is a social somnambulist who believes, dreams, and acts at the order of the mob or of its leader. Man belongs to those somnambulists who become artificial, suggested, automatic personalities with their eyes fully open, seeing and observing nothing but what is suggested to them.

The hypnoidic states, observed and described by me in the classical Hanna case, belong to the same category. The hypnoidic states are essentially fear cataleptic states of a vivid character, closely related to hypnotic conditions of primitive life.[11]

FOOTNOTES:

[10] Dr. Morton Prince and Dr. H. Linenthal coöperated with me in the study of the case published in full in the "Boston Medical and Surgical Journal."

[11] See my works, "The Psychology of Suggestion," "Multiple Personality," and others.

CHAPTER XXIII

APHONIA, STAMMERING, AND CATALEPSY

S. R. Age 25. Russian Jewess; married; has four children. Patient was brought to me in a state of helplessness. She could not walk, and was unable to utter a word. When spoken to she replied in gestures. When challenged to walk, she made unsuccessful attempts. The step was awkward, the gait reeling, the body finally collapsing in a heap on the floor. When I shut her eyelids, the eyeballs began to roll upwards, the lids soon became cataleptic, and the patient was unable to open them. When I insisted that she should open the lids, she strained hard,—the muscles of the upper part of the body became painfully tense,—wrinkled her forehead, and contorted violently her face. After long insistence on her replying to my questions, and after long vain efforts to comply with my request, she at last succeeded in replying in a barely audible voice. When whispering she kept on making incoordinate movements with jaws and lips, began to shut her eyelids, rolled up the eye-balls, forced the tongue against the teeth, stammered badly on consonants, uttering them with great difficulty after long hesitation, the sound finally coming out with explosive force.

I insisted that she must stand up, she raised herself slowly and with effort, took a couple of steps, and sat down at once on the chair. During the period of effort there was marked tremor in her left arm. When she sat down, she threw her head backward, rolled up her eyeballs, and began gradually to close her eyelids. She remained in this position for a couple of minutes, and then began spasmodically to open and shut the eyelids. When taken to her room, the patient walked up, though with some difficulty, three flights of stairs without the nurse's support.

The patient was greatly emaciated,—she lived in extreme poverty. She was married five years, and had given birth to four children. Patient was suffering from severe headaches which set in soon after the birth of the second child. At first the headaches came at intervals of a few weeks, and lasted about a day, then with the birth of the other children the headaches grew more severe and more frequent, and finally became continuous. From time to time the attacks were specially exacerbated in violence, she then complained of violent pains in the head, excruciating agony toward the vertex. The face was deadly pale, the hands and feet were ice-cold, the pulse weak and sluggish. During the attack the head had to be raised, since in any other position the pain was unbearable. The pain was originally unilateral, starting on the left side of the head. Of late the pain spread from left to right. The whole head felt sore, like a boil, the scalp was highly sensitive. The intense attacks, sweeping over the patient unawares, were accompanied by twitchings of the eyelids, rolling of the eyeballs, dizziness, sparks before the eyes, pains in the left side of the chest, and by numbness and hypoaesthesia of the face, arms and legs. The patellar reflex was markedly exaggerated, no clonus was present; the pupils reacted well to light and accommodation.

The patient was admitted to a local hospital, and was allowed to nurse her one year old baby. Three days after admission, while nursing her baby, she was seized with a violent attack of headache and pain in the left side. The arms felt numb and "gone." The patient was seized with a panic that the child might fall; hugging the baby to her left breast she screamed for help in agony and terror.

Immediately following this seizure the patient lost her voice, speech, and power of walking.

After staying in the hospital for two weeks, the patient was put under my care.

The patient was an extremely timid creature. She lived in Russia in a small town where the religious persecutions of the neighbors were persistent and unremittent. To this were joined the petty annoyances by the village police, the representatives of which acted with all the cruel tyranny characteristic of the old Russian regime. The patient's family was in constant terror. In childhood the patient has undergone all the horrors of the *pogromi* with all the terrors of inquisitorial tortures. A highly sensitized impulse of self-preservation and intense easily stimulated fear instinct were the essence of the patient's life. She was afraid of everything, of her very shadow, of anything strange, more so in the dark, and at night. With this morbid self-preservation and intensified fear instinct there were associated superstitions to which her mind was exposed in early childhood, and in her later life. The patient lived at home in the fear of the most savage superstitions and prejudices, characteristic of the poor ignorant classes of Eastern European countries, and outside the house she was in fear of her life. The patient was brought up on fear and nourished on fear. No wonder when she was run down, and met with a fear shock, that the fear instinct seized on her and gave rise to the symptoms of physical and mental paralysis.

To this life of terror we may add the extreme poverty in which the patient lived in Russia and afterwards in this country. The hard work in a sweat-shop and the ill nutrition ran down the patient and further predisposed her to disability and disease. Patient lived in constant dread of actual starvation, with fear of having no shelter, with fear of no roof over her head. She was so timid that she was scared by any sudden movement, or by a severe, harsh, threatening voice. She was extreme suggestible, imitative, and credulous. She was like a haunted animal, like a scared bird in the claws of a cat. Fear often threw her into a state of rigidity.

The patient suffered from a fear of fatigue, from fear of exhaustion, from fear of disability, from fear of paralysis, pain, sickness, and death, fear of the negative aspect of the most primitive, and most fundamental of all impulses, the impulse of self-preservation. The fear psychosis, based on an abnormally developed fear instinct which formed the main structure of her symptom complex, had a real foundation in the psycho-physiological condition of her organism. The patient actually suffered from fatigue due to exhaustion, underfeeding, and overworking.

Married at the age of twenty, she bore four children in succession. This was a drain on the poor woman, and further weakened her feeble constitution. Her husband was a poor tailor working in a sweat-shop, making but a few dollars a week. The family was practically kept in a state of chronic starvation. The wolf was hardly kept away from the door. The family was in constant dread of "slack time" with its loss of employment and consequent privations and suffering.

The husband was a hard worker, did not drink, but the long hours of work, the low wages, the poor nutrition, the vicious air, and the no less vicious environment, cheerless and monotonous, sometimes gave rise to moods, discontent, anger, and quarrels, of which the patient with her timidity stood in utter terror.

The patient's dream life was strongly colored by a general underlying mood of apprehension. The fear instinct of self-preservation formed the soil of the whole emotional tone of the psychosis, waking, sub-waking, dreaming, conscious, and subconscious. Again and again did the nurses and attendants report to me that, although the patient was aphonic and it was hard to elicit from her a sound, in her sleep she quite often cried out, sometimes using phrases and words which were hard to comprehend, because they were indistinct, and because they were sometimes in her native language. When awakened immediately, it was sometimes possible to elicit from her shreds of dreams in regard to scares and frights about herself, about her children, about her husband, relatives, and friends. When she came under my care the patient often used to wake up in the morning in a state of depression due to some horrible hallucinatory dreams in which she lived over again in a distorted form, due to incoordination of content and to lack of active, guiding attention, dreams in which the dreadful experience of her miserable life kept on recurring under various forms of fragmentary association and vague synthesis, brought about by accidental, external and internal stimulations.

The patient was taken to her room in the evening, and put to bed. During the night she was somewhat restless, kept on waking up, but on the whole, according to the nurse's account, she slept quite well. In the morning the patient had a hearty breakfast, and felt better than the day before when she was brought to me. The voice improved somewhat in strength and volume. During the day she rested, felt well, and enjoyed her meals. Speech was still in a whisper barely audible, but there was no stammering, no muscular incoordination, no twitchings of the face. About four in the afternoon patient sat up in bed, her voice became somewhat stronger, though speech was still in a whisper. This improvement lasted but a few minutes. When her arms were raised, the left hand manifested considerable tremor and weakness as compared with the right arm. After having made a few remarks which apparently cost her considerable effort, she had a relapse, she again lost her voice, and was unable to whisper. I insisted that she should reply to my questions; she had to make a great effort, straining her muscles and bringing them into a state of convulsive incoordination before she could bring out a few sounds in reply. A little later, about ten or fifteen minutes after I left the room, the nurse came in and quietly asked her a question, the patient answered in a whisper, with little strain and difficulty. An hour later the patient regained her speech for a short period of a few minutes. These changes went on during the patient's waking period. Once towards evening the patient regained her voice and speech to such an extent that she could talk with no difficulty and little impediment; the voice was so resonant and strong that it could be heard in the hall adjoining the room. This however lasted but a few moments.

After having had a good night's sleep the patient woke up in good condition; appetite was good. Voice was clear, though low. She was in a state of lassitude and relaxation. I attempted to examine her and kept testing her condition, physical and mental. I was anxious to make a psychognosis of the patient's case. The tests and the questions strained her nervous system by requiring to hold her attention, and by keeping her in a state of nervous and mental agitation. She looked scared, anxious,—the scared, haunted look in her face reappeared. The patient was no more than about twenty to twenty-five minutes under experimentation when a severe headache of the vertex and of the left side of the head set in. The eyeballs began to roll up, eyelids were half closed; lids and eyeballs were quivering and twitching. The hands were relaxed and looked paralyzed. When raised they fell down by her side in an almost lifeless condition. There was marked hypoaesthesia to pain and heat sensations. The anaesthesia was more marked on the left than on the right side. The left arm when raised and kept for a few seconds showed marked tremor as compared with the right arm. This is to be explained by the fact that the exacerbations of the headache, of pain, and the general cataleptic seizures set in usually during or after the nursing periods. The infant while nursing was kept by the mother on the left arm, the left side thus bearing the pressure, weight, and strain,—it was with the left side that fear became mainly associated.

During the height of the attack the patient was quietened, her fears allayed, and a five-grain tablet of phenacetine was given her with the authoritative remark that the drug was sure to help her. As soon as she swallowed the tablet the patient opened her eyes, and said she felt better. About an hour later, when another attempt at an examination was made, patient had an attack of headache, cried, said she was afraid, but she answered in a whisper when spoken to. She talked slowly, in a sort of staccato way. I insisted that she should talk a little faster and pronounce the words distinctly. She made violent attempts to carry out my command, but got scared, began to hesitate, and stammer, her voice and speech rapidly deteriorating with her efforts, ending in complete mutism.

During the day I tried from time to time to keep up the experiment of insisting that the patient should speak, and every time with the same result of bringing about an attack.[12] The patient began to stammer and stutter, becoming more and more frightened the more the nurse and myself insisted that she should make an effort and reply to our questions. Still, when the patient's attention became distracted, when she was handled gently, when her fears were allayed, the speech and sound improved in quality and in loudness, and at times her sentences were quite fluent, her enunciation quite distinct.

This state of instability lasted for several days until the patient became somewhat familiar with the surroundings. In one of her better moments the patient told me that she thought her stammering began with a definite event. One evening when she was fatigued with the labors of the day for her family, a stammerer came in to see her. The stammering made a strong impression on her. She felt the strain of the stammerer; she could not control the sympathy and the strain, and involuntarily began to imitate stammering. She began to fear that she might continue to stammer and be unable to enunciate sounds and words. The more she feared the harder it was for her to speak or even to use her voice.

A few days later the patient began to improve, she began to adapt herself to her surroundings, and did not get so easily scared.

About eight days after the first examination the patient woke up one morning in a state of depression; she cried a good deal. She did not sleep well the night before, dreamt and worried on account of her children. She was afraid that something might have happened to them in her absence, perhaps they were sick, perhaps the husband could not take good care of them. She talked in a whisper, her eyes were shut. When I insisted on opening the eyelids, she opened them, but did it with difficulty. I put her into a hypnotic state. In about a minute her eyes rolled up, and the eyelids shut spasmodically. There was present a slight degree of catalepsy. Mutism was strongly marked. Upon sudden and unexpected application of an electric current, the patient opened her eyes, cried out, but soon relapsed into a state of lethargy. Gradually patient was brought out of the lethargic state.

A couple of hours later, after she had a good rest a few more experiments as to her sensori-motor life were attempted. I asked her to raise objects, tested her sensitivity to various stimulations, her concentration of attention, asked her questions about her life, about her family, took again her field of vision. All that was a great effort to her. While I was taking her field of vision the patient's eyes began to close, and it took about twenty seconds before she could open them. She opened them with effort, but shut them again. This time it took her about 45 seconds before she could open the lids. Fatigue, or rather fear fatigue, set in sooner with each repetition of experiment and test, and lasted a longer time.

For several days the patient kept on improving slowly. She then had another relapse. She slept well the night before, but woke up early about six in the morning; she began to worry about her family, and complained of headache. About half past eight the headache became severe, there was again pain in the left side, the left hand began to tremble, and felt anaesthetic, the eyelids closed, and could not open, aphonia returned, in fact she fell into a state of mutism. About ten o'clock patient opened her eyes, but she was unable to talk. After long insistence on her reply to my question as to how she was, she finally replied in a whisper: "Well," then added "I have a bad headache." She had great difficulty in replying to my questions, moved her jaws impotently before she was able to emit a sound, her muscles were strained, the face was set, tense, and drawn, the brow was corrugated, the eyeballs rolled up, and the eyelids shut tightly. The patient was unable to raise her hands, they lay powerless at her side. When raised the arms were found to be lethargic, fell to her side, only the left hand manifested light, fibrillary twitchings and a gross tremor. When insisted upon that she must raise her arms, she became agitated, scared, began to moan and cry. Claimed severe pain in head, in chest, in heart. "Pain in heart, in head, I am afraid," she moaned in a whisper. There was loss of kinaesthetic sensibility, patient complained that she did not feel her arms, "they are not mine." She had to look at the arm in order to find it. There was also present anaesthsia to other sensations such as pain, touch, heat, and cold. After a couple of hours' rest the sensibility returned. The sensibility was affected more on the left side than on the right, and also returned earlier on the right side.

When the fatigue and the scare subsided the patient was tested again. This time the reactions to sensory stimulations were normal. The patient was touched, pinched, and pricked, she reacted to each stimulus separately, and was able to synthesize them and give a full account of their number. Kinaesthetic sensibility was good,—she was fully able to appreciate the various movements and positions in which her limbs and fingers were put.

The patient was left to rest, quietened, treated carefully, avoiding sudden stimulations, allaying her fears and suspiciousness of danger, lurking in the background of her mind. After a few hours she sat up, made an attempt to raise herself from bed, got up with some effort, and sat down in an easy rocking chair next to her. Her eyes were wide open. Asked how she was, she replied in a whisper that she felt quite well. The effort however fatigued her, her head began to drop, eyelids began to close, and the eyeballs began to roll up. Twitchings were observed in the eyelids, and tremors in the left arm. She was again put to bed and given a rest of a few hours. She opened her eyes, and told me that she was weak. This statement she herself volunteered. I found that she could move her hands easily, and that the numbness was completely gone.

For a whole week the patient kept on growing in health and in strength, her sensori-motor reactions improved, she walked round the room for a few minutes, talked in a low voice for a quarter of an hour at a time without manifesting her symptoms of fatigue; her appetite and sleep improved accordingly. At the end of the week there was again a relapse,—she did not sleep well the night before, dreamt of being hunted and tortured, woke up depressed, had no appetite for breakfast, complained of headache, pains, worries, and fears. The headaches have abated in their virulence during last week, but now they seemed to have reappeared in their former vigor. When I began to examine her she looked frightened, her eyeballs rolled up, her eyelids closed. The aphonia was severe, patient lost speech and voice. When spoken to she could not answer. Asked if she heard me, she nodded her head affirmatively. There were slight twitchings of her left hand and also of the muscles of her face. When attention was attracted to the arm the twitchings increased in violence and rapidity. With the distraction of the attention the twitchings disappeared. When the left hand was put in the patient's field of vision, thus making her attention concentrate on that limb, the tremors increased again, becoming finally convulsive in character.

I insisted she should try to open her mouth, and say something,—she made fruitless efforts, moving incoordinately the muscles of the face and of the forehead, but she could not utter a sound. She could not move her arms on command, could hardly wriggle the fingers of her hand. She appeared like a little bird paralyzed by fear. When the arm was raised passively it fell down slowly being in a cataleptic state.

I allayed the patient's fear. I strongly impressed her with the groundlessness of her fears, and also with the fact that everything was well with the children, and that her husband will be good and gentle with her. The patient was permitted to see her family. The husband was made to realize that he must treat her with more consideration. He came often to visit her, and learned to treat her well. He soon found a better position, was advised to remove to a healthy locality and to more cheerful surroundings. The children were well cared for. The patient found deep satisfaction in the midst of this family happiness. The fear state abated,—the patient became more confident, more hopeful for the future, and began to improve. The infant was weaned so that the strain of nursing was removed. The patient's appetite began to improve; she gained several pounds in a few days. Long periods of examination and investigation of her nervous and mental state no longer exhausted or terrified her. Her concentration of attention could be kept up from a quarter to half an hour at a stretch without giving rise to fatigue, headache, or to a seizure with its consequent psychomotor effects. The haunted look of fear disappeared, and along with it were also gone the fatigue and dread of physical and mental exercise or work. She could work and walk with ease the whole length of the room and of the hall. She began to take more and more interest in her appearance and in dress. For many minutes at a time she looked out on the street taking an interest in all that was done and what was going on.

The case was discharged, and was sent home. She continued to stay well.

FOOTNOTE:

[12] In fact from my long experience with cases of stammering, stuttering and mutism I may say that where no organic lesion may be suspected, the disturbance is one of self and fear.

CHAPTER XXIV

SUGGESTED HALLUCINATIONS

The servility, the state of fear of the subconscious, the source of neurosis, in its relation to the master hypnotizer is well brought out in the mechanism of hypnotic and post-hypnotic hallucinations.

Before we proceed with our discussion it may be well to give an analysis, however brief, of the normal percept, of the abnormal percept or hallucination, and then compare them with hypnotic and post-hypnotic hallucinations. The understanding of perception, normal and abnormal, is, in fact, at the basis of normal and abnormal psychology.

We may begin with the percept and its elements. In looking at the vase before me I see its beautiful tints, its rounded shape, its heavy pedestal with its rough curves, its solidity, weight, brittleness, and other experiences which go to make up the perception of the vase. The visual elements are given directly by the visual perceptive experience; but whence come the seemingly direct experiences of weight, heaviness, roughness, smoothness, and others of the like kind? They are evidently derived from other senses. The whole perceptive experience is of a visual character. We take in the whole with our eye. In the organic structure of the percept then, besides the experiences directly given by the stimulated sense-organ, there are other experiences, sensory in character, indirectly given, and coming from other sense organs which are not directly stimulated.

The percept is a complicated dynamic product, and its elementary processes are never derived from one isolated domain of sensory experience. The activities of all the sensory domains co-operate in the total result of an apparently simple percept. Along with sensory processes directly stimulated, a mass of other sensory processes becomes organized and helps to contribute to the total result. The direct sensory elements are termed by me *primary sensory elements*; the indirectly given experiences are termed *secondary sensory elements*. The secondary sensory elements may be figuratively said to cluster round the primary sensory elements as their nucleus.

The whole perceptual experience is tinged by the character of the primary elements which constitute the guiding nucleus, so to say. Thus, where the primary sensory elements are visual, the whole mass, no matter from what domain the sensory experiences are derived, appears under the form of the visual sense, and the percept is a visual percept. While the primary sensory elements form, so to say, the dynamic center of the total perceptual experience, the secondary sensory elements mainly constitute its content. Both primary and secondary elements are sensory and are induced peripherally; the primary directly, the secondary indirectly. The percept then is sensory and is constituted by primary sensory elements, or primary sensations, and by secondary sensory elements, or secondary sensations.

The character of the secondary sensory elements stands out clear and independent in the phenomena of synaesthesia, of secondary sensations. In the phenomena of synaesthesia we have a sensation of one sense organ followed, without an intermediary direct stimulation, by a sensation coming from another sense organ. Thus, when a sensation of light instead of giving rise to a subsequent idea gives rise to a sensation of sound, for instance, we have the phenomenon of secondary sensation. Here the secondary sensations stand out free and distinct, but they are really always present in our ordinary perceptive experiences as bound up secondary sensory elements, as secondary sensations grouped round primary sensations.

When the phenomena of synaesthesia were first brought to the notice of the scientific world, they were regarded as abnormal and exceptional, and only present in special pathological cases. Soon, however, their field became widened, and they were found not only in the insane and degenerate, but in many persons otherwise perfectly normal. We find now that we must further widen the field of secondary sensory elements, and instead of regarding them as a freak of nature existing under highly artificial conditions, we must put them at the very foundation of the process of perception.

Secondary sensations are at the basis of perception. We have become so accustomed to them that we simply disregard them. When, however, the conditions change, when the secondary sensations stand out by themselves, isolated from the primary nuclear elements with which they are usually organically synthesized into a whole, into a percept, when they become dissociated, it is only then that we become conscious of them directly and declare them as abnormal.

Secondary sensations are always present in every act of perception; in fact, they form the main content of our perceptual activity, only we are not conscious of them, and it requires a special analysis to reveal them. Secondary sensations *per se* are not something abnormal—just as hydrogen present in the water we drink or the oxygen present in the air we breathe are not newly created elements,—it only requires an analysis to discover them. If there be any abnormality about secondary sensations, it is not in the elements themselves, but rather in the fact of their dissociation from the primary nuclear elements.

When the secondary sensory elements come to the foreground and stand out clearly in consciousness, a full-fledged hallucination arises. In the phenomena of synaesthesia we have hallucinations in the simplest form, inasmuch as only isolated secondary sensory elements dissociated from their active primary central elements stand out in the foreground of consciousness. This very simplification, however, of hallucinations reveals their inner character. The most complex hallucinations are only complex compounds, so to say, of secondary sensory elements. Hallucinations are not anything mysterious, different from what we find in the normal ordinary processes of perception; they are of the same character and have the same elements in their constitution as those of perception. Both hallucinations and percepts have the same secondary as well as primary elements. The difference between hallucinations and percepts is only one of relationship, of rearrangement of elements, primary and secondary. When *secondary sensory elements become under conditions of dissociation dynamically active in the focus of consciousness we have hallucinations.*

From this standpoint we can well understand why a hallucination, like a percept, has all the attributes of external reality. A hallucination is not any more mysterious and wonderful than a percept is. We do not recognize the humdrum percept, when it appears in the guise of a hallucination, and we regard it as some strange visitant coming from a central, or from some supersensory universe. Hallucinations, like percepts, are constituted of primary and especially of secondary sensory elements, and like percepts, hallucinations too are induced peripherally.

How is it with suggested[13] or hypnotic hallucinations? Do we find in hypnotic or suggested hallucinations, as in the case of hallucinations in general, the requisite primary and secondary sensory elements directly and indirectly induced? Binet makes an attempt to establish a peripheral stimulus in the case of hypnotic hallucinations, claiming that there is a *point de repére*, a kind of a peg, on which the hypnotic hallucination is hung. It is questionable whether Binet himself continued to maintain this position. However the case may be, this position is hardly tenable when confronted with facts. Hypnotic hallucinations may develop without any peg and prop.

Furthermore, granted even that now and then such a peg could be discovered, and that the alleged hypnotic hallucination develops more easily when such a peg is furnished, still the fact remains that even in such cases the peg is altogether insignificant, that it is altogether out of proportion and relation to the suggested hallucination, and that on the same peg all kinds of hallucinations can be hung, and that finally it can be fully dispensed with. All this would go to show that the peg, as such, is of no consequence, and is really more of the nature of an emphatic suggestion for the development of the alleged hypnotic or post-hypnotic hallucinations.

The arbitrariness of the hypnotic hallucinations, showing that the whole thing is simply a matter of representations, or of what the patient happens to think at that particular moment, is well brought out in the following experiments: Mr. F. is put into a hypnotic state, and a post-hypnotic suggestion is given to him that he shall see a watch. The eyeball is then displaced, the watch is also displaced; now when the eyeball returns to its normal condition we should expect that the hallucinatory watch would return to its former place; but no, the watch is not perceived in its previous place,—it appears in a displaced position. The hallucinatory watch could thus be displaced any distance from its original position. The patient evidently did not see anything, but simply supplied from his stock of knowledge as to how a seen watch would appear under such conditions, and he omitted to observe the fact that with the normal position of the eye the watch should once more return to its former position. Such inconsistencies are often found in hypnosis.

More intelligent and better informed patients would reason out the matter differently, and would give different results. If the subject knows of contrast colors and if a color is suggested to him he will without fail see such contrast colors. If his eyes have been fixed on some hallucinatory color, such as red, for instance, he will even give you a detailed account of the green he sees, but if he does not know anything of the effects of contrast colors no amount of fixation on hallucinatory colors will bring out the least contrast effects. The reason is the patient does not know anything about it and cannot think of it.

We tried to mix by suggestion different hallucinatory colors, and as long as he knew nothing of the real results his replies were uniformly wrong; no sooner did he find out what the right mixture *should* be than he gave correct results. The hypnotic subject really does not perceive anything; he tells what he believes the master wants him to see under the given conditions. The subconscious fear instinct makes the hypnotized subject obey and please the hypnotizer, as the dog obeys his master.

CHAPTER XXV

TRANCE SERVILITY

Dr. C., a known psychoanalyst, on whom I carried on a series of experiments, goes into a deep somnambulistic state. He is an excellent visualizer and takes readily visual hallucinations. Being a physician and psychiatrist the subject's account is all the more valuable. Now Dr. C. describes his hypnotic hallucinations as "mental pictures," as "auditory memories," which "lack exteriority, are not located in space." He aptly characterizes his hallucinations, visual, auditory, and others, as *"fixed ideas."*

Mr. M. goes into deep hypnosis. When in one of the deep trance-states a suggestion is given to him that on awakening he shall see a watch. When awake he claims he sees a watch. He was asked: "Do you really see it?" He replied, "Yes." The interesting point here was the fact that the subject did not even look in the direction where the suggested hallucinatory watch was supposed to be placed and where he himself claimed that the watch was located. When tested by automatic writing the hand wrote: "Yes, I see the watch." The subconscious then was also under the influence of the suggested hallucination. It is well to bear in mind this point.

Re-hypnotized, and suggested that on awakening he would see *two* watches. One was a real silver watch and the other was suggested hallucinatory. The subject claimed he saw both, but he only handled the hallucinatory one, and when asked which of the two he would prefer he pointed to the hallucinatory watch. When asked why, he replied that the suggested watch was bigger. He was really indifferent to the chosen watch and paid no further attention to it, as if it did not exist for him. He tried to please the master hypnotizer of whom he was subconsciously in awe.

He was again put into the hypnotic state and was suggested to see a flower. On awakening he claimed he saw a flower and smelled it in an indifferent, perfunctory fashion. The subconscious was then tested by automatic writing and the writing was to the effect that he saw it. "I see a flower." The subconscious then had also the same hallucination. A series of similar experiments was carried out with the same results. *The subconscious claimed in automatic writing that the suggested hallucination was real.*

The subject was again put into hypnosis and was given the suggestion that he would see a watch on awakening, but here I made some modification. "When you wake up you will be sure to see a watch," I said, emphatically. "Look here; I want you to write what you really see and not what you do not see." When awake he saw a watch, but he immediately wrote: "I do not see anything." *Here the subconscious disclaimed the suggested hallucinations which it had claimed and insisted on before.*

Re-hypnotized, and was given the suggestion that on awakening he would see three watches. He was awakened and a real silver watch was put before him; the other two were suggested hallucinatory. He claimed he saw all three. Meanwhile, in automatic writing he wrote: "One silver watch, real, the others golden, not real; nothing there." A series of similar experiments was made and with the same results. *The automatic writing disclaimed the hallucinations, although before, under the same conditions, it most emphatically insisted on their reality.*

The subject was put into hypnosis and a post-hypnotic suggestion was given to him that he would see his wife and child. When awake, he began to smile. When asked why he smiled he said: "I see my wife and child"; but he wrote "I see nobody." When put again in hypnosis he still continued to smile and said: "I see my wife and child"; but he wrote (in hypnotic state): "I really do not see them; I see nothing; I see my child, but I really see nothing." That was when the psychopathic patient got the inkling that I wished to know the truth rather than to be misled by his slavish obedience and fears by complying with my orders. "What do you mean," I asked, "by 'I see my child, but I really see nothing?'" To which he replied in automatic writing: "I mean that I see my child in my mind only, but I don't see anything."

I then gave him a post-hypnotic suggestion to see a snake. He claimed on awaking that he saw a snake. He manifested little fear. He certainly did not behave as if he really saw a snake and instead wrote "I see a snake. I see it in my mind." A great number of similar experiments were carried out by me, varying the suggestions, and all with the same results. I shall not burden the reader with a detailed account, as they all gave identical results.

At first the automatic writing claimed emphatically the presence of the hallucinatory object and when the truth of the automatic writing was insisted on, the writing disclaimed fully the perception of the hallucinatory object. Finally we came on the real character of the suggested hallucination; "I see my child, but *honestly*, I do not see anything; I see my child in my mind only, I don't see anything." In other words, if we take the facts plainly and do not play hide and seek with the subconscious, we come to the conclusion that in the suggested hallucinations the subject does not perceive anything as is the case in an actual hallucination. He does not *perceive*, but he simply *thinks* of the suggested hallucination.

As long then as the automatic writing was regarded by the subject as independent, for which he was not responsible, as long as the suggestion of the hallucination was not taken as directly addressed to it, the subject himself frankly acknowledged the fact that he did not see anything. When this truth of automatic writing was brought home to the subject he was bound by suggestion to claim that he actually saw the suggested hallucination, although he really did not see anything at all.

This clearly shows that the hypnotic consciousness, from the very nature of its heightened suggestibility, clings most anxiously to the given suggestion, and insists on the reality of its fulfillment. We must, therefore, be on our guard and not trust the subject's introspective account, unless it is well sifted by good circumstantial evidence. It is because such precautions have not been taken in the close interrogation of the subject's actual state of mind, and because of the deep-rooted psychological fallacy as to the relation of ideational and perceptual activities, that the prevalent belief in the validity of suggested hallucinations has passed unchallenged. If not for those factors, it would have been quite evident that the *hypnotic and post-hypnotic suggested hallucinations are not genuine, but are essentially spurious. Hypnotic hallucinations, unlike actual hallucinations, are not really experienced. Hypnotically suggested hallucinations are only forms of delusions*, attempts to appease the master hypnotizer of whom the subconscious stands in awe and fear.

The state of hypnotic subconsciousness is a state based on the will to conform to the master hypnotizer's commands. At bottom the subconscious trance-will is one of slavish obedience to the authoritative, fear-inspiring will of the master hypnotizer, whom the hypnotic subconscious attempts to please and obey slavishly. The hypnotic state is a fear state of a primitive type. It is the fear state of the Damara ox obeying the herd, or the leader of the herd.

Man is hypnotizable, because he is gregarious, because he is easily controlled by *self-fear*, because he easily falls into a *self-less* state of complacent servility. Man, subconscious man, is servile, in fear of his Lord. The independent, free man is yet to come.

FOOTNOTE:

[13] I use the term "suggested hallucination" to indicate the character and origin of the latter. The term seems to me convenient and may prove acceptable.

CHAPTER XXVI

THE HYPNOIDAL STATE AND SUPERSTITIONS

The hypnoidal state into which man is apt to fall so easily, is well adapted to fear suggestions, since the fear instinct and the impulse of self-preservation are present in the subconsciousness, exposed during trance states to all sorts of fear suggestions and superstitions. It is during these brief periods of primitive hypnoidal states that the animal is exposed to attacks of enemies whose senses become sharpened to detect the weak spots in the armor of their victims, immersed in the momentary rest of the hypnoidal state.

During these periods of repose and passivity or of sleep stage, the animal can only protect itself by all kinds of subterfuges, such as hiding in various inaccessible places, or taking its rest-periods in shady nooks and corners, or in the darkness of the night. Each hypnoidal period closely corresponds to the larval stage of the insect, reposing in its cocoon,—the most critical time of the insect organism, most exposed to the depredations of its enemies. And still the hypnoidal state is requisite to the animal in order to restitute its living matter and energy which have been wasted during the active moments of its life activities. Hence the weakness of the animal depends on the very constitution of its organism.

The hypnoidal state, although absolutely necessary in the process of metabolism, is also the moment of its greatest danger, and the fear instinct is specially intense at the onset of that hypnoidal moment, the lowest point of the weakness of the organism. The animal, after taking all precautions, is finally paralyzed into temporary immobility at the risk of its own existence.

The fear instinct determines the nature and character of rest and sleep. The lower the animal, the scantier are its means of defense in the ceaseless struggle for its preservation. The simpler the animal, the greater and more numerous are the dangers menacing it with total extinction,—hence it must be constantly on its guard. A state of sleep such as found in the higher animals is rendered impossible. The sleep must be light, and in snatches, rapidly passing from rest into waking,—the characteristic of the hypnoidal state. The fear instinct is the controlling factor of sleep and rest. When we are in danger the sleep is light and in snatches, and we thus once more revert to an ancient form of rest and sleep.

The insomnia found in cases of neurosis is a reversion to primitive rest-states, found in the lower animals. The insomnia is due to the fear instinct which keeps dominating the conscious and subconscious mental activities, a state which has prevailed in the early stages of animal life. That is why the sleep of neurotics is unrefreshing and full of dreams of dangers and accidents, and peopled with visions of a terrorizing nature. Hence the neurotic fear of insomnia which is itself the consequence of the obsession, conscious and subconscious, of the fear instinct.

In my work on sleep I was greatly impressed with the place fear holds in animal life existence. From the lowest representative, such as the insect to the highest, such as man, fear rules with an iron hand. Every animal is subject to cataplexy of fear and to the hypnoidal state itself, the consequence of fear-adaptations to the external conditions of a hostile environment. Cataplexy and the consequent hypnoidal state which paralyze the animal, depriving it of all defense, are grounded in the imperfections of living protoplasm.

Man is subject to the hypnoidal periods of primitive life. It is during those periods that the shafts of suggestion are most apt to strike his subconsciousness, divorced as it is during those moments from the nodding self consciousness. During these nodding moments of his life he is exposed to harmful suggestions, since they are apt to arouse the fear instinct, the most sensitive of all human instincts. It seems as if the fear instinct is never fully asleep, and is the easiest to arouse. It seems to be watchful or semi-watchful during the most critical moments of man's helplessness.

Fear of darkness and fear of invisible foes are specially strong in man, because of the deeply rooted fear instinct, but also because of his memories of accidents and dangers that have befallen him, and which may befall him. Man's fears hang round dark places, gloomy corners and nooks, caves and forests, and more especially during the darkness and shades of night, appearing as treacherous visions and specters of lurking dangers. And still from the very nature of his being man must rest and sleep, hence the association of terrors with night time. He can only overcome his night terrors by living and sleeping in more or less secure corners, in the neighborhood of his fellow-beings who by the mere fact of numbers multiply not only the means of defense, but actually increase susceptibility for the scent of danger and possible speedy defense. In the society of his fellows the sense organs of the individual are increased by the presence of others who are in various stages of vigilance, and hence there is greater protection against dangers and invisible foes that lurk in the darkness of night, foes of which primitive man is in terror of his life.

The fear of the unknown, the mysterious, and the dark, peoples the mind of primitive man with all sorts of terrible spectres, ghosts, spirits, goblins, ghouls, shades, witches, and evil powers, all bent on mischief, destruction and death. *Primitive man suffers from chronic demonophobia.* Fear states are specially emphasized at night when the "demons" have the full power for evil, and man is helpless on account of darkness and sleep which paralyze him. Hence the terrors of the night, especially when man is alone, and defenseless.

The fear of solitude comes out strongly in the intense fear that obsesses man in the gloomy darkness of the night horrors. Fire and fellow-beings can alone relieve his night terrors. The fear of foes, of demons, of evil powers does not abate in the day, only it is relieved by reason of light, of association, and of wakefulness. Man, more than any other animal, is the victim of the fear instinct. Many tribes, many races of men perished, due to superstitions and fear obsessions.

The *Homo sapiens* is rare. We may agree with Tarde that *Homo somnambulis* would be a proper definition of the true mental condition of most specimens of the human race. For the human race is still actuated by the principle of *"Credo, quia absurdum est."* I need not go far to substantiate the fact that this principle still guides the life of the average specimen of civilized humanity. Spiritualism, theosophy, telepathy, ghost hunting, astrology, oneiromancy, cheiromancy, Christian Science, psychoanalytic oneiroscopy employed in events and situations of individual and social life, and many other magical practices whose name is legion, based on the mysteries of communication with ghosts, spirits, demons, and unknown fearsome powers, still haunt the credulous mind, obsessed with conscious and subconscious horrors of the terrible, invisible spirit world.

Against the fears of diseases, the scares of the day and terrors of night, civilized man still uses the magic arts and mysterious, miraculous powers of the magician, the wizard, the witch, the mental healer, the shaman, the medicine man, the miracle man, and the psychoanalyst. Just at present under my own eyes I witness the pitiful credulity of man, driven by the terrors and horrors of the fear instinct. In San Jose, San Diego, in Los Angeles, and in many other Western "culture" centers mystic cults hold high carnival, swaying the minds of fear-crazed, deluded humanity. As typical specimens of superstitious fears and absurd beliefs, due to the fear instinct, we may take as illustrations the following occurrences in the centers of the far West, obsessed by the aberrations of the fear instinct (I quote from Los Angeles papers):

"Faith Healer at Los Angeles, Venice, California, after several wonder cures, orders sun's rays to be darkened. 'Brother Isaiah,' called by thousands the 'Miracle Man,' claimed to have repeated the marvel of dimming the sun at Venice yesterday evening.

"At 6 o'clock the disciple of healing by faith raised his hands and announced that as evidence of his power he would blot out the brilliant solar rays. He gazed at the dazzling red ball above the waters of the Pacific, and his lips moved in low murmurs.

"'It is done,' he said. 'I have clouded the sun. All those who have seen this miracle raise your hands.' Hundreds of hands waved in the air.

"The first time 'Brother Isaiah' claimed to have dimmed the sun's rays was at Miracle Hill, when he had been in Los Angeles but a few days.

"Brother Isaiah stepped to one side of his wooden platform on the Venice Beach yesterday. He placed a silver police whistle to his lips and blew. The piercing crescendo sent a shiver through the tense mass of humanity which stretched from the sand back to the ocean walk." Similar miracles and cures were carried on by Mrs. Amy McPherson in San Diego, San Jose, and all along the Pacific coast.

The self-impulse and the fear instinct, in their intensified forms, are the bane of deluded, neurotic humanity.

CHAPTER XXVII

NEUROSIS AND HEREDITY

The following discussion in the form of questions and answers may prove of interest to the physician and to the intelligent layman. The discussion occurred in the course of correspondence. A friend of mine thought the subject of sufficient importance to have it brought to the attention of the cultured public.

The questions are as follows:

"Are not all neuropathic conditions the results of a morbid, unstable nervous organism, the basis of which lies in a faulty heredity?

"Are not weak nerves the cause of hysterical, neurasthenic and neuropathic affections in general?

"Is not all neurosis due to defective parent stock?

"If the occasions for fear, as some psychopathologists claim, were more frequent in primitive times than now, then the cave men must have had more psychopathic affections than civilized man."

To these questions the following answers are given:

Psychopathic diseases are not hereditary—they are *acquired* characteristics, having their origin in the abnormal, hypertrophied growth of the fear instinct which is at the root of the primal impulse of self-preservation. This is proved by psychopathological studies of clinical cases; and it can be further demonstrated by experimental work in the laboratory even in the case of animals. "Weak nerves," "a run down, exhausted nervous system," whatever the terms may mean, may overlap psychopathic conditions, but the two are by no means equivalent, much less identical. Psychopathic, psychoneurotic states are not "weak nerves" or "fatigued nerves." Above all, there is no need to obscure the matter and resort to the much abused, mystical and mystifying factor of heredity. It is easy to shift all blame on former generations, when, in most cases, the fault is close at hand, namely, a debased environment, a defective training, and a vicious education.

There is good reason to believe that primitive man had a far greater tendency to dissociation, to subconscious psychopathic states than modern man. Even the Middle Ages teem with psychopathic mental epidemics of the most puerile type. In the course of evolution, social and individual, this neurotic, psychopathic tendency has gradually diminished, but has never been completely eliminated. Increase of knowledge, better education, the increase of social safeguards, sanitary and hygienic conditions with consequent increase of safety from dangers, have all helped materially in decreasing the occasions for the cultivation of the fear instinct.

Under the rigorous conditions of primitive life individuals who have been unfortunate and have become affected with mental troubles and emotional afflictions of the fear instinct are mercilessly exterminated by the process of tribal and social selection. Each generation weeds out the individuals who have been unfortunate enough to fall under unfavorable circumstances and have become mentally sick, suffering from acquired psychopathic disturbances. In primitive life the crippled, the maimed, the wounded, the sick fall by the way, and are left to perish a miserable death. In fact, the less fortunate, the wounded and the stricken in the battle of life, are attacked by their own companions,—they are destroyed by the ruthless, social brute. The gregarious brute has no sympathy with the pains and sufferings of the injured and the wounded. The faint and the ailing are destroyed by the herd.

Civilization, on the other hand, tends more and more towards the preservation of psychopathic individuals. We no longer kill our sick and our weak, nor do we abandon them to a miserable, painful death,—we take care of them, and cure them. Moreover, we prevent pathogenic factors from exercising a harmful, malign social selection of the "fit." We do our best to free ourselves from the blind, merciless, purposeless selection, produced by pathogenic micro-organisms and by other noxious agencies. We learn to improve the external environment.

We do not condemn people to death because they are infected with smallpox, typhus, typhoid bacilli, or because of an infected appendix. We no longer regard them as sinful, unclean, accursed, and tabooed. We vaccinate, inoculate, operate, and attempt to cure them. By sanitary and prophylactic measures we attempt to prevent the very occurrence of epidemics. Our valuation of individuals is along lines widely different from those of the stone age and cave man. We value a Pascal, a Galileo, a Newton, a Darwin, a Pasteur, and a Helmholtz far above a Milo of Croton or an African Johnson.

Civilization is in need of refined, delicate and sensitive organizations, just as it is in need of galvanometers, chronometers, telephones, wireless apparatuses, and various chemical reagents of a highly delicate character. We are beginning to appreciate delicate mechanisms and sensitive organizations. We shall also learn to train and guard our sensitive natures until they are strong and resistant to the incident forces of an unfavorable environment. The recognition, the diagnosis, and the preservation of psychopathic individuals account for the apparent increase of neurotics in civilized communities.

It may be well to add that, although occasions for sudden, intense, overwhelming fears are not so prevalent in civilized societies as they are in primitive savage communities, the worries, the anxieties, the various forms of slow grinding fears of a vague, marginal, subconscious character present in commercial and industrial nations, are even more effective in the production of psychopathic states than are the isolated occasions of intense frights in the primitive man of the paleolithic or neolithic periods.

CHAPTER XXVIII

NEUROSIS AND EUGENICS

In my work on Psychopathology I lay special stress on the fact that the psychopathic individual has a predisposition to dissociative states. Early experiences and training in childhood enter largely into the formation of such a predisposition. Still, there is no doubt that a sensitive nervous system is required—a brain susceptible to special stimuli of the external environment. This, of course, does not mean that the individual must suffer from stigmata of degeneration. On the contrary, it is quite possible, and in many patients we actually find it to be so, that the psychopathic individual may be even of a superior organization. *It is the sensitivity and the delicacy of nervous organization that make the system susceptible to injurious stimulations, to which a lower form of organization could be subjected with impunity.*

An ordinary clock can be handled roughly without disturbance of its internal workings, but the delicate and complicated mechanism of a chronometer requires careful handling and special, favorable conditions for its normal functioning. Unfavorable conditions are more apt to affect a highly complex mechanism than a roughly made instrument. It is quite probable that it is the superior minds and more highly complex mental and nervous organizations that are subject to psychopathic states or states of dissociation. Of course, unstable minds are also subject to dissociative states, but we must never forget the fact that highly organized brains, on account of their very complexity, are apt to become unstable under unfavorable conditions. A predisposition to dissociation may occur either in degenerative minds or in minds superior to the average. *Functional psychosis requires a long history of dissociated, subconscious shocks, suffered by a highly or lowly organized nervous system, a long history dating back to early childhood.*

As Mosso puts it: "The vivid impression of a strong emotion may produce the same effect as a blow on the head or some physical shock." We may, however, say that no functional psychosis, whether somatopsychosis or psychoneurosis, can ever be produced simply by physical shocks. *In all functional psychoses there must be a mental background, and it is the mental background alone that produces the psychosis and determines the character of the psychopathic state.*

Fear is an important factor in the etiology of psychopathic affections which include somatopsychoses and psychoneuroses.

To regard fear as "error," as do some sectarians, is absurd, and is certainly unscientific. Abnormal fear which is the basis of all functional nervous or psychopathic maladies, is essentially a pathological process affecting the organs in general and the nervous system in particular in as definite a way as the invasion and infection of the organism by various species of bacteria, bacilli, and other micro-organisms which attack the individual during his lifetime.

Like infectious diseases, the deviations, abnormalities, and excesses of the fear instinct are *acquired* by the individual in the course of his relations with the external environment, and are as real and substantial as are syphilis, smallpox, diphtheria, cholera, and the bubonic plague. To regard them as imaginary or to relegate them to the action of Providence or to heredity is theoretically a misconception, and practically a great danger to humanity.

There is nowadays a veritable craze for heredity and eugenics. Biology is misconceived, misinterpreted, and misapplied to social problems, and to individual needs and ailments. Everything is ascribed to heredity, from folly and crime to scratches and sneezes. The goddess Heredity is invoked at each flea-bite—*in morsu pulicis Deum invocare.*

Even war is supposed to be due to the omnipotent deity of Heredity. Superior races by their patriotism and loyalty destroy the weak and the helpless, and relentlessly exterminate all peaceful tribes. Such warlike stock comes of superior clay. The dominant races have some miraculous germ-plasm, special "unit characters," wonderful dominant "units" which, like a precious heritage, these races transmit unsullied and untarnished to their descendants.

Wars, carnage, butcheries make for progress, culture, and evolution. Our boasted civilization with its "scientific" business thoroughness and its ideal of "efficiency" attempts to carry into effect this quasi-evolutionary doctrine—this apotheosis of brute force under the aegis of science. The eugenic belief is really a recrudescence of the ancient savage superstition of the magic virtues of noble blood and of divine king stock.

All nervous, mental, neuropathic, and psychopathic maladies are supposed to be a matter of heredity. If people are poor, ignorant, superstitious, stupid, degraded, brutal, and sick, the eugenists unhesitatingly put it all down to poor stock.

The eugenic remedy is as simple as it is believed to be efficacious: Introduce by legislation "efficient" laws favoring "eugenic" marriage, and teach the masses control of births. The select and chosen stock alone should multiply—the millennium is then bound to come. Such is the doctrine of our medico-biological sages.

"Scientific" farmers and breeders of vegetables, fruits, and cattle are regarded as competent judges of human "breeders." Agriculturists and horticulturists set themselves up as advisers in "the business of raising good crops of efficient children." Bachelors, spinsters, and the childless generally, are specially versed in eugenic wisdom and pedagogics.

All social ills and individual complaints are referred to one main source—heredity. With the introduction of eugenic legislation, with the sterilization of the socially unfit, among whom the greatest men and women may be included, with the breeding of good "orthodox, common stock," and with eugenic Malthusian control of births, all evil and diseases on earth will cease, while the Philistine "superman" will reign supreme forevermore.

In the Middle Ages all diseases and epidemics, all wars, all social and private misfortunes were considered as visitations of Divine wrath. The fear instinct held sway, terrorizing poor, deluded humanity. In modern times our would-be eugenic science refers all ills of the flesh and woes of the mind to an outraged Heredity. The dark ages had resort to prayers, fasts, and penitence, while our age childishly pins its faith to the miraculous virtues and rejuvenating, regenerative powers of legislative eugenic measures, and to the eugenic Malthusian control of births.

Our scientists in eugenics gather hosts of facts, showing by elaborate statistical figures that the family history of neurotics reveals stigmata of degeneration in the various members of the family. The eugenic inquirers do not stop for a moment to think over the fact that the same sort of evidence can be easily brought in the case of most people. In fact, the eugenists themselves, when inquiring into the pedigree of talent and genius, invariably find somewhere in the family some form of disease or degeneration. This sort of "scientific" evidence leads some eugenic speculators, without their noticing the *reductio ad absurdum*, to the curious conclusion or generalization that degeneration is present in the family history of the best and the worst representatives of the human race.

The so-called scientific method of the eugenists is faulty, in spite of the rich display of colored plates, stained tablets, glittering biological speculations, brilliant mathematical formulae, and complicated statistical calculations. The eugenists pile Ossa on Pelion of facts by the simple method of enumeration which Bacon and the thinkers coming after him have long ago condemned as puerile and futile. From the savage's belief in sympathetic, imitative magic with its consequent superstitions, omens, and taboos down to the articles of faith and dogmas of the eugenists, we find the same faulty, primitive thought, guided by the puerile, imbecile method of simple enumeration, and controlled by the wisdom of the logical *post hoc, ergo propter hoc*.

What would we say of the medical man who should claim that measles, mumps, cholera, typhoid fever, yellow fever, malaria, tetanus, and various other infectious diseases are hereditary by quoting learnedly long tables of statistics to the effect that for several generations members of the same family suffered from the same infectious diseases? What would we say of the medical advice forbidding marriage to individuals whose family history reveals the presence of exanthemata? We stamp out epidemics not by eugenic measures, but by the cleansing of infectious filth, and by the extermination of pathogenic micro-organisms.

Every human being has a predisposition to smallpox, cholera, tetanus, bubonic plague, typhus fever, malaria, and to like infectious diseases, but there is no inherent necessity for everyone to fall a victim to the action of pathogenic organisms, if the preventive and sanitary conditions are good and proper. No one is immune against the action of bullets, cannon balls, shells, and torpedoes, or to the action of various poisons, organic and inorganic, but one is not doomed by fate to be killed by them, if one does not expose himself to their deadly action.

Every living organism is, by the very nature of its cellular tissues, predisposed to wounding by sharp instruments, or to the burning action of fire, but this does not mean an inherent organic weakness to which the organism must necessarily submit and perish. We are all of us predisposed to get injured and possibly killed, when we fall down from a high place, or when we are run over by an automobile or by a locomotive, but there is no fatalistic necessity about such accidents, if care is taken that they should not occur.

We may be predisposed to neurosis by the very nature of complexity, delicacy, and sensitivity inherent in the structure of a highly organized nervous system, and still we may remain healthy and strong all our life long, provided we know how to keep away from noxious agencies. The creed of the inevitable fatality of neurosis is as much of a superstition as the Oriental belief in the fatalism of infectious diseases, plagues, and accidents of all kinds. Such fatalistic superstitions are dangerous, fatal, because they distract the attention from the actual cause and from the requisite prophylactic measures.

We go far afield in search for the remote source of our troubles, when the cause is close at hand. We need only open our eyes to see the filth of our towns, the foul, loathsome slums of our cities, the miserable training, the wretched education given to our children, in order to realize at a glance the source of our ills and ailments. We should lay the guilt at the door of our social order. We starve our young. We starve our children physically and mentally. We piously sacrifice our tender children and the flower of our youth to the greedy, industrial Moloch of a military, despotic, rapacious plutocracy.

Witness semi-civilized Europe with its lauded culture brutally shedding the blood of its youth and manhood on the altar of commercial patriotism! It is not heredity, it is the vicious conditions of life that stunt the physical, nervous, and mental growth of our young generation. When we are confronted with the miserable, degraded, crippled forms of our life, we fall back cheerfully on some remote grandparent, and credulously take refuge in the magic panacea of eugenics.

The practical aspect is clear. Psychopathic neurosis in its two varieties, somatopsychosis and psychoneurosis, is not hereditary, but *acquired*. We should not shift the blame on former generations and have resort to eugenics, but we must look to the improvement of mental hygienic conditions of early childhood, and to the proper education of the individual.

It is easy to put the blame on grandparents,—they are dead and cannot defend themselves. Could they arise from their graves, they could tell some bitter truths to their descendants who are ready to shift responsibility to other people's shoulders. It is about time to face the truth fairly and squarely, a truth which is brought out by recent investigations in psychopathology, that no matter where the *fons et origo* of neurosis be, whether in self-preservation and its accompanying fear instinct, the condition of life primordial, or in the other forms of self-preservation, *the formation of psychopathic neurosis with all its characteristic protean symptoms is not hereditary, but acquired. Neurosis arises within the life cycle of the individual; it is due to faulty training and harmful experience of early child life.*

Future medicine will be largely prophylactic, preventive, sanitary, hygienic, dietetic. What holds true of medicine in general holds true of that particular branch of it that deals with neurosis. The treatment will become largely prophylactic, preventive, educational, or pedagogic. It is time that the *medical and teaching profession should realize that functional neurosis is not congenital, not inborn, not hereditary, but is the result of a defective, fear-inspiring education in early child life.*

The psychopathic diathesis can be overcome by dispelling the darkness of ignorance and credulity with their false fears and deceptive hopes, above all, by fortifying the critical, controlling, guiding consciousness. Let in sun and air into the obscure cobwebbed regions of the child and man. The gloom and the ghosts of the fear instinct are dispersed by the light of reason.

As the great Roman poet, Lucretius, well puts it:

"Hunc igitur terrorem animi tenebrasque necessest
Non radii solis neque lucida tela diei
Discutiant, sed naturæ species ratioque."[14]

FOOTNOTE:

[14] Darkness and terror of the soul are not dispelled by the rays of the sun and glittering shafts of the day, but by the rational aspect of nature.

CHAPTER XXIX

PRIMITIVE FEARS

Various authorities in Ethnology and Anthropology concur in their description and testimony as to the superstitious fears that obsess primitive man.

Professor Baldwin Spencer, the anthropologist, writes of the Australian aborigines that they have "an intense belief in evil magic. The natives have no idea of disease or pain as being due to anything but evil magic, except that which is caused by an actual accident which they can see.... Anything they do not understand they associate with evil magic.... You have only to tell a native that he is the victim of evil magic, and he succumbs at once, and can only be cured by the exercise of counter magic.

"The number of supernatural beings feared by aborigines of Australia is exceedingly great. For not only are the heavens peopled with such, but the whole face of the country swarms with them; every thicket, most watering places abound with evil spirits. In like manner, every natural phenomenon is believed to be the work of demons, none of which seem to be of a benign nature, one and all apparently striving to do all imaginable mischief to the poor black fellow."

The same is true of the negro. "The negro is wont to regard the whole world around him as peopled with envious beings, to whom he imputes every misfortune that happens to him, and from whose harmful influence he seeks to protect himself by all kinds of magic means." "The religion of the Bolok (of the Upper Congo River)," writes an observer, "has its basis in their fear of those numerous invisible spirits which surround them on every side, and are constantly trying to compass them in their sickness, misfortune and death; and the Boloki's sole object in practising their religion is to cajole, or appease, cheat or conquer or kill those spirits that trouble them, by their Nganga (medicine men), their rites, their ceremonies, and their charms. If there were no evil spirits to circumvent there would be no need of medicine men and their charms.... The Boloki folk believe that they are surrounded by spirits which try to thwart them at every twist and turn, and to harm them every hour of day and night.... I never met among them a man daring enough to go at night through the forest that divided Monsembe from the upper villages even though a large reward was offered. Their invariable reply was: 'There are too many spirits in the bush and forest.' The spirits whom the people dread so much are the mingoli, or disembodied souls of the dead; the life of the Boloki is described as 'one long drawn out fear of what the mingoli may next do to them.' Those dangerous beings dwell everywhere, land and water are full of them; they are ever ready to pounce on the living and carry them away, or to smite them with disease, and kill them.... The belief in witchcraft affects their lives in a vast number of ways. It regulates their actions, modifies their mode of thought and speech, controls their conduct towards each other, causes cruelty and callousness in a people not naturally cruel, and sets the various members of a family against each other.... Belief in witches is interwoven into the very fiber of every Bantu speaking man and woman; and the person who does not believe in them is a monster, a witch to be killed."

The fear of evil spirits, the fear of witchcraft, and the fear of malicious spiritual agencies have been the pests of credulous, fear-obsessed humanity in all the ages of its existence. The crusades, and religious wars have shown us the blight suffered by humanity, obsessed by the impulse of self-preservation and the fear instinct. *Fear* or *pretended Love* of the great spirit, under whatever name, is used for the avoidance of fears and evils.

Sir E. F. im Thurn describes the Indian of Guiana as haunted by the omnipresence of malicious ghosts and spirits. "The whole world of the Indian swarms with these beings. If by a mental effort, we could for a moment revert to a similar mental position, we should find ourselves surrounded everywhere by a host of harmful beings.... It is not therefore, wonderful that the Indian fears to move beyond the light of his camp-fire after dark ... nor is it wonderful that occasionally the air round the settlement seems to the Indian to grow so full of beings, that a sorcerer is employed."

The Indians of Paraguay "live in constant dread of supernatural beings and if nothing else contributed to make their life miserable, this ever present dread would be in itself quite sufficient to rob it of most of its joys."

Professor Powell writes of the Indians: "The Indians believed that diseases were caused by unseen evil beings and by witchcraft, and every cough, every toothache, every headache, every fever, every boil and every wound, in fact all their ailments were attributed to such a cause. Their so-called medical practice was a horrible system of sorcery and to such superstition human life was sacrificed on an enormous scale...."

Similarly, the malignant spirits of the Maori are "so numerous as to surround the living in crowds." The Maori claims: "the spirits throng like mosquitoes, ever watching to inflict harm." The Melanesian "sees himself surrounded at every step by evil spirits and their influences." The Papuans "people land and sea with mysterious, malignant powers which take up their abode in stones and trees or in men, and cause all kinds of misfortunes, especially sickness and death." The Bakua of New Guinea are in constant fear of spirits.... "Of forest spirits the number is infinite; for it is above all in the mysterious darkness, the tangled wilderness of the virgin forests that the spirits love to dwell.... The spirits are never bent on good, they live in evil places. At night-fall the native hears the voices of the spirits, they make inroads into human habitations, and drive man crazy."

In Java, the people are firmly convinced that "the number of spirits is innumerable, they are a source of fear and anxiety." The natives of Sumatra are possessed of "fear of unknown powers.... Every misfortune bespeaks the ill-will of hostile spirits. The whole world is a meeting place of demons." The Batakas "live in perpetual fear of evil spirits."

Professor M. Williams writes of the Hindoos: "The great majority of the inhabitants of India are, from the cradle to the burning ground, victims of a form of mental disease which is best explained by the term *demonophobia*. They are haunted and oppressed by a perpetual dread of demons. They are firmly convinced that evil spirits of all kinds, from malignant fiends to mischievous imps and elves, are ever on the watch to harm, harass and torment them, to cause plague, sickness, famine, and disaster, to impede, injure and mar every good work. The worship of at least ninety per cent of the people of India in the present day is a worship of fear. The simple truth is that evil of all kinds, difficulties, dangers and disasters, famines, diseases, pestilences and death, are thought by an ordinary Hindoo to proceed from demons, or more properly speaking, from devils, and from devils alone." "The underlying principle (of the religion of the Kacharis of Assam) is characteristically one of fear or dread."

"The Thibetans," writes an observer, "are thorough-going demon worshippers. In every nook, path, big tree, rock, spring, waterfall and lake there lurks a devil,—for which reason few individuals will venture out alone after dark. The sky, the ground, the house, the field, the country, have each their special demons; and sickness is always attributed to malign demoniacal influence."

The Burmese, the Laosians of Siam, the Thay of Indo-China are in all their activities controlled by the fear instinct which is at the bottom of all their beliefs. "The Thay cannot take a single step without meeting a demon on the path.... Spirits watch him, ready to punish negligence, and he is afraid. *Fear is not only for him, the beginning of wisdom, it is the whole of his wisdom.*"

The Koreans may be regarded as the most superstitious people among the Orientals. Before me lies a Korean book full of superstitions which can only be matched in their absurdities with those of Australian aborigines who, in their savage culture, belong to the paleolithic period. The whole course of the Korean's life is controlled to the very minutiae by the terrors and horrors of demoniacal, invisible, deadly, malignant powers of demons, spirits, ghosts, hobgoblins, specters, and witches. According to the Korean belief the earth is a pandemonium in which witches and evil spirits hold high carnival.

J. M. de Groot writes "In Korean belief, earth, air, and sea are peopled by demons. They haunt every umbrageous tree, shady ravine, spring and mountain crest.... They make a sport of human destinies. They are on every roof, ceiling, oven and beam. They fill the chimney, shed, the living room, the kitchen, they are on every shelf and jar. In thousands they waylay the traveler as he leaves his home, beside him, behind him, dancing in front of him, whirring over his head, crying out upon him from air, earth, and water. They are numbered by thousands of billions, and it has been well said that their ubiquity is an unholy travesty of Divine Omnipresence. This belief, and it seems to be the only one he possesses, keeps the Korean in a perpetual state of nervous apprehension, it surrounds him with indefinite terrors, and it may be truly said of him that he passes the time of his sojourning here in fear.... The spirits keep the Korean in bondage from birth to death."

Im Bang, a Korean writer on Korean beliefs, has a characteristic story of a poor relative of some Korean dignitary. This poor relative of the high official once a year gathered hundreds of thousands of spirits whom he checked off, so as to keep their malignant disposition under control. And this gentleman was but one of the many clerks; he was but one census man of the vast bureaucratic spiritistic machinery for the regulation and control of evil demons.

The same holds true of the other tribes in Asia. Thus the Gyliaks think that all the places on earth are filled with malicious demoniacal agencies. Similarly, the Koryaks on the Amoor are terrorized by the malignancy of evil spirits that dog their steps. W. Jochelson tells of the Koryaks that "when visiting the houses to cause diseases and to kill people, they (the spirits or demons) enter from under the ground.... They are invisible to human beings, they are sometimes so numerous in houses that they sit on the people, and fill up all corners.... With hammers and axes they knock people over their heads and cause headache. They bite, and cause swellings. They shoot invisible arrows which stick in the body causing death. The demons tear out pieces of flesh from people, thus causing sores and wounds to form on the body." The same spirit of fear of the invisible and of the mysterious, fear of evil powers, controlling the fate of man, constitutes the central belief of almost every primitive tribe, semi-civilized, ancient, as well as modern nation. They are all controlled by the fundamental instinct of life—the fear instinct.

The Semitic scholar, R. H. Harper, writes of the Assyrians and Babylonians as follows: "There is no place in the universe where evil spirits can not penetrate. Every manner of evil and disaster is ascribed to them, from pestilence, fever, and the scorching wind of the desert, down to the trifles of life,—a quarrel, a headache, a broken dish, or a bad dream. They walk the street, slip into the door, get into the food, in short, are everywhere, and the danger from their presence is always imminent.... Corresponding to a widespread belief in demons was a similar belief in witchcraft. It was not at all strange that the demons, who worked in every possible corner of the universe, should take possession of human beings...."

The tablets excavated in the imperial library of Ashurbanipal show the spirit of the people even of the highest classes debased with delusions and religious hallucinations due to self-preservation and fear instinct, so dominant in man who, when common-sense departs from him, may be regarded as the *irrational animal par excellence*.

We may give the following illustration taken from one of the many tablets of the Shurpu series:

"The evil spirits like grass have covered the earth. To the four winds they spread brilliancy like fire, they send forth flames. The people living in dwellings they torment, their bodies they afflict. In city and country they bring moaning, small and great they make to lament. Man and woman they put in bonds, and fill with cries of woe. Man they fall upon and cover him like a garment. In heaven and earth like a tempest they rain; they rush on in pursuit. They fill him with poison, his hands they bind, his sides they crush."

According to the ancient rabbis, a man should not drink water by night, for thus he exposes himself to the Shavriri, demons of blindness. What then should he do if he is thirsty? If there be another man with him, let him rouse him up and say: "I am thirsty," but if he be alone, let him tap upon the lid of the jug (to make the demon fancy there is some one with him), and addressing him by his own name, let him say: "Thy mother bid thee beware of the Shavriri, vriri, riri, ri." Rashi, a mediaeval commentator, says that by this incantation the demon gradually contracts and vanishes as the sound of the word Shavriri decreases.

The ancient rabbis instruct that "no one should venture out at night time on Wednesday or Saturday, for Agrath, the daughter of the demon Machloth, roams about accompanied by eighteen myriads of evil demons, each one of which has power to destroy." The rabbis claim that the air, land and sea are full of demons, all bent on evil and destruction of man. In this respect the learned rabbis differ but little from the superstitious Koreans and Australian savages. The rabbis warn the pious Jew that "should he forget to fold his prayer cover, he is to shake it thoroughly next morning, in order to get rid of the evil spirits that have harbored there during the night." The evil spirits are infinite in number. Thus the Talmudic authorities are in full accord with the ancient Babylonians, Assyrians, and with the lowest savages, ancient and modern, obsessed by the fear of spirits, by Demonophobia.

One cannot help agreeing with the English anthropologist, Frazer, who after his study of the subject, arrives at the following conclusion: "In India from the earliest times down to the present day the real religion of the common folk appears always to have been a belief in a vast multitude of spirits of whom many, if not most, are mischievous and harmful. As in Europe beneath a superficial layer of Christianity a faith in magic and witchcraft, in ghosts and goblins has always survived and even flourished among the weak and the ignorant (and apparently cultivated) so it has been and so it is in the East (and we may say also in the West). Brahmanism, Buddhism, Islam may come and go, but the belief in magic and demons remains unshaken through them all, and, if we may judge of the future from the past, it is likely to survive the rise and fall of other historical religions. For the great faiths of the world, just in so far as they are the outcome of superior intelligence, of extraordinary fervor of aspiration after the ideal, fail to touch and move the common man. They make claims upon his intellect and his heart, to which neither the one nor the other is capable of responding. With the common herd who compose the great bulk of every people, the new religion is accepted only in outward show.... They yield a dull assent to it with their lips, but in their heart they never abandon their old superstitions (and fears of evil and mysterious miraculous agencies); in these they cherish a faith such as they can never repose in the creed which they nominally profess; and to these, in the trials and emergencies of life, they have recourse as to infallible remedies." And he quotes Maxwell to the effect that "The Buddhists in Ceylon, in times of sickness and danger ... turn to demons, feared and reverenced in the same way as do 'the Burmese, Talaings, and Malays.'"

The Jews firmly believed in demoniacal agencies. "When the even was become, they brought unto Him many that were possessed with devils; and He cast out the spirits with His word, and healed all that were sick." "And in the synagogue there was a man which had a spirit of an unclean devil; and he cried out with a loud voice." "And devils also came out of many ..., and He rebuking them suffered them not to speak." "And there was a herd of many swine feeding on the mountains.... Then went the devils out of the man, and entered into the swine, and the herd ran violently down a steep place, and were choked." "Casting out devils" was a sure proof of divine mission.

Perhaps a quotation from the Talmud will make clear the fear of demons which obsesses the Jew: Abba Benjamin says, "if the eye were permitted to see the malignant spirits that beset us, we could not rest on account of them." Abai, another sage, says: "They outnumber us, they surround us as the heaped up soil in our garden plots." Rav Hunna says: "Every one has a thousand on his left side and ten thousand on his right." Rava claims: "The crowding at the schools is caused by their (demons) pushing in; they cause the weariness which the rabbis experience in their knees, and even tear their clothes by hustling against them. If one would discover traces of their presence, let him sift some ashes upon the floor at his bedside, and next morning he will see their footmarks as of fowls on the surface. But if one would see the demons themselves, he must burn to ashes the afterbirth of a first born black kitten, the offspring of a first-born black cat, and then put a little of the ashes into his eyes, and he will not fail to see the demons."

In the words of Lord Avebury, the archeologist, "the savage is a prey to constant fears.... Savages never know but what they may be placing themselves in the power of these terrible enemies (the demons); and it is not too much to say that the horrible dread of unknown evil hangs like a thick cloud over savage life and embitters every pleasure."

In our modern times the preachers, the revivalists, the pulpit, appeal to fear and to hell in order to keep their flock in the fold. Fear of eternal damnation for infidels is the war cry of religion.

Professor Dreslar elicited from 875 California normal school students four-fifths of whom were young women, 3225 confessions of belief in superstitions.... "How thin is the veneer of culture over that great mass of irrational predisposition which in the hour of fear and excitement resumes control of the popular mind, and leads on to folly and ruin!" (Ross).

Buckle is right in pointing out the significant fact that superstition is found in any walk of life in which risk or danger predominates. Sailors are more superstitious than landsmen, while farmers and business people, especially gamblers and speculators, are more superstitious than industrial workers. Similarly Cumont is right in ascribing the superstitions of soldiers as due to risks and dangers of war.

After the great world war one notices the rise of all sorts of superstitions. Superstitions and fear are close companions. A modern historian does not hesitate to declare that "Europe is held in hate, because the nations fear each other.... What sentiment has dug the ditch separating Russia from the rest of the world? It is fear. The states of Western Europe, which the Soviets regard as their persecutors, think themselves menaced in their turn by the Soviet republic." The Great War was produced by self-preservation and fear. The world is still in the grip of the fear instinct.

The Bible claims: Fear of the Lord is the beginning of wisdom. The Latin poet declares: *Primus in orbe deos fecit timor*. The real state of things is: *Self and fear are the Lords of life*, individual and social.

Bacon in his essay "On the Wisdom of the Ancients," with his clear insight has stated the matter succinctly: "In the Panic terrors there is set forth a very wise doctrine; for by the nature of things *all living creatures are endued with a certain fear and dread*, the office of which is to preserve their life and existence, and to avoid or repel approaching mischief. But the same nature knows not how to keep just measure,—but together with salutary fears ever mingles vain and empty ones; insomuch that *all things (if one could see into the heart of them) are quite full of Panic terrors; human things most of all*; so infinitely tossed and troubled as they are with superstition (which is in truth nothing but a Panic terror), especially in seasons of hardship, anxiety, and adversity."

CHAPTER XXX

THE HERD AND THE SUBCONSCIOUS

Superstitious terrors are by no means confined to race; they are common to all races. For example, among the aborigines of Australia a native will die after the infliction of even the most superficial wound, if he is scared by the suggestion that the weapon which inflicted the wound has been sung over, and thus endowed with magical virtue. He simply lies down, refuses food, and pines away.

Similarly among some of the Indian tribes of Brazil, if the medicine-man predicted the death of anyone who had offended him, "the wretch took to his hammock instantly in such full expectation of dying, that he would neither eat nor drink, and the prediction was effectually executed."

Speaking of certain African races Major Leonard observes: "I have seen more than one hardened old Haussa soldier dying steadily and by inches, because he believed himself to be bewitched; so that no nourishment or medicines that were given to him had the slightest effect either to check the mischief or to improve his condition in any way, and nothing was able to divert him from a fate which he considered inevitable.

"In the same way, and under very similar conditions, I have seen Kru-men and others die, in spite of every effort that was made to save them, simply because they had made up their minds, not (as we thought at the time) to die, but that being in the clutch of malignant demons they were bound to die."

The gregarious individual must obey the master leader on pain of death. In gregarious life the whole pack attacks the disobedient individual for challenging the chief, king, priest, the god-man, the lord of the horde. Obedience is a virtue, disobedience is a mortal sin, affecting the whole horde, hence a horrible death of the sinner is the sole punishment. The independent personality is inhibited, the individual falls into a state of social somnambulism, and the will-less, self-less subconscious, a semblance of personality, charged with self-preservation and fear instinct, obeys the commands of the master leader who is often a brutal type, a Nero, a Domitian, a Caracalla, a Caligula, a John the Terrible.

In a society where the socio-static press is always at work, where political pressure is far stronger than even in the ancient despotic monarchies, where a class government is in possession of all modern improvements, where gray uniformity and drowsy monotony reign supreme, obedience must be the rule. Blind, stupid obedience, that slavish obedience which is peculiar to somnambulic subjects, characterizes such societies.

Servility is well illustrated by the following historical incident: Prince Sougorsky, ambassador to Germany in 1576, fell sick *en route* in Courland. The duke of the province often inquired as to his health. The reply was always the same: "My health matters nothing, provided the sovereign's prospers." The duke, surprised, said, "How can you serve a tyrant with so much zeal?" He replied, "We Russians are always devoted to our Czars, good or cruel. My master (Ivan the Terrible) impaled a man of mark for a slight fault, who for twenty-four hours, in his dying agonies, talked with his family, and without ceasing kept repeating, 'Great God, protect the Czar!'"

The same is true of modern class societies where the Demos is the despot. God preserve the Demos! When the business demon of the Demos requires sacrifice, self immolation, anticipate his order. Pray for the Demos; Great God, protect the greedy Demos! The Demos is my Lord, to him is due my servile loyalty.

It is interesting to observe that the superstitious, the savage, the negro, and the soldier are excellent subjects for hypnotic purposes. Soldiers as experiments show, have a strong predisposition to hypnotic states. I was told by Professor Münsterberg that the hypnotic predisposition was strongly developed in the German soldier. M. Liebault experimented on ten hundred and twelve persons, and found only twenty-seven refractory. Berenheim remarks on this that "It is necessary to take into account the fact that M. Liebault operates chiefly upon the common people."

The great pressure exerted on the lower social strata, and especially on soldiers, the dull monotony of their life, the habit of strict obedience to command, predisposes them to social subconscious automatisms,—to the formation of mobs, clubs, unions, lodges, associations, parties, clans, sects, mobocracies. In all such organizations there is present the same servile spirit—the impersonal self and the gregarious fear instinct—the basis of subconscious, social somnambulism.

Man is a social somnambulist, he lives, dreams, and obeys with his eyes open. Whenever the impulse of self-preservation gets a special grip on the gregarious individual, when he becomes wild with terror in the bosom of the herd, then he may be regarded as a psychopathic victim.

The historian of the future will represent our age as dark, barbaric, savage, an age of the cruel Napoleonic wars, of commercial crises, financial panics, religious revivals, vicious, brutal, savage world wars,—mobs, crazes, plagues, social pests of all sorts and description....

A herd of sheep stand packed close together, looking stupidly into space.... Frighten them,—and if one begins to run, frantic with terror, the rest are sure to follow,—a stampede ensues, each sheep scrupulously reproduces the identical movements of the one in front of it. This susceptibility to imitation is but what we, in relation to man, term suggestibility, which consists in the impressing on the person of an idea, image, movement, however absurd and senseless, which the person in his hypnotized state reproduces like an automaton,—although he or she thinks it is done quite voluntarily. Suggestibility is natural to man as a social animal. Under specially favorable conditions this suggestibility which is always present in human beings may increase to an extraordinary degree, and the result is a stampede, a mob, an epidemic.

It is sometimes claimed that somnambulic persons are asleep. Sleep and somnambulism have been identified. This is a misuse of words since there are a whole series of subconscious states in which not one symptom of sleep appears. *Extreme susceptibility to suggestions and mental automatisms are the chief traits of the subconscious.*

Gregarious men and women carry within themselves the germs of the possible mob, or of mental epidemics. As social creatures men and women are naturally suggestible. When this susceptibility or sensitivity to suggestions becomes abnormally intense, we may say that they are thrown into a social subconscious, somnambulic state.

We know by psychological and psychopathological experiments that limitation of voluntary movements and inhibition of free activities induce a subconscious state. This subconscious state is characterized by inhibition of the will power,—memory remains unaffected;

consciousness appears intact; the subject is aware of all that goes on.

Keeping this in mind, we can understand social life, and especially morbid, social movements, mob life of all ages.

A subconscious state is induced in the organized individual by the great limitation of his voluntary activities and by the inhibition of his free critical thought. Bound fast by the strings of tradition and authority, social men and women are reduced to subconscious automata. The subconscious rises with the growth of organized civilization, while the critical, independent powers of the individual correspondingly fall. Hence the apparent social paradox that the growth of society tends to destroy the mental forces which helped to build up civilization.

In such societies the individual staggers under the burden of laws and taboos. Individuality is stifled under the endless massive excretions of legislators. Recently even the lawgivers or law manufacturers began to object to the labor involved in the work on the ever growing mass of bills introduced into the legislature of one state alone. Thus a senator of a Western state complained that in *one* year over 1700 bills passed through the mill of his Legislature. Multiply that figure by the number of states, add the municipal edicts, and the endless laws turned out by the Federal Government, and one can form some faint idea of the vast burden laid on the shoulders of the individual citizen.

The Los Angeles Times, which no one will accuse of radicalism, pointedly remarks: "The State has just issued a reference index to the laws of California since 1850—it is of itself a bulky volume of more than 1300 pages. When it takes a book of that size merely as an *index* it would seem that the lawmakers had about done their worst."

Over-production of laws is one of the great evils of modern civilization. Civilized society is apt to be obsessed by a state of law-mania which is a danger and a menace to the free development of the individual citizen.

The Roman legal thinkers left us two significant sayings: *Ex Senatus consultis et plebiscitis, crimina execrentur*,—(Senatorial decisions and popular decrees give rise to crimes) and: *Ut olim vitiis, sic nunc legibus laboramus*,—(As we formerly suffered from vices and crimes so we suffer at present from laws and legislation)....

In describing the gregariousness of the Damara oxen Francis Galton writes: "Although the ox has so little affection for, or interest in, his fellows, he cannot endure even a momentary severance from his herd. If he be separated from it by stratagem or force, he exhibits every sign of mental agony; he strives with all his might to get back again, and when he succeeds, he plunges into the middle to bathe his whole body with the comfort of closest companionship. This passionate terror is a convenience to the herdsman." ... When an animal accustomed to a gregarious life is isolated from the herd, it is agitated with extreme terror. The same holds true of man who is a social animal. Man must go with the herd or with the pack, and he is terrified to stand alone, away from the crowd,—and still more terrorized when the crowd disapproves of him. Man is gregarious, and as such he must go with the mass, with the crowd. He is in mortal fear of social taboo. As a gregarious animal man lives in fear of external danger, and is in terror of social authority.

As Galton writes: "The vast majority of persons of our race have a natural tendency to shrink from the responsibility of standing and acting alone: they exalt the *vox populi*, even when they know it to be the utterance of a mob of nobodies, into the *vox Dei*; they are willing slaves to tradition, authority and custom. The intellectual deficiencies corresponding to these moral flaws are shown by the rareness of free and original thought as compared with the frequency and readiness with which men accept the opinions of those in authority as binding on their judgment." This slavish obedience is intimately bound up with one of the most fundamental of all instincts,—the fear instinct.

The individual is so effectively trained by the pressure of taboo based on self and fear, that he comes to love the yoke that weighs him down to earth. Chained to his bench like a criminal galley slave, he comes to love his gyves and manacles. The iron collar put around his neck becomes a mark of respectability, an ornament of civilization. Tarde finds that society is based on respect, a sort of an alloy of fear and love, fear that is loved. A respectable citizen is he who is fond of his bonds, stocks, and shekels, and comes to love his bonds, stocks, and shackles of *fears and taboos*.

Human institutions depend for their existence and stability on the impulse of self-preservation and its close associate,—the fear instinct.

CHAPTER XXXI

MYSTICISM, PRAYER, CONVERSION, AND METAPHYSICS

The psychology of mysticism and conversion is a fascinating subject. This is not the place to go into detail or even adequately cover the subject which is as extensive as it is important. I can only touch the matter in a superficial way—enough to answer the present purpose.

The state of mysticism is essentially a hypnoidal trance state, and its traits are the characteristics of the hypnoidal consciousness. Like the hypnoidal state, that of the mystic state may pass into waking, sleep, or into the hypnotic condition.

James marks off mystic states, by the traits of Ineffability, Transciency, Passivity, and Noetic Quality. These traits are just the ones found in the deeper states of the hypnoidal consciousness, especially the ones which approximate and pass into the hypnotic condition. In the mystical state, as in the hypnoidal state, there is a delicious languor, a lack of tension to the stimulation of the external environment which retreats in the distance; there is the instability of the hypnoidal consciousness which soon passes into the other forms such as sleep, hypnosis, or waking. There is also present the refreshing, invigorating condition of the whole individuality on emerging from those peculiar subconscious states. The lethargic and cataleptic states often present in states of ecstasy, in which the mystics fall, depend entirely on states of the hypnoido-hypnotic trance.

The mystic consciousness and the hypnoidal one are not identical. The mystic consciousness is a species of the hypnoidal consciousness. What are then its special features? In the first place, the mystic consciousness has a negative and a positive aspect, depression and exaltation. In the second place, mysticism expresses a definite reaction of the individual to the conditions of his external environment. This reaction is one of retraction from the miseries and fears of life.

If we examine closely the type of consciousness characteristic of the state preceding the onset of the mystic condition, we find that it is essentially that of suffering, of misery, of disappointment, of despair, of inability to meet fairly, squarely, and courageously the experiences of life. There is a strong feeling of insecurity, a feeling of anxiety as to self and the world. A feeling of intense anguish seizes on the individual that he and the world are going to perdition, that on such terms life is not worth living. The instinct of fear penetrates every pore of his being, and inspires the individual with dread, horror, and terror. Terrorized by the wild evils of life, the personality becomes benumbed and paralyzed, and ready to succumb. This state of intense depression is not simply related to fear, *it is fear*. It is the *status melancholicus* often preceding states of exaltation. The individual reaches a critical condition where life becomes impossible. The whole universe holds for him nothing but terrors and horrors.

Carlyle expresses this attitude when he makes Teufeldroeckh say: "I live in a continual, indefinite, pining fear; tremulous, pusillanimous, apprehensive of I know not what: it seems as if things, all things in the heavens above and the earth beneath would hurt me; as if the heavens and the earth were but boundless jaws of a devouring monster, wherein I, palpitating, lie waiting to be devoured."

In this state of agony of fear, the individual looks for salvation in fleeing from the terrors of the world to the arms of the divinity.

In his terror the individual passes through a second stage, he becomes "converted," he turns with prayers to the divine power to which he looks for shelter from the dangers of life. He appeals to the divinity for protection from the evils of the day and from the terrors of the night. This second stage is often preceded by a period of subconscious incubation which sometimes gives rise to sudden conscious explosions, conscious conversions, or sudden onset of mystic state of ecstasy.

In the library of Ashburbanipal, king of Assyria, there are found "penitential psalms" much alike to our own, but some millenniums older than the Biblical psalms. These Assyro-Babylonian penitential psalms, inscribed in cuneiform script on clay tablets, clearly express the attitude of the worshipper or suppliant:

> "O Goddess, in the anguish of my heart have I raised cries of anguish to thee; declare forgiveness.
> May thy heart be at rest.
> May thy liver be pacified.
> The sin which I have committed I know not.
> The Lord in the anger of his heart hath looked upon me.
> The goddess hath become angry and hath stricken me grievously.
> I sought for help, but no one taketh my hand.
> I wept, but no one cometh to my side.
> I utter cries, but no one harkens to me.
> I am afflicted, I am overcome.
> Unto my merciful god I turn.
> I kiss the feet of my goddess.
> How long, known and unknown god, until the anger of thy heart be pacified?

> How long, known and unknown goddess, until thy unfriendly heart be pacified?
> Mankind is perverted, and has no judgment,
> Of all men who are alive, who knows anything?
> They do not know whether they do good or evil.
> O Lord, do not cast aside thy servant!
> He is cast into the mire; take his hand.
> The sin which I have sinned turn to mercy!
> Known and unknown goddess, my sins are seven times seven;
> Forgive my sins!
> Forgive my sins, and I will humble myself before thee.
> May thy heart, as the heart of a mother who hath borne children, be glad!
> As a father who hath begotten them, may it be glad!"

In this respect we agree with Ribot. "Depression," says Ribot, "is related to fear.... Does not the worshipper entering a venerated sanctuary show all the symptoms of pallor, trembling, cold sweat, inability to speak—all that the ancients so justly called *sacer* horror? The self abasement, the humility of the worshipper before the deity supposed to be possessed of magic power, is essentially one of fear." With the anthropologist we may refer this awe or fear to the terror which the savage mind feels in the presence of the magician, the witch, the medicine man, the man-god, and the woman-deity.

The Mithraic religion, which for some time has been the great rival of Christianity for the salvation of the individual from the terrors of the world, played a great rôle in the mystic ceremonies of the cult. In fact, the dying and the resurrection of a god-man for the salvation of the worshippers constituted a cardinal principle in the actual practices or rites of barbarous nations and savage tribes. The man-god or woman-deity had to die, had to be sacrificed by the community. The sins of the savages were redeemed by the divine flesh and blood of "the man-god."

In describing the life and theological doctrines of St. Paul, Professor Pfleiderer says: "Perhaps Paul was influenced by the popular idea of the god who dies and returns to life, dominant at that time in the Adonis, Attis, and Osiris cults of Hither Asia (with various names and customs, everywhere much alike). At Antioch, the Syrian capital, in which Paul had been active for a considerable period, the main celebration of the Adonis feast took place in the spring time. On the first day, the death of 'Adonis,' the Lord, was celebrated, while on the following day, amid the wild songs of lamentations sung by the women, the burial of his corpse (represented by an image) was enacted. On the next day (in the Osiris celebration it was the third day after death, while in the Attis celebration it was the fourth day) proclamation was made that the god lived and he (his image) was made to rise in the air. It is noteworthy that the Greek Church has preserved a similar ceremony in its Easter celebration down to our own day.

"During the joyous feast of the resurrection of the god in the closely related Attis celebration, the priest anointed the mouths of the mourners with oil, and repeated the formula:

'Good cheer, ye pious! As our god is saved,
So shall we, too, be saved in our distress.'

"The rescue of the god from death is the guarantee of a like rescue for the adherents of his cult. In the mysteries of Attis, Isis, and Mithra, the fact that the worshippers partook of the god's life by the mystical participation in his death, was visualized by such rites, which employed symbols showing the death of the initiate, his descent into Hades, and his return. Hence, this ceremony was called the 're-birth to a career of new salvation,' a 'holy birthday.' In one Mithra liturgy, the newly initiated pray: 'Lord, reborn, I depart; in that I am lifted up, I die; born by that birth which produces life, I will be saved in death, and go the way which thou hast established, according to thy law and the sacrament which thou hast created.'"

In all those mysteries the central note is the salvation of the worshipper from the "perils of the soul."

In some cases the terrorized individual is driven to the mystic state. He falls into a sort of trance. The world of fears becomes veiled from him, and recedes in a mist, and even completely disappears from his view. He finds repose in his god. This is the positive stage of mental exaltation, of ecstasy; it figures as "the union" of the worshipper with his god or goddess. It is this oblivion in the depths of the hypnoidal and the hypnotic states, it is this relapse into the regions of the subconscious that brings about relief from all fears of life. The bliss felt in these dim regions of mental life refreshes and invigorates the wearied soul. The coming in contact with new vast stores of subconscious reserve energy may once more vitalize and supply with new energy the fear stricken personality. This is the inspiration of those who have experienced the mystical power of "conversion."

In a later chapter I take up the subject of subconscious reserve energy advanced by James and myself, independently. Meanwhile, we may say that the phenomena of prayer, conversion, and especially of mysticism belong fundamentally to the manifestations of self-preservation and the fear instinct on the one side and to subconscious reserve energy on the other.

Of course, we must add the fact that certain historical and social conditions are apt to give rise to phenomena of mysticism, the conditions of social unrest being especially favorable. When social life begins to decay, when the protection of society is weakened, and the individual is set loose, and left to stand alone, something that especially terrorizes the social brute, then nothing is left to the individual bereft of his social stays and social stimulants, but to turn *inward* and *upward*, that is to turn mystic. In his states of desolation and fear-obsession the individual is inclined to turn to the stimulating, narcotizing influence of the deity which puts the soul in a state of transcendental bliss, thus hiding the terrorized soul in a misty and mystic cloud, so that he no longer sees the terrors and horrors of life.

Such mystic states are found in periods of social and moral decay. Instance the decaying Roman empire, the Hellenistic period, the Middle Ages, and in fact, any period in which security, safety, and social stability are on the ebb, while fears and perils are on the increase. Mysticism, Salvation of the soul, under all their guises, are interrelated with the primordial fear instinct which dominates the hunted beast and the terror-stricken neurotic patient.

If we turn to philosophical and metaphysical speculations, we find, on examination from a pragmatic point of view, that their essential differences revolve on the *security and safety of the world scheme*. From Plato and Aristotle to Seneca, Epictetus, Marcus Aurelius, down to Schopenhauer, Hegel, and our American thinkers Royce and James, as well as from the Bible to Brahmanism and Buddhism, we find the same valuation of world safety, based on the vital impulse of self-preservation and its fundamental fear instinct. The *Salvation* of the World and the Individual is the fundamental keynote of theological metaphysics and metaphysical religion.

Professor Royce, the representative of transcendental, monistic idealism in America, thus summarizes his philosophical and religious attitude: "It is God's true and eternal triumph that speaks to us 'In this world ye shall have tribulations. But fear not; I have overcome the world.'" This reminds one of the ancient Assyrian cuneiform oracles addressed to the Assyrian kings: "To Esarhaddon, king of countries, Fear not! I am Ishtar of Arbela. Thine enemies I will cut off, fear not!" "Fear not, Esarhaddon, I, Bel, am speaking with thee. The beams of thy heart I will support." "Fear not, you are saved by Faith. Fear thy Lord only, He is your Rock and Salvation," says the Bible. "Fear not!" teaches the Buddhist, "Nirvana, the Absolute, is your refuge."

Professor James in his inimitable way summarizes the difference between his pluralism and idealistic monism: "What do believers in the Absolute mean by saying that their belief affords them comfort? They mean that since in the Absolute finite evil is 'overruled' already, we may, therefore, whenever we wish, treat the temporal as if it were potentially the eternal, be sure that we can trust its outcome, and, without sin, dismiss our fear and drop the worry of our finite responsibility.... The universe is a system of which the individual members may relax their anxieties...." James contrasts his empirical, pragmatic pluralism with the idealistic monism.

In another place James says: "Suppose that the world's author put the case before you before creating, saying: 'I am going to make a world not certain to be saved, a world, the perfections of which shall be conditioned merely, the condition being that each several agent "does his level best." I offer you the chance of taking part in such a world. Its safety, you see, is unwarranted. It is a real adventure, with real danger, yet it may win through.... Will you join the procession? Will you trust yourself and trust the other agents enough to face the risk?' Should you in all seriousness, if participation in such a world were proposed to you, feel bound to reject it as not safe enough? Would you say that rather than be part and parcel of so fundamentally pluralistic and irrational a universe, you preferred to relapse into the slumber of nonentity from which you had been aroused by the tempter's voice?

"Of course, if you are normally constituted, you would do nothing of the sort. There is a healthy-minded buoyancy in most of us which such a universe would exactly fit.... The world proposed would seem 'rational' to us in the most living way.

"Most of us, I say, would, therefore, welcome the proposition, and add our *fiat* to the *fiat* of the creator. Yet perhaps some would not; for there are morbid minds in every human collection, and to them the prospect of a universe with only a fighting chance of safety would probably not appeal. There are moments of discouragement in us all, when we are sick of self, and tired of vainly striving. Our own life breaks down, and we fall into the attitude of the prodigal son. We mistrust the chance of things. We want a universe where we can just give up, fall on our father's neck, and be absorbed into the absolute life as a drop of water melts into the river or the sea.

"The peace and rest, the security desiderated at such moments is security against the bewildering accidents of so much finite experience.

"Nirvana means safety from this everlasting round of adventure of which the world of sense consists. The Hindoo and the Buddhist, for this is essentially their attitude, are simply *afraid, afraid* (my italics) of more experience, afraid of life....

"Pluralistic moralism simply makes their teeth chatter, it refrigerates the very heart within their breast."

Thus we find that at the bottom of philosophical, metaphysical, and religious speculations there are present the same primitive impulse of self-preservation and fear instinct.

While there are some other important factors in that theological and metaphysical problem which has agitated humanity for ages, a problem which I expect to discuss some other time in another place, there is no doubt that James with his great psychological genius has laid his finger on fundamental factors of human life,—self-preservation and the fear instinct.

CHAPTER XXXII

FEAR SUGGESTIONS

In my psychopathological and clinical work of the various manifestations and symptoms of psychopathic and functional diseases I come to the conclusion that the principal cause of all those morbid affections is the fear instinct, rooted in the very impulse of life, the impulse of self preservation. Fears are not secondary effects, they are due to one of the most fundamental of all instincts, the instinct of fear which is primary and elemental.

Anything which arouses the fear instinct in the inhibitory or paralyzing stages will necessarily give rise to psychopathic functional psychosis or neurosis. The fear instinct and the impulse of self-preservation, inherent in all life, are the alpha and omega of psychopathic maladies.

The fear instinct is usually cultivated by a long history of events of a fearsome character so that fear instinct and the impulse of self-preservation become easily aroused on various occasions of external stimulation, producing general fear, mental or emotional, and often accompanied by sensory, motor, and intestinal derangements of various organs with their secretions and hormones, as well as with general morbid, functional changes of the central nervous system, sympathetic and parasympathetic systems. This in its turn gradually cultivates a disposition to formation of hypnoidal states, that is, the brief momentary formation of trance states, in which the subconscious becomes through dissociation exposed to fear suggestions or fear stimulations, which arouse in the morbidly cultivated subconscious morbid fear symptoms, motor, sensory, intestinal, emotional in their various combinations and associations.

The cultivated predisposition to lapses into hypnoidal states is a prerequisite of psychopathic disturbances. We may, therefore, say that the three factors, namely, Self-preservation, Fear instinct, Hypnoidal states form the triumvirate of psychopathic, functional neurosis.

Charcot with his sharp eye for observation as well as his long clinical experience observed, in what he termed hystericals, a brooding period which precedes the manifestations of the hysterical attacks and symptom complex of the hysterical manifestations. These brooding periods are of the utmost consequence, although Charcot and his disciples as well as the psychopathologists generally, hardly paid any attention to this important phenomenon.

These brooding periods preceding the onset of the malady afterwards recur regularly before each attack of the malady, only the period is brief, and is hardly noticeable except by the one who looks searchingly. Psychopathologists pass this important stage without noticing its full significance. *The period appears as a sort of a psychic aura, a sort of* momentary attack of epileptic *petit mal.* This brooding state is a modification of the hypnoidal state.

It is during such hypnoidal states, when the conditions which I have shown to be requisite for the induction of trance or subconscious states, happen to be specially strong and the hypnoidal state is prolonged, that the unprotected subconscious becomes subject to fear suggestions or to stimuli arousing the fear instinct and the impulse of self-preservation.

"Many patients," says the famous physiologist and physician, Mosso, "die in the hospital from fear and depression who would probably have recovered had they been tended in their own homes.... In their morning round the physicians find that the serious cases have grown worse, while those who are better beg to be dismissed.... The physician, who has the night watch must walk up and down the whole night, and is kept busy preventing convulsive attacks, or fainting fits.

"Fear attacks nullify every effort of the will.... Even Alexander of Macedon had to count with fear in his courageous army of select Macedonians. In order to insure victory he offered sacrifices to Fear before he joined battle."

Physical maladies become worse during the night, and especially during the early morning hours when the energy of the body is at its lowest level,—conscious and subconscious fears reaching their highest intensity. This holds specially true of nervous cases, and particularly of psychopathic patients, who are dominated by the impulse of self-preservation and the fear instinct. The fears and worries keep the patient awake, and the subconscious fears become emphasized by concentration of attention, monotony, limitation of field of consciousness, limitation of voluntary movements, and other factors favorable to dissociation and the induction of the hypnoidal state, in which the patient becomes sensitive to the awakening of the fear instinct, with all its horrible fear suggestions.

The symptoms of the disease which are more or less under his control during the day become often so intensified in the dark, that the patients become demoralized with fear, suffering as they do the anxiety and anguish induced by the terrors of the night. Even medical men, professors of medical colleges, who have come under my care, have confessed to me that, when in a state of insomnia, the terrors of the night are so intense that they had to resort to morphine to still the anguish of the fear instinct.

For years I lived in close relation with neurotic, psychopathic patients. I watched them day and night. I have been called by patients for medical aid in the late hours of the night, and more so during the vigil hours of the darkness of the night. I had to relieve and soothe the fears, the terrors of the night. It is in the night, when in a low state of neuron energy that patients feel the grip of horrors oppressing them with nightmares of the relentless and merciless instinct, the fear instinct. To be relieved of the night terrors many patients are willing to risk anything, even the consequence of deadly narcotics, the plagues of mental healers, and the sexual phantasms of Psychoanalysis.

The hypnoidal state is induced artificially, often brought about by intoxication, as in the case of holy Soma drink among the Hindoos, or by fasting, as among the American Indians during the initiation periods, or by dancing, such as the corrobboree among the aborigines of Australia, or by singing, or by praying. All the conditions of disjunction of consciousness with the manifestations of subconscious activities are brought into play, in order to come in contact with demons, spirits, totems, and find among them guides and protectors.

In prolonged hypnoidal states, the fear instinct and the impulse of self-preservation are calmed under appropriate conditions. Illusions and hallucinations which easily appeared in the twilight states of hypnoidal subconscious states became manifested as beneficent spirits, as agents favorable to the life existence of the individual, the spirit appearing as the totem, the guardian of the individual. Prayer and singing, which are the most successful of all the methods of inducing subconscious subwaking, twilight states, have survived to our present day.

Of all the methods of utilization of subconscious subwaking, twilight states the most effective is prayer, especially, the individual form of prayer. Prayer admirably fulfills the conditions requisite for the induction of the hypnoidal state and for the getting access to the subconscious activities, the formation of subconscious personalities, subconscious illusions and hallucinations. Such subconscious states have been shown, on experimental evidence, to be not of a sensory, but of a purely delusional character, strong enough to affect the individual with an intense belief in its external reality.

The deluded human mind in its craven fear of the unseen and the mysterious spirit-forces helps itself to any soporific or anaesthetic, narcotic stimulant, to bring about a scission of the conscious self from the subconscious activities. The induction of the hypnoidal state is brought about by all kinds of intoxicants, narcotics, fasting, dancing, self-mortification, sex excesses which exhaust the devotee, and leave him in a state of trance. All such practices and rites seek blindly for some trance-state to still the morbid fear instinct.

The psychoanalysis of Freud, Jung, Adler, Stoekel, with their sexual love, belongs to this category of *narcotic sexual religions* which inhibit the critical self.[15]

FOOTNOTE:

[15] The popular novelists try to disclose "the secrets of the heart" by means of Freudian sex phantasies, psychoanalytic mother complexes, and Jungian mystic sex libido. It is only in an era of philistinism and vulgarity with a literature of decadence and commonplace mediocrity that psychoanalysis can take root and flourish.

"Die Theorie behauptet mit ausschliessender Sicherheit (?), das es nur sexuelle Wünschregungen aus dem Infantilen sein können, welche in den Entwicklungsperioden der Kindheit die Verdrängung (Affectverwandlung) erfahren haben, in späteren Entwicklungsperioden dann einer Erneuerung fähig sind, sei es in folge der sexuelle Konstitution, die sich ja aus der ursprünglichen Bisexualität herausbildet, sei es in folge ungünstiger Einflüsse des sexuellen Lebens, und die somit die Triebkräfte für alle psychoneurotische Symptombildung ab geben." (S. Freud, "Die Traumdeutung," p. 376, zweite Auflage 1909.) In other words, slippery and mutable as Freud's statements are, he clearly declares in his *magnum opus* the far-reaching generalization that neurosis is based on infantile sexual wishes, either due to bisexuality or to unfavorable influences of sexual life. Suppression of sexual experiences can be easily observed (by competent observers, of course), in infants a few months old. If you miss the process of suppression in the baby, you can easily trace it by means of psychoanalysis to the early recollections of tender infancy. It is certainly lack of comprehension that induces Ziehen to dub Freud's speculations as Unsinn (nonsense). Freud's admirers with a metaphysical proclivity delight over the theory of suppressed wishes. The wish is fundamental and prior to all mental states. This piece of metaphysical psychologism is supposed to be based on clinical experience. If wishes were horses, beggars would ride. The Freudist manages to ride such horses.

The following speculation of Jung's well represents the metaphysico-religious character of psychoanalysis: "By entering again into the mother's womb he (Christ) redeems in death the sin of life of the primitive man, Adam, in order symbolically through his deed to procure for the innermost and most hidden meaning of the religious libido its highest satisfaction and most pronounced expression.... In the Christian mysteries the resurrected one becomes a supermundane spirit, and the invisible kingdom of God, with its mysterious gifts are obtained by his believers through the sacrifice of himself on his mother. In psychoanalysis the infantile personality is deprived of its libido fixations in a rational manner. The libido which is thus set free serves for the building up of a personality matured and adapted to reality, a personality that does willingly and without complaint everything required by necessity. (It is, so to speak, the chief endeavor of the infantile personality to struggle against all necessities, and to create coercions for itself where none exist in reality.)" Such metaphysico-religious lucubrations parade under the term psychoanalysis.

"Man," says James, "believes as much as he can," but the credulity of the psychoanalyst is limitless. The psychoanalyst with his allegories, symbolism, sublimation, incest phantasies, bi-sexuality, sexual suppression, mother complexes, Oedipus and Electra phantasms, and all the other complex psychoanalytic instrumentalities is an excellent example of sex obsessed, delusional dementia praecox. Psychoanalysis is a sort of sexual mysticism. All mental life is reduced by psychoanalysis to "creation" or "procreation."

CHAPTER XXXIII

LIFE ENERGY AND THE NEUROTIC

The subject of fear may be considered from a somewhat different point of view, namely from a purely physiological and biological aspect. The cell in general, the nerve cell, or neuron, is a reservoir of energy. In fact the great biologist Sachs proposed to term the cell, *energid.*

For we must look at the organism as a store of energy which is used up in the course of the adjustments of the individual to his environment. The organism stores up energy and uses the energy during the course of its life activity.

Life energy is physiological, bio-chemical, electrical, mechanical, etc. The mental and emotional activities are intimately related with the expenditure of energy accumulated by the cells of the organism, which discharge that energy in response to the various stimulations of the external world. In its activities the organism keeps on taking in energy, and once more discharging energy in its life reactions. The storing up of energy falls under the anabolic or building up processes, while the discharging or liberating processes of the amount of the stored up energy are classed under the katabolic processes.

The total cycle of energy from the start of storage to the end of liberation of energy, starting once more with the storing of energy, may be regarded as the cycles of organic functional activity which is classified under metabolism.

We deal here with a reservoir of vital energy whose life activities or reactions depend on the amount of energy contained in the cell or the neuron, and whose functioning and reactions vary with the level of energy in the reservoir.

The neuron is but a highly differentiated cell or reservoir for the intake and outgo of energy. In this respect the nerve cell is entirely like other cells of humbler function. Every cell is a storage cell, accumulating energy and then liberating it at an appropriate occasion of a given stimulus, all cells working for the preservation of the organism as a whole. The rise and fall of the level of energy in the reservoir regulate the various manifestations, sensory, motor, emotional, mental which the individual displays to the various stimulations coming from his environment.

Within certain limits the fall of energy is normal,—when it reaches a certain level the organism once more replenishes the store and once more the level of energy rises. This energy is *Dynamic* under certain conditions. However, the discharge of energy must go on, and the organism must draw further on its store of energy, on the accumulated store of energy put away for safety and emergency. This stored up energy is *Reserve Energy*.[16]

The late Charles S. Minot, the American histologist, points out this reserve energy present in the organism, a reserve energy of growth called forth under special emergencies of life.

By a striking series of instructive facts, Dr. Meltzer points out that "all organs of the body are built on the plan of superabundance of structure and energy." Like Minot, Meltzer refers to the significant fact that most of our active organs possess a great surplus of functioning cells. This surplus is requisite for the safety of the individual.

If, however, the drain of energy still goes on without replenishing the total store, the energy drawn on the region of the danger zone is entered. *This energy is Static.* The concomitant symptoms are various psychomotor and psycho-secretory disturbances of a psychopathic or psycho-neurotic character. This energy is drawn from the upper levels of energy. Under such conditions restitution of the total amount of energy to its normal level is still possible.

Should the process of liberation of energy go on further without restitution, the energy drawn is taken from the lower levels of static energy, and the symptoms are *functional, neuropathic.* The lower-most levels of static energy are the last the cell can dispense with to save itself from total destruction. With further increase of discharge of energy the cell must give its very life activity, the energy is drawn from the breaking up of cell tissue; this energy is organic or necrotic.

Thus the total energy of the nerve cell or the neuron may be divided into normal dynamic energy, reserve energy, static energy, and organic or necrotic energy. The various nervous and mental diseases may thus be correlated with the flow and ebb of neuron energy, with the physiological and pathological processes that take place in the neuron in the course of its activity and reactions to the stimuli of the external and internal environment.

The various levels of neuron energy may be represented by the diagram on page 336.

Static energy is indicated by the diagram NWFI. By *organic energy* is meant that energy contained in the very structure of the tissues of the neuron, not as yet decomposed into their inorganic constituents. This is indicated by diagram IFGH.

These phases of neuron energy are not different kinds of energy, in the sense of being distinct entities; they merely represent progressive phases or stages of the same process of neuron activity.

Liberation of neuron energy is correlative with active psychic and physical manifestations. Hence states of the nervous system corresponding to liberations of energy are designated as *waking states*. *Restitution* of expended energy or arrest of liberation of neuron energy goes hand in hand with *passive* conditions of the nervous system; hence states of restitution or arrest of energy are termed collectively *sleeping states*.

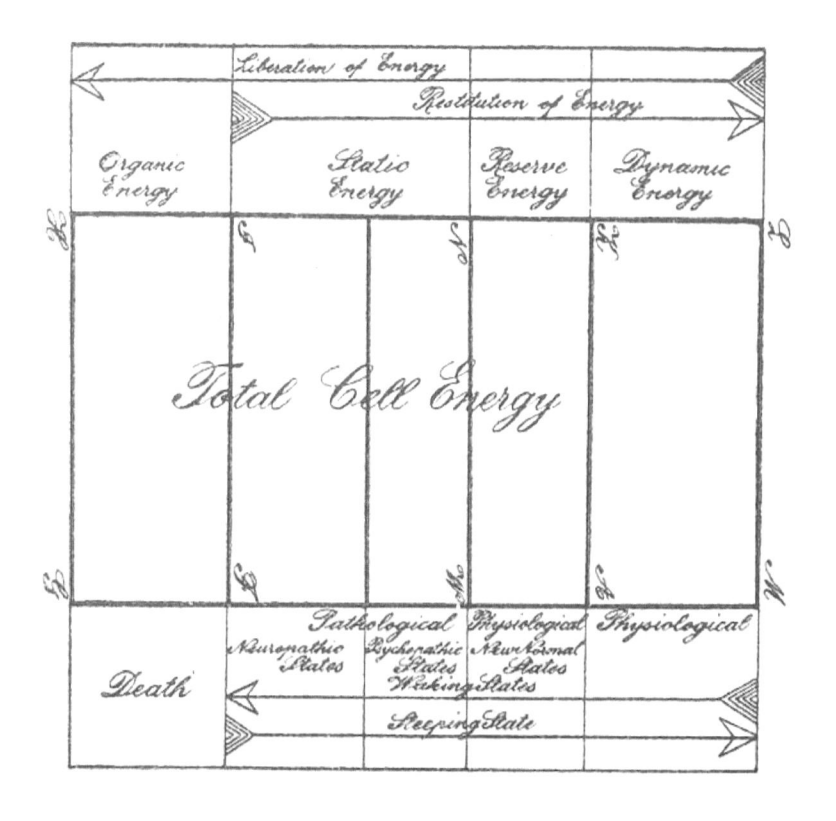

Organic Energy	Static Energy	Reserve Energy	Dynamic Energy
← Liberation of Energy		Restitution of Energy →	
Death	Neuropathic Psychopathic States	Pathological States Waking States	Physiological Neurohormonal States	Physiological
		Sleeping State	

Total Cell Energy

DIAGRAM IV

The ascending arrow, indicating the process of restitution of energy, corresponds to the ascending arrow on the right, indicating the parallel psychomotor sleeping states. The descending arrows indicate physiological and pathological processes of liberation of energy, and also their concomitant psychomotor waking states.

"Ascending" and "descending" mean the rise and fall of the amount of neuron energy, taking the upper level of dynamic energy as the starting point. Briefly stated, *descent* means *liberation* of energy with its concomitant, psychomotor, waking states. *Ascent* means *restitution* of energy with its parallel sleeping states.

The cycles in dynamic energy correspond to the physiological manifestations of the nervous system in the activity and rest of the individual in normal daily life. Concomitant with the expenditure of dynamic energy of the neurons, the individual passes through the active normal waking state, and hand in hand with the restitution of this expended energy, he passes through the sleeping states of normal daily life.

When, however, in the expenditure of energy, the border line or margin is crossed, dynamic and reserve energies are used up. In crossing KA the ordinary normal energies of everyday life are exhausted, and reserve energy has to be drawn upon. If this reserve energy is not accessible, the static energy is used, or in case the reserve energy is exhausted, then once more the static energy has to be drawn upon; in either case the individual enters the domain of the abnormal, of the pathological.

When the upper levels of static energy are used, the symptoms are of a psychopathic or neurotic character. When the use of energy reaches the lower levels of static energy, affecting the very nutrition of the neuron, neuropathic manifestations are the result. When the neuron itself is affected, that is the organic structure is being dissolved, then organopathies result. It means the death of the nerve cell.

FOOTNOTE:

[16] The principle of reserve energy was developed independently by my friend, William James, and myself.

CHAPTER XXXIV

DYNAMIC ENERGY

Whenever the dynamic energy is exhausted and the levels of reserve energy are reached, the individual affected begins to feel restless, and if there is no access to the levels of reserve energy, the individual gets scared. The fear instinct becomes awakened, giving rise, after repeated unavailing attempts, to the states of psychopathic neurosis. In states of depression, such as hypochondria and more especially in states of melancholia, the fear instinct is potent. The fear instinct is brought about in the darkness of the night, when the individual is fatigued from his day's labor, when the external stimuli are at a minimum, and reserve energy is not available. The fear instinct rises from the subconscious regions to the surface of conscious activities.

Convalescent states as well as exhaustion from pain and disease, such as fever or a shock from some accident, war-shock, shell-shock, surgical shock predispose to the manifestation of the fear instinct. Hence the caution of surgeons in the preparation of the patient for a serious operation. For the result may be a shock to the system due to the subconscious activities of the fear instinct present in subconscious mental life, no longer protected by the guardianship of the upper consciousness. And it may also be shown, both by experiment and observation, that during the subconscious states when the lower strata of dynamic energy are reached, such as hypnoidal, hypnoid states, and sleep, that the individual is more subject to fear than during the waking states. We know how a sudden noise, a flash of light during drowsy states or sleep startles one, and the same holds true of any stimulus. I have observed the same condition of fright during hypnoidal states.

We must agree with the French psychologist, Ribot, when he comes to the conclusion that "every lowering of vitality, whether permanent or temporary, predisposes to fear; the physiological conditions which engender or accompany it, are all ready; *in a weakened organism fear is always in a nascent condition.*"

The fear instinct becomes morbid when the individual has to draw on his reserve energy, and finds he is unable to do it. The cure consists in the release of the reserve energy which has become inaccessible. This can be done by various methods, but the best is the method of induction of the hypnoidal state under the control of a competent psychopathologist. The whole process consists in the restitution of the levels of dynamic energy and the building up of the patient's active personality.

From our point of view, fear is not necessarily due to pain previously experienced, it may be purely instinctive. The fear instinct may be aroused *directly*, such for instance is the fear of young children who have never before experienced a fall. In fact we claim that the fear instinct and the restlessness which expresses it antedate and precede pain. The fear of pain is but one of the forms under which the fear instinct is manifested. The fear instinct appears long before pain and pleasure come into existence. This holds true not only of the lower animal life, but also of the vague fear found in many a case of neurasthenia and functional neurosis and psychosis. Ribot also calls attention to pantophobia. "This is a state in which the patient fears everything, where anxiety instead of being riveted on one object, floats as a dream, and only becomes fixed for an instant at a time, passing from one object to another, as circumstances may determine."

It is probably best to classify fears as *antecedent* and *subsequent* to experience, or fears as *undifferentiated* and *differentiated*.

When the dynamic energy is used up in the course of life adaptations, and reserve energy is drawn upon, there may be danger that the energy may be used up until the static energy is reached, and neuropathic conditions are manifested. These conditions are preceded by psychopathic disturbances. Associative life becomes disturbed, and emotional reactions become morbid. There is a degeneration or reversion to earlier and lower forms of mental activity, and to lower instinctive life. The primitive instincts, the impulse of self-preservation and the fear instinct, come to the foreground, giving rise to the various forms of psychopathic affections.

This process of degeneration and simplification is characteristic of all forms of psychopathic conditions, though it may be more prominent in some cases than in others. The type of mental life becomes lowered and there is a reversion, a sort of atavism, to simpler and more childish experiences, memories, reactions of earlier and less complex forms of mental life. I have laid special stress on this feature of psychopathic reactions in all my works on the subject. What I emphasize in my present work is the fact that psychopathic reactions are dominated by self and fear, which are laid bare by the process of degeneration.

The patient in psychopathic states is tortured by his fears, he is obsessed by wishes which are entirely due to his fear and deranged impulse of self-preservation.

As the static energy is reached, and with lack of functional energy of the dynamic character, the energy habitually used in the ordinary relations of life, the patient experiences a monotony, a void in his life activity. He has a feeling of distress, as if something is haunting him, and possibly something terrible is going to happen to him or his family. He may have a feeling of some depression, and may suffer from a constant unquenchable craving for new stimulations, run after new impressions and excitements which pale in a short time on his fagged mind. He is restless, demanding new amusements and distractions. He is distracted with fear, conscious and more often subconscious,—which he is unable to dispel or shake off. He seems to stand over a fearful precipice, and he is often ready to do anything to avoid this terrible gap in his life. Life is empty, devoid of all interest; he talks of ennui and even of suicide; he is of a pessimistic, gloomy disposition, his state of mind approaching a state of melancholia. He asks for new sensations, new pleasures, new enjoyments which soon tire him. He is in the condition of a leaking barrel which never can be filled.

Psychopathic individuals are in a state of the wicked "who are like the ocean which never rests." This misery of ever forming wishes and attempting to assuage the inner suffering, this craving for new pleasures and excitements, in order to still uneasiness, distress, and the pangs of the fear instinct with its gnawing, agonizing anxieties, brings the patient to a state in which he is ready to drink and use narcotics. The patient seeks ways to relieve his misery. The patient has used up all his available dynamic energy, and being unable to reach the stores of reserve energy looks for a key or stimulant to release his locked up reserve energies. The patient is unable to respond to the stimuli of life, so he attempts then the use of his static energy. This can only result in producing psychopathic and neuropathic symptoms.

The patient needs to be lifted out of the misery of monotony and ennui of life, he needs to be raised from his low level of vitality, to be saved from the listlessness into which he has fallen. The low level of energy makes him feel like a physical, nervous, and mental bankrupt. This bankruptcy is unbearable to him. He is in a state of distraction, distracted with the agony of fear. Something must be done to free himself from the depression of low spirits and from the low level of energy which keeps him in a state devoid of all interest in life, accompanied by physical, mental and moral fatigue. He is like a prisoner doomed to a life long term.

This constant craving for stimulation of energy, this reaction to the anxiety of the morbid fear instinct is the expression of exhaustion of available dynamic energy for the purpose of normal life activity. The patient attempts to draw on his latent reserve energy. Since this form of energy is not accessible to the stimulations of common life, he tries to release the energy by means of artificial stimulations, be it morphine, alcohol, mysticism, Freudism, sexual and religious "at-one-ments" or by other stimuli of exciting character. Unable to release energy by fair means the patient is driven to the employment of foul means for the stimulation of new sources of energy. The psychopathic patient is driven by fear, by fears of life and death.

The morbid fear instinct in all cases is brought about by exhaustion of energy, whether sudden or gradual. Fear is due to exhaustion of lower levels of dynamic energy and to the inability of liberation of stored up reserve energy. The more intense this incapacity of utilization of reserve stores of energy be, the more intense is the fear. When this condition is prolonged the psychopathic symptoms become unendurable.

The experienced, thinking surgeon has learned the danger of this condition in his operating room. Thus it is told of Porta, the great surgeon of Pavia, when his patients died under an operation, he used to throw his knife and instruments contemptuously to the ground, and shout in a tone of reproach to the corpse: "Cowards die of fear."

The great physiologist Mosso gives a graphic description of the effects of fear in a pathetic case that has come under his personal observation: "As army surgeon, I had once to be present at the execution of some brigands. It was a summary judgment. A major of the *besaglieri* put a few questions to one or two, then turning to the captain said simply: 'Shoot them.' I remember one lad, of scarcely twenty years of age, who mumbled replies to a few questions, then remained silent, in the position of a man warding off a fatal blow, with lifted arms, extended palms, the neck drawn between the shoulders, the head held sideways, the body bent and drawn backwards. When he heard the dreadful words he emitted a shrill, heart-rending cry of despair, looked around him, as though eagerly seeking something, then turned to flee, and rushed with outspread arms against a wall of the court, writhing and scratching it as though trying to force an entrance between the stones, like a polyp clinging to a rock. After a few screams and contortions, he suddenly sank to the ground, powerless and helpless like a log. He was pale and trembled as I have never seen anyone tremble since. It seemed as though the muscles had been turned to a jelly which was shaken in all directions."

CHAPTER XXXV

FEAR VARIETIES

The great psychologist Ribot classifies fears into pain fears, and disgust fears. To quote from Ribot: "I propose to reduce them (fears) to two groups. The first is directly connected with fear and includes all manifestations, implying in any degree whatever the fear of pain, from that of a fall or the prick of a needle, to that of illness or death. The second is directly connected with disgust, and seems to me to include the forms which have sometimes been called pseudophobia (Gelineau). Such are the fear of contact, the horror of blood and of innocuous animals, and many strange and causeless aversions. Let us remark furthermore that fear and disgust have a common basis, being both instruments of protection or defense. The first is the defensive-conservative instinct of relative life, the second the defensive-conservative instinct of organic life. As both have a common basis of aversion, they show themselves in equivalent ways: fear of withdrawal, departure, flight, disgust by vomiting and nausea: The reflexes of disgust are the succedanea of flight; the organism cannot escape by movement in space from the repugnant object which it has taken into itself, and goes through a movement of expulsion instead."

I hesitate to accept Ribot's classification, inasmuch as we have pointed out that fear is prior to pain. In most lower animals it is hardly probable that not having representations that there is present a fear of pain in advance of the pain itself. Fear under such conditions can only be awakened by an actual sensory experience whether it be painful or not. In fact Ribot himself agrees to the fact that "There is a primary, instinctive, unreasoning fear preceding all individual experience, a hereditary fear."

Perhaps a word may be said in regard to the factor of disgust as having a common basis with fear. It is only by a stretch of imagination, if not by a stretch of words, that fear and disgust can be identified. There may be fear where there is no disgust, and there may be disgust where there is no fear. The two are independent variables, and can hardly be referred to as one and the same fundamental reaction, such as withdrawal and flight. The object of disgust does not preclude approach. The avoidance or aversion, the nausea and vomiting are all subsequent phenomena. Disgust may even follow after an abuse of food, of pleasant or necessary objects of nutrition, such as satiety.

The reactions of the fear instinct run the contrary way, approach is precluded from the very start. Fear is not associated with useful objects or events, unless it be in morbid states of fear.

And still fear and disgust may become intimately associated when disgust and its objects awaken the fear instinct, and the fear becomes the fear of disgust or of the disgusting object. Disgust is more of a specialized character, and is associated with particular events or specific objects, while fear, in its primitive form at least, is more of a generalized character.

In the higher forms of life disgust may be so intimately related to fear that the two become synthesized, so to say, and are felt like one emotional state, the state becoming one of fear disgust. In such cases the fear instinct, fear disgust, is a determining factor of the morbid state. This is confirmed by clinical experience of the various cases of psychopathic functional neurosis and psychosis.

In the various morbid states of the depressive types fear is awakened long before any pain is actually suffered, or any particular cause is found by the patient to account for the terror that dominates his mental life. The fear comes first while the representative cause is assigned by the sufferer as the cause of the fear.

Similarly in the functional psychosis and neurosis the object, experience, event, may be quite ordinary without any suggestion of pain or distress in it. In fact, the experience may be indifferent or even pleasant, but when associated with the fear instinct may become the nucleus of a very distressing pathological state. The experience is the *occasion*, while the fear instinct, the intimate companion of the impulse of self-preservation, is the only cause of functional psychopathic maladies.

The fear instinct in its primitive state is anterior to all experiences of danger, pain, and suffering, as is the case in most of the lower animals. In the higher animals where memory is developed, the fear instinct is associated with some form of representation, however vague, and then fear becomes posterior to experience. In man both forms of fear are present. The anterior form is specially found in children, while in adults the posterior form is, under normal conditions, predominating. The primitive anterior type of the fear instinct is by no means absent, in fact, it is more overpowering, its effects are overwhelming when it comes forth from the subconscious regions to which it is confined, and is manifested under conditions of lowered vitality.

When the strata of dynamic energies are passed and the strata of reserve energies are reached, the reserve energy not being accessible, the fear instinct is elemental, fundamental, while the fear of pain and of some definite representation of danger, or of suffering is a secondary consequence. People may suffer from pain, disease, and even danger, and still have no fear, while others may have never experienced the pain or disease, and still be obsessed by intense pangs of fear. Fear is *sui generis*, it is at the foundation of animal life.

The fear instinct may be awakened directly by a sensory stimulus, when, for instance, one finds himself in darkness and feels some creeping, slimy thing, or when attacked suddenly with a club or a knife. The fear instinct may again be aroused by an expectation, by something to which his dynamic energies cannot respond adequately, while the reserve energies are in abeyance, such for instance as the expectation of some threatening event either to himself or to the objects bound up with his life existence. When one is threatened with some misfortune, with torture, death, or with a mortal disease, or with a serious operation, or when confronted with great danger against which his energies prove inadequate, in such cases the fear is ideational. These types of fear may in turn be either conscious or subconscious.

We may thus classify the fears as follows:

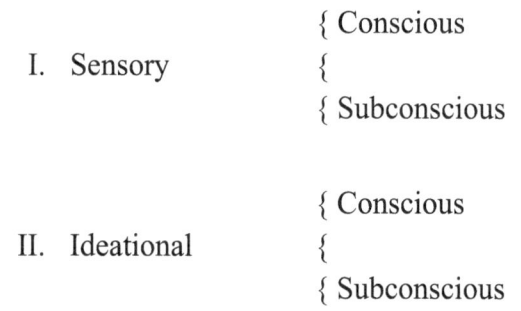

    I. Sensory   { Conscious
                            {
                            { Subconscious

    II. Ideational   { Conscious
                            {
                            { Subconscious

The fear of the etherized or chloroformed patient is entirely of the subconscious type. It is the arousing of subconscious fear which, from the nature of the case, cannot be reached and alleviated that gives rise to functional psychosis and neurosis.

From this standpoint it may be said that *psychopathic diseases are subconscious fear states, in other words functional psychosis or neurosis is essentially a disease of subconscious activities.* This is, in fact, confirmed by my clinical experience and by my psychopathological research work.

Dr. L. J. Pollock, professor of nervous diseases at Northwestern University Medical School, made an extremely interesting "Analysis of a Number of Cases of War Neurosis." This analysis fully conforms to the results obtained by me in my work on functional psychosis and neurosis carried on for a great number of years. It fully confirms the results of my studies, clinical and psychopathological, that the causation, or etiology of functional psychopathic states depends on fluctuations of the levels of neuron energy, or physical exhaustion, fatigue, hunger and thirst, or shock to the system, and more especially on the ravages of the fear instinct, aroused during the dangers and horrors of war.

"Of several hundred cases which I observed in base hospitals in France, copies of about 350 records were available. From these 200 of the more detailed ones were selected to determine the relative frequency of some of the factors.... From the numerical group has been excluded cases of emotional instability, timorousness, hospital neuroses occurring as an aftermath of an illness or a wound, the phobic reactions of gassed patients and constitutional neuroses, and those not directly related to the war.

"Heredity as a factor plays but a small part, and the incidence of neuropathic taint constituted little over 4 per cent.

"Of these 43 per cent followed shell fire, 36 per cent after concussion as described by the soldier.... A definite history of fatigue and hunger was obtained in 30.5 per cent. Both probably occurred in a greater percentage, but were frequently masked by other symptoms which occupied the patient's attention to a greater extent. Fatigue and hunger are important factors, not only because they prepare the ground for an ensuing neurosis by breaking down the defensive reactions, but also in that when the patient is more sensitive and impressionable, the natural physical consequences of fatigue are misinterpreted by him as an evidence of an illness, and give rise to apprehension and fear.

"As frequently as fear is seen in some form or other in the neuroses of civil life, so does it manifest itself in the war neuroses. Fifty per cent of the cases admitted considerable fear under shell fire. Concussion was the immediate precipitating cause of the neuroses in 31 per cent of the cases. The symptoms of the neuroses could be divided into those of the reactions of fear and fatigue."

These results corroborate my work on neurosis as due to exhaustion of Neuron Energy and Self-Fear.

In fact, in one of my works written at the beginning of the war, I predicted the wide occurrence of what is known as shell shock, war shock or war neurosis. The prediction was fully corroborated by the facts.

Fear, Self, Reserve Energy, and Fatigue are the main factors in the formation of the psychopathic or neurotic condition. Janet, in a recent article of his, lays stress on the fear states in psychopathic affections and refers these conditions to the levels of vital energy. There is no doubt that Janet lays his finger on the very heart of the psychopathic diathesis.

In my work I come to a similar conclusion only I lay more stress on the fear states, being referred to the fundamental instinct present in all animal life as a primordial condition of existence. This instinct is intensified and extended in the psychopathic diathesis.

The level of energy and the fear instinct are vitally interdependent. A low level of energy, especially a dissociation or inhibition of the store of reserve energy, arouses an excess of reaction of the fear instinct, and *vice versa* the excessive reaction of the fear instinct locks up the stores of reserve energy, thus intensifying and extending the psychopathic states with their fear-fatigue conditions. Janet refers indirectly to the impulse of self-preservation which is of the utmost consequence in psychopathic affections. On the whole, I may say that my work and clinical experience are in accord with that of the great French psychopathologist.

Where the fear instinct, self, and inhibition of reserve energy are present, then any emotion, even that of love, and devotion, will give rise to psychopathic states. This psychopathic state is not produced, because of the intensity or repression of the emotion, but because of the underlying subconscious predisposition to fear-instinct, self-preservation, and inhibition of reserve energy.

The feelings of inhibited reserve energy produced by fear and self, make the individual hesitate in decision, in action, and finally demoralize and terrorize him. These conditions take away from him all assurance and security of life and action, and hold him in a perpetual state of anxiety until he becomes completely incapacitated for all kinds of action and reaction.

Events that threaten the impulse of self-preservation of the individual, such as misfortunes, shocks, losses, tend to bring about psychopathic states, on account of the aroused fear instinct, on account of the impulse of self-preservation, and sudden inhibition of the stores of reserve energy. Events that may lead to dissolution of personality are, hence, attended with intense anxiety.

As we have seen, an intense state of fear, conscious or subconscious, produces a state of aboulia, a state of indecision, a state of incompletion of action, a state of insufficiency, a paralysis of will power, and a sense of unreality, all of which are intimately interrelated. For the fear instinct, when intense, inhibits and arrests the will and paralyzes action. *The patient fears, not because he is inactive, but he is inactive, because he fears.*

The impulse of self-preservation, the fear instinct, and the principle of subconscious reserve energy give an insight into the multiform symptomatology of the psychopathic diathesis.

The following classes of people are subject to psychopathic affections:

(I) Childless people.

(II) People who had been afflicted with various diseases in childhood.

(III) Children of sickly, nervous, psychopathic parents who have kept their progeny in a constant state of anxiety, full of terrors and troubles of life.

(IV) People who had been affected by a series of shocks and fears in childhood and youth.

(V) People whose parents suffered long from various systemic diseases, especially cardiac and tubercular troubles.

(VI) In a large family of children the first, or last child, or sickly child of psychopathic parents.

(VII) The only child, or sickly child, especially of a widowed parent who is of a psychopathic diathesis.

In all these cases the psychopathic state is due to early cultivation of the fear instinct, self-impulse, and low level or dissociated state of vital reserve energy.

CHAPTER XXXVI

CONTROL OF THE NEUROTIC[17]

The first thing in the examination and treatment of neurosis is the elimination of any physical trouble. It is only after such an elimination that one should resort to psychotherapeutic treatment.

In psychopathic or neurotic diseases one should take into consideration the fact that the patients are characterized by the tendency of formation of habits which are hard to break. The patients are apt to ask that the same thing be done again and again for the simple reason that it has been done several times before. In other words, *psychopathic neurosis is characterized by automatism and routine.* This tendency to *recurrence* is characteristic of all forms of primitive life as well as of mental activities which are on the decline,—it is the easiest way to get along.

Effort is abhorrent to the patient. He is afraid of change in the same way as the savage is afraid of any novelty or of any change in custom. Tradition is holy, and in a double sense, because it has been handed down by former generations, regarded as divine and superior, and because the new is strange and, therefore, may prove dangerous and of evil consequence. What has not been tried may prove harmful, pernicious, and even deadly. The old has been tried and approved by generations and the consequences are known, while the new may be in alliance with evil powers. This holds true in all cases obsessed by the impulse of self-preservation and the fear instinct. What the patients have tried several times and what has proved good and pleasant is demanded by the patient to be repeated; the new is not known and may be risky, dangerous. I have great difficulty in making changes in the life of advanced psychopathic cases, because of the fear of the new, *neophobia*. Once the change is made, and the patient becomes adapted to the new way, then the old way is shunned. In short, *neophobia is an essential trait of psychopathic patients*.

The physician must take this trait of neophobia into account, and as the patient begins to improve, he must gradually and slowly wean the patient of this phobia, inherent in the very nature of the malady. The patient must learn to do *new* things, and not simply follow mechanically a régime, laid out by the physician.

The patient's life must become personal. The patient should be made to change many of his ways, and above all he should learn to follow reason, rather than habit and routine. Everything, as much as possible, should be reasoned out,—he should be able to give a rational account of his habits and actions. Whatever appears to be a matter of routine, irrational and unaccountable habit, simply a matter of recurrence, of repetition of action, should be discarded, should be changed to actions and adaptations for which the patient could give a rational account.

We must remember that the patient lives in the condition of recurrent mental states, that his mental activity, as I have pointed out, follows the laws of recurrence, characteristic of the type of recurrent moment consciousness.[18] It is, therefore, the physician's object to lift the patient out of this low form of mental activity to the higher types of rational, personal life in which the patient can rise above the perturbations of life, above the pettiness of existence with its worries and fears. This procedure is essential.

We can realize how pernicious are those schemes which physicians and many people in sanitariums lay out for the patients just to keep them busy for the time of their stay under special care. As soon as the patients leave, they are in the same predicament as before. The patients wish to have their lives conducted in the same mechanical, automatic routine. In this way they are really on the same low plane of mental life, on the plane of recurrent moment consciousness, a type which forms the pathological web and woof of the patient's life.

Unless the patient is lifted out of this low, mean, and animal form of conscious activity, he cannot be regarded as cured. Instead of having the patient's life saturated and controlled by the recurrent automatisms of the fear instinct, he should learn to be controlled by the light of reason. "A free man is he," says Spinoza, "who lives under the guidance of reason, who is not led by fear." Epicurus and the ancient Epicureans laid special stress on the necessity of getting rid of fear through reason, enlightenment, and education. Thus the great poet Lucretius:

"The whole of life is a struggle in the dark. For even as children are flurried and dread all things in the thick darkness, thus we in the daylight fear things not a whit more to be dreaded than those which the children shudder at in the dark and fancy future evils. This terror, therefore, and darkness of mind must be dispelled not by the rays of the sun and glittering shafts of day, but by knowledge of the aspect and law of nature."

As Carlyle tersely puts it: "The first duty of a man is still that of *subduing Fear*. We must get rid of Fear; we cannot act at all till then. A man's acts are slavish, not true but specious (we may add psychopathic); his very thoughts are false, he thinks too as a slave and coward, till he has got Fear under feet.... Now and always, the completeness of his victory over Fear will determine how much of a man he is."

The patient complains of lack of confidence. This is a pathognomonic symptom of psychopathic states. At the same time there is confidence in the symptom complex which is often described by him with microscopic minuteness. The patient has no doubt about that. He is in search of some one who can overcome this symptom complex in a way which he specially approves. The patient matches his morbid self-will against the physician's control. The physician is not to be subdued by the authority of the diseased personality, he should not let himself be controlled by the ruling symptoms of the patient's life. Either the physician meets with *opposition*, and after some time, must give up the treatment of the case, or he is victimized by the patient's demands, and must comply with them. In the latter case the patient may stick to the physician for some time. In both cases the patient is not really cured. It is only when the *diseased self* becomes subdued and falls under the physician's control, it is only then that a cure is really possible, it is only then that the normal healthy self may come to the foreground.

The first and foremost characteristic of psychopathic states is the narrowing down of the patient's life interests. He begins to lose interest in abstract problems, then in that of his own profession or occupation, then he loses interest in the welfare of his party or his country, and finally, in his family, wife, and children. Even in the case of love, the psychopathic patient seeks to utilize the person he loves for his own, neurotic benefit, namely, his neurotic comfort and health. He loves the person as a glutton likes his meal, or as a drunkard his liquor. The self becomes narrowed down to health, the key to his supposed spiritual life. Self-preservation and fear permeate the patient's life.

We notice that the patient's life activity, especially his mental functions, becomes narrowed down. His attention becomes circumscribed to a few subjects and objects. This is the limitation of the *extent* of attention. There is afterward a limitation of the *temporal span* of attention. The patient cannot keep his attention on any subject for any length of time. This span of attention becomes more and more limited with the growth and severity of the psychopathic malady. If the patient is educated and has had an interest in various subjects, the latter become more and more limited in scope. Finally the patient becomes reduced to the least amount of effort of the attention, and that only for a brief period of time. When the trouble reaches its climax, the patient loses all interest and capacity of reading and of studying. He cannot think, he becomes less and less original in his thoughts, he becomes even incapable of thinking. The patient's whole mind becomes limited to himself and to the symptoms of his disease.

Along with it the fear instinct grows in power, inhibiting all other activities. There is a limitation of the patient's personal self. The personality becomes reduced to the lowest levels of existence, caring for his own selfish pains and small pleasures, which are exaggerated and magnified to an extraordinary degree. In other words, the *personal* life of the patient becomes more and more limited as the pathological process goes on. It becomes harder and harder for the patient to take an active interest in life.

It is clear that under such conditions the tendency of the patient is to rest and brood about himself, and keep indulging his limited interests, which get still more narrowed as the pathological process becomes more extensive and intensive. Under such conditions it is suicidal to indulge the patient and suggest to him a *rest cure*, a cure which lies along the line of the disease process, thus tending to intensify the disease. What the patient needs is to change his environment, and be put under conditions in which his interests of life can be aroused. His life activities should be stimulated to functioning on the right lines, laid out by physicians who understand the patient's condition. *Rest is harmful to the neurotic. What the patient needs is work, work, and work.*

What we must remember in the treatment of psychopathic patients is the fact that we deal here with the aberrations of the impulse of self-preservation, the most powerful, the most fundamental, and the least controllable of animal impulses, accompanied with the fear instinct, which is the most primitive of all animal instincts. This morbid state of the impulse of self-preservation must be fully realized before any treatment is begun. The physician must also see and study closely the line on which the self-preservation impulse is tending, and comprehend the associations along which the impulse takes its course in the history of the patient and in the symptom complex.

What one must especially look after is the elusive feeling of self-pity which manifests itself under various garbs, and hides itself under all kinds of forms. As long as the patient is introspective and has the emotional side of self-pity present, so long is his condition psychopathic.

The extreme selfishness and the uniqueness with which psychopathic patients regard their own condition should be eradicated from their mind. It must be impressed on them that their case is quite common, and that there is nothing exceptional about them. It must be made clear to them that the whole trouble is a matter of mal-adjustment, that they have developed inordinately the impulse of self-preservation and the fear instinct until their mental life has become morbid and twisted. The whole personality has to be readjusted. It is the special tendency of psychopathic patients to regard themselves as unique, privileged above all other patients, they are a kind of geniuses among the afflicted, possibly on account of the special endowments possessed by them, gifts of quite exceptional and mysterious a character. "Have you ever met with a case like mine?" is the stereotyped phrase of the psychopathic, neurotic patient. As long as the patient entertains that conception of *nobility*, the impulse of self must still be regarded as morbid.

The neurotic must be made to understand clearly that there is no aristocracy in disease, and that there is no nobility of the specially elect in the world of morbid affections, any more than there is in the domain of physical maladies.

The egocentric character of the psychopathic patient puts him in the position of the savage who takes an animistic, a personal view of the world and of the objects that surround him. Natural forces are regarded as dealing with man and his fate, often conspiring against man. Magic is the remedy by which the savage tries to defend himself, and even to control the inimical or friendly natural forces or objects, animate and inanimate, with which he comes in contact. This same attitude, animistic and personal, of the primitive man is present in the psychopathic patient. The patient is afraid that something fearful may happen to him. Against such accidents he takes measures often of a defensive character which differ but little from the magic of the savage and the barbarian. That is why these patients are the victims of all kinds of fakes, schemes, panaceas of the wildest type, unscrupulous patent medicines, absurd régimes, mental and religious, whose silliness and absurdity are patent to the unprejudiced observer. The mental state of the psychopathic or neurotic patient is that of the savage with his anthropomorphic view of nature, with his fears based on the impulse of self-preservation. *The psychopathic patient is in a state of primitive fear and of savage credulity with its faith in magic.*

The emotional side of the impulse of self-preservation and of the fear instinct should always be kept in mind by the physician who undertakes the treatment of psychopathic cases. The physician must remember that the emotions in such cases are essentially of the instinctive type, that they therefore lie beyond the ken of the patient's immediate control and action of the personal will. The physician should not, therefore, be impatient, but while protecting the invalid against the fears that assail the latter, he should gradually and slowly undermine the violence of the impulse of self-preservation and the anxiety of the fear instinct. For in all psychopathic maladies the main factors are the impulse of self-preservation and the fear instinct.

FOOTNOTES:

[17] The discussion here is necessarily brief. The reader is referred for details to my work "The Causation and Treatment of Psychopathic Diseases," Ch. XVII, General Psychotherapeutic Methods.

[18] See Sidis, "The Foundations," Part II, Moment-Consciousness.

CHAPTER XXXVII

REGAINED ENERGY AND MENTAL HEALTH

The *principle of reserve energy*, developed independently by Professor James and myself, is of the utmost importance to abnormal psychology. The principle is based on a broad generalization of facts—psychological, physiological and biological—namely, that far less energy is utilized by the individual than there is actually at his disposal. A comparatively small fraction of the total amount of energy, possessed by the organism, is used in its relation with the ordinary stimuli of its environment.

The energy in use may be regarded as *kinetic or circulating energy*, while the energy stored away is *reserve energy*. There must always be a supply of reserve energy requisite for unusual reactions in emergency cases. Those organisms survive which have the greatest amount of reserve energy, just as those countries are strong and victorious which possess the largest amount of reserve capital to draw upon in critical periods.

As life becomes more complex, inhibitions increase; the thresholds of stimulations of a complex system rise in proportion to its complexity. With the rise of evolution there is a tendency to increase of inhibitions, with a consequent lock-up of energy which becomes *reserve*. Now there are occasions in the life of the individual, under the influence of training and emotional trauma, when the inhibitions become unusually intense, tending to smother the personality, which becomes weakened, impoverished in its reactions, and is unable to respond freely to the stimuli of its environment. The inhibited system becomes inactive and may be regarded as *dissociated* from the cycle of life.

In case of an emotional trauma there is often a breach in the continuity of association. The affected system becomes dissociated from the rest of the personality, and is like a splinter in the flesh of the individuality. Its own threshold, when tapped, may be very low, but it is not directly accessible through the mediacy of other systems; hence its threshold appears unusually or pathologically high. When the inhibitions are very high they must be removed. This removal of inhibitions brings about an access to the accumulated energy of the inhibited systems. In case of disjunction or break of continuity we must stimulate the dormant reserve energy of the systems, and thus assist the process of repair and bridge the breach of associative continuity. A new, fresh, active life opens to the patient. He becomes a "reformed" personality, free and cheerful, with an overflow of energy.

The hypnoidal state is essentially a rest-state characterized by anabolic activity. There is a restitution of spent energy; inhibitions become removed, and access is gained to "dormant" systems or complexes. The awakened "dormant" complex systems bring with them a new feeling-tone, a fresh emotional energy resulting in an almost complete transformation of personality.

As an illustration of the transformation effected I take at random the following extracts from some of the letters written to me by patients who have experienced this welling up of reserve energy: "Indeed, were I to fill this entire sheet with expressions of the gratitude which wells up from my inmost heart it would be only a beginning of what I feel. Surely the darkness of the world has been dispelled since this *new light* has illuminated my soul, and *I feel that this wondrous light will never fail me*. It were vain to attempt to thank you for this wonderful transformation."

A letter from a patient reads: "You will be glad to know that all is well with me. Life is one happy day. I am a marvel to my friends in the way of happiness and cheer. I have to confess that I feel almost wicked to be so happy."

Another letter runs as follows: "Next to the gladness in my own restoration, I am rejoiced at the wonderful transformation that has come to my dear friend T—— from your treatment. She writes me most enthusiastically of her steady and sure progress toward the goal of perfect health, of her strength to take up the home duties which had been so burdensome, and she now finds a delight in the doing of them, and of her husband's and friends' joy in the transformation that has been wrought in her."

A patient writes: "Your treatments cut a deep channel in my subconscious life, one from which if I do happen to wander astray is for only a short time; then I am carried right back in the trend. In fact, there exists a deep indelible, happy and cheerful impression incorporated in my subconscious life that it is impossible to eradicate.... You have laid a concrete foundation upon which I am building, little by little, a structure that some day you will be proud of, and for which words are insufficient to express my profound gratitude."

Another patient writes: "The big result of your treatment was restoring my faith and arousing my ambitions. I never think of suicide. I only want to live and work and redeem myself. I have never been so happy and I have never worked harder.... I feel the most extraordinary eagerness; a strange, irrepressible enthusiasm; and an absolute conviction of the truth and beauty of work, of my work. I dare not think of failure, and yet success as I conceive it is too wonderful ever to come. The brave will of life in me permitting, I shall some day approximate my prayer, my dream, my vision; and then I must let the earth know you are responsible."

The following extract of a letter, written to me by a patient, an experienced English surgeon, now in charge of a hospital in England, whose case was severe and chronic, dating from early childhood, is valuable, both on account of his medical training and his mental abilities which make him an excellent judge as to the fundamental change and cure effected:

"It is now exactly two years since I was undergoing treatment at your kindly and sympathetic hands. I remember that you once told me that the seed sown by you would probably take this length of time to come to fruition. Therefore, it may not be without interest to you to receive a supplement to many other letters in which I will endeavor to summarize my progress—for the last time.

"I have no longer even the least lingering doubt that you can count me among your most brilliantly successful cures. I say this after many—too many—heart searchings which are probably characteristic of my somewhat doubting temperament. At first, I was disappointed with the whole business: I suppose I looked for strange and dramatic events to occur which would change my whole personality and temperament in a short time. Nothing so exciting happened; I left Portsmouth still feeling that I owned the same name, and very much the same 'ego' that I arrived with. I was unaware that any profound psychological operation had taken place. To be candid, I did not think it had—the beginnings, no doubt, were there—but no more. But now when I carry my mind back to the type of obsession which used to assail me—is there any change? Good God! I behold a miracle, although it has come about so silently that I can only realize the difference by comparing the present with the past. In conclusion I can only send you my undying gratitude.... You have saved me from what, I honestly believe, would have one day resulted in deliberate suicide which I often contemplated as the one solution of my trouble...."

These extracts are typical of many others, and clearly show the enjoyment of new strength and powers until now unknown to the patient. Fresh reservoirs of reserve energy have been tapped and have become available in an hour of dire need. The patient has light and strength where there were darkness and depression. We are confronted here with the *important phenomenon of liberation of dormant reserve energy*. The patient feels the flood of fresh energies as a "marvelous transformation," as a "new light," as a "new life," as "a something worth more than life itself."

The hypnoidal state helps us to reach the inaccessible regions of dormant, reserve energy, helps to break down inhibitions, to liberate reserve energies and to repair the breaches or dissociation of mental life. The painful systems become dissociated, disintegrated and again transformed, reformed, and reintegrated into new systems, full of energy and joy of life.

The banishment of credulity, the cultivation of the upper, critical consciousness, the rational control of the subconscious, the moderation of the self-impulse, the regulation of the fear-instinct, and the access to the vast stores of subconscious reserve energy, all go to the formation of a strong, healthy-minded personality, free from fear and psychopathic maladies.

INDEX

Affections, neurotic, 59

Aphonia, 234, 248

Aristotle, 320

Automatic writing, 258, 260, 262

Automatic state, 121

Bacon, 301

Bain, 39, 56

Bernheim, 306

Binet, 255

Bramwell, 112

Carlyle, 49, 314

Catalepsy, 212, 218, 234, 244

Cataplexy, 67, 96

Characteristics of morbid states, 73, 74

Charcot, 325

Civilization, 273, 274

Claperède, 95

Compayré, 40

Consciousness, 77
will-, 77

Conversion, 312, 319

Crile, 53

Dämmerzustände, 220, 221

Darwin, Ch., 47, 57, 274

Demoor, 131

Diathesis, psychopathic, 285

Differentiation of neurotic states, 113

Disturbances, neurotic, 58

Donley, John, 102, 103

Dormant systems, 371

Dostoevsky, 25

Egocentric, 366

Energy,
circulating, 369
dynamic, 335, 339
kinetic, 369
neuron, 333, 339, 354

organic, 335
reserve, 334, 354, 369
restitution of, 336
static, 334, 335

Epictetus, 320

Eugenics, 276, 285

Fear, attacks, 226
instincts, 23, 24, 26, 42, 48, 55, 128, 164, 325, 354, 364
stages of, 27

Fear suggestion, 324
symptoms and description, 57, 60
types of, 351

Frazer, 297

Functional psychosis, 42, 43

Galton, 74, 146, 310

Hall, Stanley, 70

Haller, 46

Hallucination, 250, 254, 255
hypnotic, 256
pseudo, 224

Health, 130

Hegel, 320

Heredity, 271, 278, 353

Hypnagogic state, 92

Hypnapagogic state, 92

Hypnoidal state, 66, 91, 93, 95, 98, 101, 102, 106, 109, 113, 176, 264, 328

Hypnoidization, 101, 102, 109, 110

Hypnosis, 93, 96
nature of, 95, 96

Individuality, struggle for, 21

James, William, 34, 320, 321

Janet, 355

Kirchner, 67

Kraepelin, 50

Liebault, 306

Life energy, 332

Maladies, 164
neurotic, 164
psychopathic, 58, 368

Meltzer, 334

Metaphysics, 312

Mitchell, T. W., 103, 106, 107

Minot, 334

Mosso, 46, 277, 326, 345

Münsterberg, 305

Mysticism, 75, 76, 139, 312, 319

Nerve cell organization, 77
    inferior, 77
    superior, 77

Neuropathies, 62, 63, 65

Neurosis, 42, 44, 60, 171, 178, 271, 276, 285
    forms of, 61

Neurotic patients, 118, 130, 160

Neurotic states, 136

Organopathies, 61, 63, 65

Parasitism, neurotic, 131

Pascal, 274

Percept, nature of, 251

Perez, 33

Personality, 86, 89

Pfleiderer, 317

Plato, 320

Pollock, 352

Prayer, 312, 319, 329

Preyer, 33

Principle of contrast, 139
of differentiation, 143
of diminishing resistance, 143
dissociation, 142
dominance, 144
dynamogenesis, 144
embryonic psychogenesis, 137
fusion or synthesis, 138
inhibition, 144
irradiation or diffusion, 142
mental contest and discord, 145
modification, 148
proliferation and complication, 138
recession, 140
recurrence, 137

Psychoanalysis, 7, 9, 192, 330

Psychognosis, 120

Psycholepsy, 216

Psychopathic affections, 65, 115, 121, 130, 161, 284, 356

Psychosis, functional, 41, 44, 277

Ribakov, 171

Ribot, 33, 75, 340, 341

Romanes, 40

Routine, 121, 358

Royce, J., 320

Schopenhauer, 320

Self-preservation, 19, 23, 26, 128, 147, 164, 182, 311, 325, 368

Self, subwaking, 86, 89, 90

Seneca, 320

Sensory elements, 251
  primary, 251
  secondary, 251

Sex, instinct, 132

Sherrington, 52, 70

Sleep, 66, 95, 96, 110

Somatopsychosis, 64

Stammering, 234, 242

States
  hypnagogic, 92
  hypnapagogic, 92
  recurrent, 223, 360
  sleeping, 337
  waking, 336

Struggle for individuality, 21

Subconscious, the, 77

Suggestibility, 79, 80, 85
   abnormal, 81
   laws of, 81, 82
   normal, 81

Suggestion, 79
   post-hypnotic, 259, 260

Sully, 41

Superstition, 38, 264, 305

Synæsthesia, 252, 254

Taboos, 281, 308, 311
   apparition, 259

Trance states, 79

Weir-Mitchell, 160
   rest treatment of, 165

Writing, automatic, 258, 260, 262

TRANSCRIBER'S NOTE

Obvious typographical errors and punctuation errors have been corrected after careful comparison with other occurrences within the text and consultation of external sources.

Except for those changes noted below, all misspellings in the text, and inconsistent or archaic usage, have been retained.

Pg 41: 'In certain types of funtional psychosis' replaced by 'In certain types of functional psychosis'.
Pg 102: 'Relaxtion of nervous' replaced by 'Relaxation of nervous'.
Pg 113: 'to the crystillization' replaced by 'to the crystallization'.
Pg 123: 'Phychoanalysis and Christian' replaced by 'Psychoanalysis and Christian'.
Pg 157: 'patient was aways' replaced by 'patient was always'.
Pg 166: 'later life developd' replaced by 'later life developed'.
Pg 187: 'who reasurred me' replaced by 'who reassured me'.
Pg 265: 'process of matabolism' replaced by 'process of metabolism'.
Pg 281: '*the reductio ad absurdum*' replaced by 'the *reductio ad absurdum*'.
Pg 336: 'Diagram IV' was sideways, and has been rotated 90°.
Pg 351: 'are in abeyanace' replaced by 'are in abeyance'.
Pg 375: 'stores of subconscous' replaced by 'stores of subconscious'.

Index:
'Münsterburg' replaced by 'Münsterberg'.

End of the Project Gutenberg EBook of
Nervous Ills, by Boris Sidis

*** END OF THIS PROJECT GUTENBERG EBOOK
NERVOUS ILLS ***

***** This file should be named 56893-h.htm
or 56893-h.zip *****
This and all associated files of various
formats will be found in:

http://www.gutenberg.org/5/6/8/9/56893/

Produced by Turgut Dincer, John Campbell
and the Online
Distributed Proofreading Team at
http://www.pgdp.net (This
file was produced from images generously
made available
by The Internet Archive)

Updated editions will replace the previous
one--the old editions will
be renamed.

Creating the works from print editions not
protected by U.S. copyright
law means that no one owns a United States
copyright in these works,
so the Foundation (and you!) can copy and
distribute it in the United
States without permission and without
paying copyright
royalties. Special rules, set forth in the
General Terms of Use part

of this license, apply to copying and distributing Project
Gutenberg-tm electronic works to protect the PROJECT GUTENBERG-tm
concept and trademark. Project Gutenberg is a registered trademark,
and may not be used if you charge for the eBooks, unless you receive
specific permission. If you do not charge anything for copies of this
eBook, complying with the rules is very easy. You may use this eBook
for nearly any purpose such as creation of derivative works, reports,
performances and research. They may be modified and printed and given
away--you may do practically ANYTHING in the United States with eBooks
not protected by U.S. copyright law. Redistribution is subject to the
trademark license, especially commercial redistribution.

START: FULL LICENSE

THE FULL PROJECT GUTENBERG LICENSE
PLEASE READ THIS BEFORE YOU DISTRIBUTE OR USE THIS WORK

To protect the Project Gutenberg-tm mission of promoting the free
distribution of electronic works, by using or distributing this work
(or any other work associated in any way with the phrase "Project
Gutenberg"), you agree to comply with all the terms of the Full
Project Gutenberg-tm License available with this file or online at
www.gutenberg.org/license.

Section 1. General Terms of Use and Redistributing Project Gutenberg-tm electronic works

1.A. By reading or using any part of this Project Gutenberg-tm
electronic work, you indicate that you have read, understand, agree to
and accept all the terms of this license and intellectual property
(trademark/copyright) agreement. If you do not agree to abide by all
the terms of this agreement, you must cease using and return or
destroy all copies of Project Gutenberg-tm electronic works in your
possession. If you paid a fee for obtaining a copy of or access to a
Project Gutenberg-tm electronic work and you do not agree to be bound
by the terms of this agreement, you may obtain a refund from the
person or entity to whom you paid the fee as set forth in paragraph
1.E.8.

1.B. "Project Gutenberg" is a registered trademark. It may only be
used on or associated in any way with an electronic work by people who
agree to be bound by the terms of this agreement. There are a few
things that you can do with most Project Gutenberg-tm electronic works
even without complying with the full terms of this agreement. See
paragraph 1.C below. There are a lot of things you can do with Project
Gutenberg-tm electronic works if you follow

the terms of this
agreement and help preserve free future access to Project Gutenberg-tm
electronic works. See paragraph 1.E below.

1.C. The Project Gutenberg Literary Archive Foundation ("the
Foundation" or PGLAF), owns a compilation copyright in the collection
of Project Gutenberg-tm electronic works. Nearly all the individual
works in the collection are in the public domain in the United
States. If an individual work is unprotected by copyright law in the
United States and you are located in the United States, we do not
claim a right to prevent you from copying, distributing, performing,
displaying or creating derivative works based on the work as long as
all references to Project Gutenberg are removed. Of course, we hope
that you will support the Project Gutenberg-tm mission of promoting
free access to electronic works by freely sharing Project Gutenberg-tm
works in compliance with the terms of this agreement for keeping the
Project Gutenberg-tm name associated with the work. You can easily
comply with the terms of this agreement by keeping this work in the
same format with its attached full Project Gutenberg-tm License when
you share it without charge with others.

1.D. The copyright laws of the place where you are located also govern
what you can do with this work. Copyright

laws in most countries are
in a constant state of change. If you are outside the United States,
check the laws of your country in addition to the terms of this
agreement before downloading, copying, displaying, performing,
distributing or creating derivative works based on this work or any
other Project Gutenberg-tm work. The Foundation makes no
representations concerning the copyright status of any work in any
country outside the United States.

1.E. Unless you have removed all references to Project Gutenberg:

1.E.1. The following sentence, with active links to, or other
immediate access to, the full Project Gutenberg-tm License must appear
prominently whenever any copy of a Project Gutenberg-tm work (any work
on which the phrase "Project Gutenberg" appears, or with which the
phrase "Project Gutenberg" is associated) is accessed, displayed,
performed, viewed, copied or distributed:

  This eBook is for the use of anyone anywhere in the United States and
  most other parts of the world at no cost and with almost no
  restrictions whatsoever. You may copy it, give it away or re-use it
  under the terms of the Project Gutenberg License included with this
  eBook or online at www.gutenberg.org. If you are not located in the

United States, you'll have to check the laws of the country where you
are located before using this ebook.

1.E.2. If an individual Project Gutenberg-tm electronic work is
derived from texts not protected by U.S. copyright law (does not
contain a notice indicating that it is posted with permission of the
copyright holder), the work can be copied and distributed to anyone in
the United States without paying any fees or charges. If you are
redistributing or providing access to a work with the phrase "Project
Gutenberg" associated with or appearing on the work, you must comply
either with the requirements of paragraphs 1.E.1 through 1.E.7 or
obtain permission for the use of the work and the Project Gutenberg-tm
trademark as set forth in paragraphs 1.E.8 or 1.E.9.

1.E.3. If an individual Project Gutenberg-tm electronic work is posted
with the permission of the copyright holder, your use and distribution
must comply with both paragraphs 1.E.1 through 1.E.7 and any
additional terms imposed by the copyright holder. Additional terms
will be linked to the Project Gutenberg-tm License for all works
posted with the permission of the copyright holder found at the
beginning of this work.

1.E.4. Do not unlink or detach or remove

the full Project Gutenberg-tm License terms from this work, or any files containing a part of this work or any other work associated with Project Gutenberg-tm.

1.E.5. Do not copy, display, perform, distribute or redistribute this electronic work, or any part of this electronic work, without prominently displaying the sentence set forth in paragraph 1.E.1 with active links or immediate access to the full terms of the Project Gutenberg-tm License.

1.E.6. You may convert to and distribute this work in any binary, compressed, marked up, nonproprietary or proprietary form, including any word processing or hypertext form. However, if you provide access to or distribute copies of a Project Gutenberg-tm work in a format other than "Plain Vanilla ASCII" or other format used in the official version posted on the official Project Gutenberg-tm web site (www.gutenberg.org), you must, at no additional cost, fee or expense to the user, provide a copy, a means of exporting a copy, or a means of obtaining a copy upon request, of the work in its original "Plain Vanilla ASCII" or other form. Any alternate format must include the full Project Gutenberg-tm License as specified in paragraph 1.E.1.

1.E.7. Do not charge a fee for access to,

viewing, displaying,
performing, copying or distributing any
Project Gutenberg-tm works
unless you comply with paragraph 1.E.8 or
1.E.9.

1.E.8. You may charge a reasonable fee for
copies of or providing
access to or distributing Project
Gutenberg-tm electronic works
provided that

* You pay a royalty fee of 20% of the gross
profits you derive from
  the use of Project Gutenberg-tm works
calculated using the method
  you already use to calculate your
applicable taxes. The fee is owed
  to the owner of the Project Gutenberg-tm
trademark, but he has
  agreed to donate royalties under this
paragraph to the Project
  Gutenberg Literary Archive Foundation.
Royalty payments must be paid
  within 60 days following each date on
which you prepare (or are
  legally required to prepare) your
periodic tax returns. Royalty
  payments should be clearly marked as such
and sent to the Project
  Gutenberg Literary Archive Foundation at
the address specified in
  Section 4, "Information about donations
to the Project Gutenberg
  Literary Archive Foundation."

* You provide a full refund of any money
paid by a user who notifies
  you in writing (or by e-mail) within 30
days of receipt that s/he

does not agree to the terms of the full Project Gutenberg-tm
License. You must require such a user to return or destroy all
   copies of the works possessed in a physical medium and discontinue
   all use of and all access to other copies of Project Gutenberg-tm
   works.

* You provide, in accordance with paragraph 1.F.3, a full refund of
   any money paid for a work or a replacement copy, if a defect in the
   electronic work is discovered and reported to you within 90 days of
   receipt of the work.

* You comply with all other terms of this agreement for free
   distribution of Project Gutenberg-tm works.

1.E.9. If you wish to charge a fee or distribute a Project
Gutenberg-tm electronic work or group of works on different terms than
are set forth in this agreement, you must obtain permission in writing
from both the Project Gutenberg Literary Archive Foundation and The
Project Gutenberg Trademark LLC, the owner of the Project Gutenberg-tm
trademark. Contact the Foundation as set forth in Section 3 below.

1.F.

1.F.1. Project Gutenberg volunteers and employees expend considerable

effort to identify, do copyright research on, transcribe and proofread
works not protected by U.S. copyright law in creating the Project
Gutenberg-tm collection. Despite these efforts, Project Gutenberg-tm
electronic works, and the medium on which they may be stored, may
contain "Defects," such as, but not limited to, incomplete, inaccurate
or corrupt data, transcription errors, a copyright or other
intellectual property infringement, a defective or damaged disk or
other medium, a computer virus, or computer codes that damage or
cannot be read by your equipment.

1.F.2. LIMITED WARRANTY, DISCLAIMER OF DAMAGES - Except for the "Right
of Replacement or Refund" described in paragraph 1.F.3, the Project
Gutenberg Literary Archive Foundation, the owner of the Project
Gutenberg-tm trademark, and any other party distributing a Project
Gutenberg-tm electronic work under this agreement, disclaim all
liability to you for damages, costs and expenses, including legal
fees. YOU AGREE THAT YOU HAVE NO REMEDIES FOR NEGLIGENCE, STRICT
LIABILITY, BREACH OF WARRANTY OR BREACH OF CONTRACT EXCEPT THOSE
PROVIDED IN PARAGRAPH 1.F.3. YOU AGREE THAT THE FOUNDATION, THE
TRADEMARK OWNER, AND ANY DISTRIBUTOR UNDER THIS AGREEMENT WILL NOT BE
LIABLE TO YOU FOR ACTUAL, DIRECT, INDIRECT, CONSEQUENTIAL, PUNITIVE OR

INCIDENTAL DAMAGES EVEN IF YOU GIVE NOTICE
OF THE POSSIBILITY OF SUCH
DAMAGE.

1.F.3. LIMITED RIGHT OF REPLACEMENT OR
REFUND - If you discover a
defect in this electronic work within 90
days of receiving it, you can
receive a refund of the money (if any) you
paid for it by sending a
written explanation to the person you
received the work from. If you
received the work on a physical medium, you
must return the medium
with your written explanation. The person
or entity that provided you
with the defective work may elect to
provide a replacement copy in
lieu of a refund. If you received the work
electronically, the person
or entity providing it to you may choose to
give you a second
opportunity to receive the work
electronically in lieu of a refund. If
the second copy is also defective, you may
demand a refund in writing
without further opportunities to fix the
problem.

1.F.4. Except for the limited right of
replacement or refund set forth
in paragraph 1.F.3, this work is provided
to you 'AS-IS', WITH NO
OTHER WARRANTIES OF ANY KIND, EXPRESS OR
IMPLIED, INCLUDING BUT NOT
LIMITED TO WARRANTIES OF MERCHANTABILITY OR
FITNESS FOR ANY PURPOSE.

1.F.5. Some states do not allow disclaimers
of certain implied

warranties or the exclusion or limitation of certain types of
damages. If any disclaimer or limitation set forth in this agreement
violates the law of the state applicable to this agreement, the
agreement shall be interpreted to make the maximum disclaimer or
limitation permitted by the applicable state law. The invalidity or
unenforceability of any provision of this agreement shall not void the
remaining provisions.

1.F.6. INDEMNITY - You agree to indemnify and hold the Foundation, the
trademark owner, any agent or employee of the Foundation, anyone
providing copies of Project Gutenberg-tm electronic works in
accordance with this agreement, and any volunteers associated with the
production, promotion and distribution of Project Gutenberg-tm
electronic works, harmless from all liability, costs and expenses,
including legal fees, that arise directly or indirectly from any of
the following which you do or cause to occur: (a) distribution of this
or any Project Gutenberg-tm work, (b) alteration, modification, or
additions or deletions to any Project Gutenberg-tm work, and (c) any
Defect you cause.

Section 2. Information about the Mission of Project Gutenberg-tm

Project Gutenberg-tm is synonymous with the

free distribution of
electronic works in formats readable by the widest variety of
computers including obsolete, old, middle-aged and new computers. It
exists because of the efforts of hundreds of volunteers and donations
from people in all walks of life.

Volunteers and financial support to provide volunteers with the
assistance they need are critical to reaching Project Gutenberg-tm's
goals and ensuring that the Project Gutenberg-tm collection will
remain freely available for generations to come. In 2001, the Project
Gutenberg Literary Archive Foundation was created to provide a secure
and permanent future for Project Gutenberg-tm and future
generations. To learn more about the Project Gutenberg Literary
Archive Foundation and how your efforts and donations can help, see
Sections 3 and 4 and the Foundation information page at
www.gutenberg.org

Section 3. Information about the Project Gutenberg Literary Archive Foundation

The Project Gutenberg Literary Archive Foundation is a non profit
501(c)(3) educational corporation organized under the laws of the
state of Mississippi and granted tax exempt status by the Internal

Revenue Service. The Foundation's EIN or federal tax identification
number is 64-6221541. Contributions to the Project Gutenberg Literary
Archive Foundation are tax deductible to the full extent permitted by
U.S. federal laws and your state's laws.

The Foundation's principal office is in Fairbanks, Alaska, with the
mailing address: PO Box 750175, Fairbanks, AK 99775, but its
volunteers and employees are scattered throughout numerous
locations. Its business office is located at 809 North 1500 West, Salt
Lake City, UT 84116, (801) 596-1887. Email contact links and up to
date contact information can be found at the Foundation's web site and
official page at www.gutenberg.org/contact

For additional contact information:

>   Dr. Gregory B. Newby
>   Chief Executive and Director
>   gbnewby@pglaf.org

Section 4. Information about Donations to the Project Gutenberg
Literary Archive Foundation

Project Gutenberg-tm depends upon and cannot survive without wide
spread public support and donations to carry out its mission of
increasing the number of public domain and licensed works that can be
freely distributed in machine readable form accessible by the widest

array of equipment including outdated
equipment. Many small donations
($1 to $5,000) are particularly important
to maintaining tax exempt
status with the IRS.

The Foundation is committed to complying
with the laws regulating
charities and charitable donations in all
50 states of the United
States. Compliance requirements are not
uniform and it takes a
considerable effort, much paperwork and
many fees to meet and keep up
with these requirements. We do not solicit
donations in locations
where we have not received written
confirmation of compliance. To SEND
DONATIONS or determine the status of
compliance for any particular
state visit www.gutenberg.org/donate

While we cannot and do not solicit
contributions from states where we
have not met the solicitation requirements,
we know of no prohibition
against accepting unsolicited donations
from donors in such states who
approach us with offers to donate.

International donations are gratefully
accepted, but we cannot make
any statements concerning tax treatment of
donations received from
outside the United States. U.S. laws alone
swamp our small staff.

Please check the Project Gutenberg Web
pages for current donation
methods and addresses. Donations are

accepted in a number of other ways including checks, online payments and credit card donations. To donate, please visit: www.gutenberg.org/donate

Section 5. General Information About Project Gutenberg-tm electronic works.

Professor Michael S. Hart was the originator of the Project Gutenberg-tm concept of a library of electronic works that could be freely shared with anyone. For forty years, he produced and distributed Project Gutenberg-tm eBooks with only a loose network of volunteer support.

Project Gutenberg-tm eBooks are often created from several printed editions, all of which are confirmed as not protected by copyright in the U.S. unless a copyright notice is included. Thus, we do not necessarily keep eBooks in compliance with any particular paper edition.

Most people start at our Web site which has the main PG search facility: www.gutenberg.org

This Web site includes information about Project Gutenberg-tm, including how to make donations to the Project Gutenberg Literary Archive Foundation, how to help produce our new eBooks, and how to subscribe to our email newsletter to hear about new eBooks.

Made in United States
Troutdale, OR
01/2023